Backpacking and Trekking in Peru and Bolivia

4th edition

Hilary Bradt

BRADT PUBLICATIONS, UK
HUNTER PUBLISHING, USA

First published in 1987 by Bradt Publications, 41 Nortoft Rd, Chalfont St Peter, Bucks SL9 0LA, England. Distributed in the USA by Hunter Publishing Inc., 300 Rariton Center Parkway, CN94, Edison, NJ 08818.

British Library Cataloguing in Publication Data

Bradt, Hilary
   Backpacking and trekking in Peru and Bolivia — 4th ed.—
   (Backpacking guide series).
   1. Bolivia — Handbooks, manuals, etc.
   2. Peru — Handbooks, manuals, etc.
   I. Title II. Series
   918.4'045   F3309.5
   ISBN 0-946983-09-7

Photos and line drawings by the author.
Maps by the author, Caroline Tanner-Crump, and Nicola Tomlin.
Cover photo: Cordillera Huayhuash.

Printed and bound in Great Britain by
A.Wheaton and Company Ltd, Exeter, Devon.

Acknowledgements

My grateful thanks to backpacking readers, whose letters and phone calls have helped me update this book. Among those whose information was particularly useful are Hessel van Hoorn, Sverre Aarseth, Robert Eckhardt, Jo Gurney, Steve Newman, Lindsey Griffin, Stephen Connelly, Norman Croucher, Charles Helm, and others whose names are lost in the mists of time.

Warm thanks are due also to the Scurrah family for their friendship and hospitality over thirteen years, and to the Shreyers and Waltons who have also ensured that I am never lonely in Lima.

The authors

The first three editions of this book were written jointly by George and Hilary Bradt. George now runs a bookshop in Boston, USA, and although he has not been involved in this re-write his 'voice' is retained in many chapters, as are his stories about our joint travels.

I (Hilary) live in Buckinghamshire and spend three months or so each year leading tours in South America for Wilderness Travel of Berkeley, California. The rest of the year is spent slaving over a hot word-processor, writing and publishing travel guides.

Contributors

Pamela Holt   A horticulturist and leader of the 1986 Anglo Scottish Womens Andean Expedition, Pamela collected plants in Bolivia for Kew and the herbarium in La Paz. Sadly, her note books were subsequently stolen in the Cordillera Apolobamba.

John Pilkington   Co-author of *Backpacking in Chile and Argentina* and the author of *Into Thin Air*, an account of a solo trek through Nepal, John is a die-hard backpacker whose most recent adventure has been to retrace the old Silk Route to China.

Christopher Portway   Chris is an established travel writer with several books and numerous articles to his credit. In 1978 he and a companion explored the Inca road from Cuzco to Quito.

Rob Rachowiecki   Author of *Climbing and Hiking in Ecuador* and co-author of *Backpacking in Mexico and Central America,* Rob has gone on to write two books *(Ecuador* and *Peru)* in the highly popular Lonely Planet series of Travel Survival Kits.

Preface

The first edition of this book, cumbersomely entitled *Backpacking along Ancient Ways in Peru and Bolivia* was written in 1973 on a river boat in Bolivia, typed in the jungle town of Trinidad while waiting for transport out, and published in America. I have a particular affection for it, since it started George Bradt's and my writing and publishing career.

In the intervening years, two other editions have been produced and sold, and George and I have gone our separate ways.

Information for this fourth edition is drawn from updates from readers and my seven years of leading treks in Peru and Bolivia. However, George's and my joint experiences in South America (we travelled and hiked there together for a total of two years), which inspired this backpacking series, still form the core of the book. So you will find a mixture of 'we' and 'I' throughout; I hope this is not irritating.

Peru, and to a lesser extent Bolivia, have become much better known in recent years and backpacking and trekking are now part of many visitors' experiences. For the newcomer, let me repeat the preface to the last edition:

Backpacking in South America is not comparable to hiking in North America where areas are set aside for exclusive use by outdoor enthusiasts. The trails described in this book serve the same purpose as England's network of footpaths and lanes: linking village to village and providing easy access to market towns.

The tourist electing to become a traveller and to journey on foot in Peru and Bolivia, finds not wilderness but the incomparable blend of man and nature — the essence of the Third World.

We hope this book helps to increase your awareness of how the rural population lives, in addition to widening your appreciation of the natural history and wild mountain scenery you'll be walking through.

Table of Contents

Preparations. 1
When to go 2, What to bring 2, Backpacking equipment 5, Making do 8, Money 9, Photography 10.

Health & Safety 13
Before you go 13, Common medical problems 14, Mountain Health 16, Medicine kit 18, Safety 19, Thefts 20,Guerrillas 22, Leaving luggage 22, Insurance 23.

On (and off) the road 25
Transport 25, Accommodation 27, Food 27, Local dishes — Peru 28, Local dishes — Bolivia 30, Natural History 31, Flora 31, Birds 35, Mammals 38, The llama family 39, Geology 40, Mother Earth 41, Indians 42, Village life 43, Fiestas 45, Inca roads 49, Backpacking — the experience 51, Guides and pack animals 53, Minimum impact 54, Language 56, Quechua and Aymara 58.

Peru 61
Exits and entrances 62, Currency 62, Miscellaneous information 62,Lima 64, Maps 65, Explorers Club 66, Useful addresses 67, National Parks 69, Cajamarca 70, Cumbe Mayo hike 71, Huaráz 79, Cordillera Blanca 79, Llanganuco to Santa Cruz 82, Q.Ulta to Colcabamba 87, Q.Honda to Chacas 89, Olleros to Chavín 91, Cordillera Huayhuash 95, Central Andes 100, Inca road 100, Pozuzo 101, The Cuzco area 103, Chinchero 105, Cordillera Vilcabamba 109, Inca Trail 109, Variations on the Inca Trail 117, Mollepata to Huayllabamba 119, Soray to Santa Teresa 122, Cordillera Vilcanota 125, Auzangate circuit 125, The Southern Route 133, Raqchi 136, Inca stone work 141, Arequipa 142, Colca canyon 144, Chalhuanca 145.

Bolivia 147
Exits and entrances 147, Currency 148, Miscellaneous information 148, La Paz 149, Pachamama 150, Maps 151, National Parks 152, Lake Titicaca 153, Cordillera Real 154, Takesi Trail 155, La Cumbre to Coroico 161, Zongo to La Cumbre 163, Huayna Potosí 165, Illimani to Chulumani 167, Sorata 170, Gold-Diggers Way 171, Cordillera Apolobamba 179, Curva to Pelechuco 180.

Trekking 183

Appendices 187
Bibliography 187, Measurements and conversions 190, Index 191, 192.

Foreword (to the third edition)

Most guide books have an aura of unreality. However accurate their information about buses, hotels and museums, you know (and often you hope) the country won't *feel* like that when you get there. But Bradt guides are different. All the accurate information a backpacker needs is there, plus practical tips such as no conventional guide ever provides. And the *feel* is there, too. Hilary and George are not standing on a podium, directing the tourist traffic. They are sharing with us their own adventures — their memories, their sometimes esoteric knowledge and the nitty-gritty lessons they have learned along the way. They don't make trekking in the Andes sound easy (it isn't), but they do make it sound fun and worthwhile, which it is.

The Bradt mixture is stimulating, sensitive, shrewd and succinct (I've always had a weakness for alliteration). Hilary and George know, respect and love the people and places they write about. If they recommend what sounds like an impossible climb to a remote 4,000 metre pass with the sort of view tourists never see, you know it can be done because they've done it with their own four feet, carrying all the necessary gear.

Any country may be visited at speed, but no country can be absorbed at speed. From train, bus, truck or car the landscape may be glimpsed, and photographed at halts, while museums, cathedrals and sights/sites are 'done' in the intervals. But truly to experience a country on a personal level one must walk, ride or cycle. Day after day, one is moved by the kindness of the locals, one curses or rejoices at the texture or gradient of the paths, one is elated by the beauty of deep valleys between grotesque peaks, by the splendours of the night sky at 4,000 metres, by the sound of the wind on the Puna. Or, occasionally, one is so badly bitten by river-gorge flies that it is hard not to throw oneself off the track onto the statutory jagged rocks far below.

Happily, more and more young people are recognising the futility of motor transport and are choosing to walk away from it all, carrying what they need for a few days, or a week, or even a fortnight. But those who have grown up in cities, and perhaps hiked only in 'tame' conditions, could at first find trekking in the Andes a trifle intimidating. That area can present a few minor problems to the beginner, all of which may be avoided or solved by reading *Backpacking and Trekking in Peru and Bolivia*. This book, however, is not only for beginners; it gives a great deal of information, not readily available elsewhere, about Indian culture, fiestas, and flora and fauna of the Andes. I just wish that my daughter and I had had it with us when we were trekking in the Andes; it would have added immensely to our enjoyment.

Enterprising travellers need no longer be rich to explore South America. Air fares — the Achilles heel of inflation — have dropped so dramatically on many international routes that nothing remains but to assemble a compact backpack (Hilary and George explain just how to keep it compact) and off you go.

Dervla Murphy

Preparations

Getting to Lima and La Paz

There are a fair number of relatively inexpensive flights to Lima from the United States and Europe. Here are a few suggestions, but you are advised to make your own enquiries since airlines offer and withdraw cheap flights with bewildering regularity.

From Europe Standard air fares from Europe to South America are high but the choice is improving. Viasa has been particularly recommended because their baggage allowance on the outward journey is double that of any other airline. They allow two bags weighing a maximum of 20kg each (but only a total of 20kg on the return journey). Their cheapest fare to Lima in 1986 was £500. An agency specialising in travel to South America, Journey Latin America (see advertisement), will arrange the best value flights and are very helpful with other travel arrangements. Other companies offering low cost flights are Trailfinders (42-48 Earl's Court Rd, London W8 6EJ) and WEXAS (45 Brompton Rd, London SW3 1DE).

Aeroflot have an inexpensive flight from Frankfurt to Lima (£400), with a stopover in Havana.

From the U.S.A. Happily 1987 saw the end of a long-standing squabble between the airlines of Peru and the United States that prevented their flying direct to each other's country. There are now plenty of flights to Peru and some to La Paz from all over the USA. AeroPeru flies from Los Angeles four times a week (cheapest fare $759; with two free stopovers in Peru) and also from other major cities, including, of course, New York and Miami. At the time of writing the best service is offered by Aerolineas Argentinas, which operate flights to Lima from eleven major U.S. cities for a flat rate of $800.

Most airlines flying from the US have the two bag system of luggage allowance, which is great for expeditions.

When to go

Peru and Bolivia share the same mountain weather pattern: the rainy season is from September to April, with most rain falling in November and December, and dry, sunny weather can be expected between May and September. In both countries, June and July are the finest months with August reasonably safe as well. However, no country is experiencing 'normal' weather these days, so you take your chances. Be prepared for rain or snow in the mountains at any time of year.

Lima and the west coast do not share these sunny months. When the Andes are bathed in sunshine, Lima sulks under perpetual low cloud, often accompanied by light drizzle. This *garua* lifts between September and April; while Lima gets its sun the highlands are soaked. All this leads to some marvellous confusions, since Peruvians and their neighbours refer to the dry months as summer (*verano*) and rainy months as winter (*invierno*). So, when the inhabitants of Huaráz and La Paz think it's summer, Limeños say it's winter, and vice versa. Confused?

Perhaps the very best month for backpacking in Peru and Bolivia is May. There may be some rain, especially during the first half of the month, but flowers are in full bloom, the grass is green, and the streams are full. The landscape is rather dried up by late August. During the wet season it doesn't rain every day, so if you have good rain-gear and a decent tent you'll enjoy some clear, sunny mornings, torrential afternoon storms, and your own company. Few gringos (foreigners) venture into the mountains during these months.

The weather in the Andes seems to be best around full moon — or so the locals say — so if possible plan your backpacking then.

What to bring

Fifteen years' experience of hiking and travelling in Peru has taught me a lot about luggage. I now know exactly what I need to keep myself happy and comfortable, but to avoid that frantic last minute search for these items I keep a large box in my room and throw things in as I come across them in the weeks leading up to a trip. Then all I have to do is make a final selection. Fully laden, my pack weighs about 20kg (44lbs), but I try to carry only 15kg or so when backpacking.

Clothes

Remember the old travellers' maxim 'bring twice as much money and half as many clothes as you think you'll need'. All of your clothes should be chosen for comfort, but select one outfit (a dress for women, a decent shirt for men) which will render you respectable for that blow-out in a good restaurant, or an invitation to visit an upper class home.

A popular saying describes a day in the Andes as including all the seasons of the year. Nights are as cold as winter, mornings are springlike, afternoon heat can be as fierce as summer, and evenings have an autumn crispness. This means extreme temperature changes, and backpackers should be prepared accordingly.

In the mountains, cold is the biggest enemy (temperatures drop to well below freezing at night). Obviously you must keep yourself really warm without adding too much weight to your pack. Thermal underwear is very useful for these freezing nights, being light but very warm. A down parka (duvet) is warm and light, or you may prefer a wool sweater and nylon windbreaker. Locally bought alpaca sweaters are ideal. You'll also need a woollen hat (again, a *chullo* like the local men wear is beautifully warm), a sun hat (with a brim or a 'Beau Geste' flap at the back), a scarf, and gloves — fingerless gloves (which can be bought locally) are useful. Several pairs of wool socks are essential.

Since you'll warm up rapidly in the sun and through exertion, you should be able to peel off successive layers of clothing during the day. (That's the problem with thermal underwear, it's lovely in the early morning when you're packing up the tent with frost-numbed fingers, but once you start walking and sweating you have to strip down to nothing to take it off. Still, it's a convenient excuse for an early rest stop). Cotton trousers over woollen tights or long underwear are more versatile than woollen trousers/pants. Corduroy is also light and warm. I used to tell people not to bring jeans, since they are too hot for the day, too cold for the night, and take ages to dry when soaked by rain or the bi-monthly wash. However, I've noticed that I no longer take my own advice, so assume that jeans are a necessary part of a traveller's luggage. Even so, *try* to take two pairs of tough cotton pants rather than denim. Shorts are comfortable during the day, but don't wear them in town where they may cause offence or ribald laughter.

Give some thought to pockets. All trousers should have deep pockets, preferably secured with a button or zip, and they're handy in shirts (and skirts) as well. You may have to add them yourself.

A jogging suit is marvellously versatile and can be used as pyjamas at night, leisure wear in hotels, and worn under other clothing gives you an extra warm layer.

Bring at least one long-sleeved shirt as protection against insects and sun.

Trainers (running shoes) or sneakers are useful for the evening around camp, for fording rivers, and wearing in towns and cities with your better clothes. Trekkers, who are not carrying a heavy pack, sometimes prefer them for hiking, but they do not provide the necessary ankle support for backpackers.

Bring rubber 'thongs' (flip-flops) to protect your feet in dubious bathrooms, and bring a swimsuit for those lovely thermal pools.

Warning Do not wear anything remotely resembling military uniform. In a country where the army is fighting guerrillas this is quite literally suicidal.

Miscellaneous useful items*

Small torch (flashlight) with spare bulb and batteries, travel alarm clock (or alarm wrist-watch), penknife (preferably Swiss Army knife), sewing kit, safety pins, large needles and strong thread for tent repairs, scissors. Masking tape, Sellotape (Scotch tape), Magic Marker (felt-tipped pens), an assortment of pencils and ballpoint pens, a small notebook, a large notebook for diary and letters home. Plastic bags ('Zip-Loc' type most useful), universal plug for baths and sinks, elastic clothesline, or cord and clothes pegs, small scrubbing brush, concentrated detergent (obtainable in tubes from camping shops) for city washing, liquid soap (in tubes) for non-polluting camp washing, shampoo, soap (in plastic container), towel, toilet roll, dental floss (excellent for repairs as well as teeth), toilet paper. Ear plugs (a godsend in noisy hotels and night buses), insect repellent, sunscreen, handcream, lipsalve, spare glasses or contact lenses, medicine kit (see *Health*). Compact binoculars, camera, plenty of film. A couple of paperback books (you can swap them with other travellers), a phrase book and Spanish dictionary, two miniature packs of cards, Scrabble and/or a pocket chess set.

A 2-litre water container, water purifying tablets, waterproof matches, slow-burning candles, compass, polaroid sun glasses, waterproofing for boots, and large plastic dustbin liners (garbage bags) for covering packs at night.

Finally, a friend doing a project in the *sierra* says her most indispensable item was a potato peeler.

Presents and bribes

You'll want to bring presents for local people, but *please* read *Village life* and *Minimum Impact* before buying gifts and distributing them to all and sundry.

Family photos and postcards of home make ideal 'show and tell' items. Bring lots of postcards of cities and be prepared to give them away; pictures of beautiful scenery are less interesting to rural Peruvians for obvious reasons. Postcards or photos of the royal family (particularly the Princess of Wales) always go down well. English language magazines are much sought after. Ballpoint pens, pencils, mirrors, fish hooks, and so on, all make acceptable presents, and how about potato peelers for those *sierra* women? Children love balloons, badges, and bubblegum.

More expensive items, such as calculators and digital watches are much appreciated by guides or *arrieros* (muleteers), and may help to get you out of a spot of trouble or ensure good service, but don't be too free with gifts in this way. It makes it much harder for more scrupulous travellers who follow you.

*Words in brackets indicates American usage.

Backpacking equipment and provisions

Experienced backpackers probably already own all the equipment necessary for a South American trip. Newcomers to backpacking should seek the advice of more experienced friends before making any purchases. A good backpacking shop should be able to advise you and climbing/ walking magazines always have good, disinterested information. If you will be doing some extensive shopping, Field and Trek (3 Wates Way, Brentwood, Essex CM15 9TB) puts out a very comprehensive outdoor equipment catalogue.

The advice below is a rough guide only; new equipment for backpackers is constantly coming on the market.

Backpack No serious backpacker these days uses a pack with an external frame; the advances made in recent years in ergonomic design enables you to have a much more comfortable and practical pack with an internal frame. Karrimor and Berghaus are the leading manufacturers in England, and Kelty and Lowe are highly recommended in the USA.

Boots Comfortable lightweight hiking boots with Vibram soles are necessary for serious backpacking. Make sure they are properly broken in before your trip. Gaiters keep you warm and dry in snow or bog, and are useful for river-crossings.

Sleeping Bag Although some very effective synthetic fillers are now on the market, you still can't beat goose-down, which is the lightest and warmest insulation around. Backpacking in the Andes poses a problem, however, in that in the valleys the nights can be quite warm and you may be too hot in the bag which is just right for four thousand metres. Your best bet is to have a sleeping bag cover — or liner — which gives you the versatility for moderate and freezing temperatures. If you have only one sleeping bag it should be rated down to -5°C or 20°F.

A sheet sleeping bag not only keeps your down bag clean, but is perfect for jungle hiking and for use in hotels which are economical with their laundering of sheets.

A tee shirt stuffed with a sweater makes a good pillow. Or bring an inflatable pillow cum cushion (see below).

Space blankets, loved by some, hated by others, are nevertheless life-saving. Norman Croucher, the legless mountaineer, recommends using adhesive tape to create an emergency survival bag from a space blanket. As I write, an injured winter climber on Ben Nevis has been praised by rescuers for avoiding death from hypothermia by using a plain plastic survival bag.

Mattress It's essential to have some sort of insulation from the cold ground as well as padding. Closed cell foam pads are the cheapest and provide perfect insulation and tolerable padding when only a centimetre thick. The best mat of all, however, is the Thermarest, a combination of air-mattress and foam pad. It's lightweight, compact — and expensive. If

you can't afford a full length Thermarest, there's a three-quarter length one, and failing that, the Sportseat, made by the same company. This square cushion is just big enough to pad your hips at night (in addition to a closed cell foam pad) and is excellent protection for your bottom on trucks and canoes.

Tent In the last edition of this book we wrote: 'Nothing fancy is needed'. Not needed, but having graduated to a good quality lightweight tent I wouldn't want to go back to cringing under a shower curtain. However, a good tent is expensive, so if you are hard up and will only camp occasionally, and in the dry season, you can make do with a simple shelter providing it doesn't weigh more than two or three kilos. If you buy a cheap tent, be sure to bring seam sealant to block those dripping seams.

Light Peruvian winter nights give you over twelve hours of darkness, so some sort of light is essential. A group will find it worth-while to bring a lantern (kerosene or Gaz), otherwise slow-burning candles are reasonably safe (they are short and squat so don't knock over) and last about nine hours. I am a recent convert to these. When John Hatt recommended them in his excellent book *The Tropical Traveller* I wrote 'rubbish! an ordinary candle is fine and can be bought all over the Third World'. I now concede that John is absolutely right, and that slow-burning candles are available in most camping shops, take up little room in your luggage, are almost unbreakable, and — at a pinch — edible!
Obviously, candles should be used with great care inside a tent.

Stove A good stove is one of the most important items on your equipment list, and worth spending some money on. Although it is just possible to get by with camp fires, these are not compatible with the minimum impact philosophy. They use scarce and valuable firewood needed by the local *campesinos* and leave ugly scars on the grass, and — worse — ancient stonework. When you see what thoughtless hikers have done to the Inca Gate of the Sun above Machu Picchu you will want to weep.
Probably the best stove for an Andean trip is the Optimus 'Camper' which burns paraffin (kerosene) — *kerosina* — which is found all over Peru and Bolivia. Even more practical are stoves that burn petrol (gasoline) as well as paraffin. The MSR stove, which runs on any fuel, is excellent.
I like the Bleuet Camping Gaz stoves because they are clean and simple to operate, but you are not allowed to take the cartridges on planes. They are quite easily bought in Peru, however.
For emergencies it's sensible to bring a tiny 'Hot Pot' — an aluminium cup and stand that burns tablets of solid fuel.
Bring 'Lifeboat' matches that don't blow out.

Pots and Pans   If you don't already own a lightweight aluminium saucepan, wait until you get to South America to buy one. Both countries sell ideal backpacking pans which are cheap and available in even the smallest towns. For those spending a long time in the mountains, Pamela Holt recommends a small pressure cooker, to reduce cooking time and fuel at altitude.

Plastic plates and mugs are more suitable than tin because the food and drink remain hot longer. A frisbee makes a fine plate and fine entertainment for you and the local kids, too. Aluminium spoons are lighter than stainless steel cutlery sets.

Dried Food   If you are coming to South America specifically for backpacking, you might as well bring much of your dehydrated food with you. However, there is a good choice of suitable pack food available in Peru and Bolivia. Trail snacks can be bought from street vendors. In Lima there are numerous stands selling chocolate, dried fruit such as raisins, dates and figs, as well as a variety of nuts. It is easy to make up your own CHORP (Chocolate, raisins and peanuts) before leaving for the mountains.

If you go to a good supermarket you'll find enough packet soups (Knorr and Maggi), noodles, sugar, oatmeal, dried milk, and so on to provide your hot meals. For lunches, cheese is excellent in both Huaráz and Cuzco; fresh bread and crackers can usually be bought in small villages, and there are powdered fruit drinks to make treated water more palatable. You can buy pumpernickel type bread in some shops in Lima which is perfect for backpacking.

Dried fruit and vegetables make excellent backpacking food, but are difficult to buy outside Lima. However, in the mountain towns the sun is so strong you can successfully dry your own, providing your hotel has a handy flat roof or balcony for the purpose. Just slice carrots, cabbage, onions and apples very finely and lay them in the sun to dry, turning them when necessary. It works!

What to bring from home? A few of your favourite freeze-dried dinners as a special treat, granola bars, powdered drink to add to that unpalatable purified water, and those handy re-usable plastic tubes filled with peanut butter, Marmite (for Brits, Vegemite for Aussies), jam, honey or whatever you fancy.

Making do

I realise that you may have bought this book in South America, and are now tearing your hair out because you haven't brought your backpacking gear with you. Don't worry, we were once in exactly the same position but managed to do several major hikes, and that was in the days before trekking became popular in the Andes. Finding equipment to rent is no longer a problem, although quality may be. Many trekking agencies and centres in Huaráz and Cuzco have equipment to rent. The South American Explorers Club in Lima often have items for sale. Also go to the most popular 'gringo hotels' and put up a notice requesting equipment. In this way you can probably acquire a sleeping bag and foam pad, a stove, and a tent. Primus stoves (heavy) can be bought in Lima or Cuzco markets. You probably won't be able to buy a backpack or boots second hand, but backpacks are sometimes sold in sports shops. Look up *Deportivo* in the telephone directory yellow pages to find the best shops. If the worst comes to the worst, you can have a backpack made. We met a girl in Ecuador with a beautiful *mochila* that a local tailor had made for her. Obviously you would have to design it yourself, and may have to omit the frame, but it would be better than nothing and inexpensive. Boots are a bigger problem because Peruvians have smaller feet than gringos, but if you're the dainty type and buy plenty of thick wool socks you'll be able to manage with a pair of locally bought canvas boots, such as volleyball or basketball players wear. These are adequate for most of the trails described in this book and less likely to hurt your feet than more expensive leather footwear.

If you don't have a tent and don't want to rent or buy one, you will survive with a large, strong sheet of plastic which you can pitch in a variety of ways. We managed with a shower curtain for fourteen months of backpacking during our first trip. One night two fighting dogs chased straight through our shelter, ripping it in half and scaring us out of our wits. We thought they were wolves. We made a proper tent after that.

Money

Information on each country's complicated money system is given in the relevent chapters. This section covers general considerations.

The only sensible currency to bring is US dollars. Other hard currencies are accepted in main cities, but will be impossible to change in smaller towns.

Bring your money in a combination of cash and travellers' cheques. Admittedly, there is a risk of the money being stolen (see *Security*), but some ingenious hiding places can be devised beforehand. A friend has just set out for Peru with $200 under the 'Odoreaters' in her hiking boots, and I travelled for eighteen months through South America with two $100 bills sewn into the hem of my trousers and skirt for emergencies (I remembered not to send them to the laundry). You will need cash for several reasons: banks and money change houses (*Casas de Cambio*) often entertain themselves by only agreeing to change dollars not travellers' cheques; anyone (taxi drivers, shop assistants, etc.) will change a small denomination bill; and many will change a high value bill at a considerably better rate of exchange than the official one. The black market comes and goes in both countries, but there is usually someone needing hard currency.

Bring travellers' cheques in denominations of $50 and up (I always seem to be waiting in a queue behind a traveller changing twenty $10 cheques; whatever your budget, you'll find you reduce the hassle of changing travellers' cheques by doing it as seldom as possible). American

Express are by far the best travellers' cheques to buy; they are quick and efficient in their refunds and are accepted everywhere. Be super-conscientious about recording the numbers of cheques changed and keeping a record of these numbers separate from your cheques. Don't sign your cheque until the bank clerk has given the go-ahead. I have been caught out by belatedly finding out that they have run out of cash, or are not changing cheques that day, or are just closing for lunch/Independence Day/Grandfather's funeral. Countersigned, your cheque is as enticing to thieves as money, and you may have difficulty in persuading the next cashier that you are not the felon.

Budgeting

Peru has always been cheap for those with hard currency, although the rise in tourism has meant sharp price rises in tourist areas. Bolivia fluctuates; one year it is ludicrously cheap and the only problem is finding a bag large enough to carry your money around in, next it is terribly expensive as the powers that be struggle to get a grip on inflation. At the time of writing prices are comparable, or a little cheaper, than Peru.

At the present rate of exchange a bare-bones budget of $10 a day is feasible — indeed, easy if you are doing a lot of backpacking in areas where there's nothing to spend your money on.

If, however, you're short of time and must really cover ground and want to enjoy yourself a little, then a budget of $20 to $30 a day, excluding air fares, is reasonable.

Backpacking is obviously the cheapest possible way of seeing a country. Your days, or weeks, in the mountains will cost almost nothing, but if you're like us you'll start having food fantasies towards the end of each hike and blow all the money you've saved on marvellous meals, hot baths and comfortable beds when you return to a city. Then it's difficult to get into the budget way of life again.

One way of making a little money is to sell your backpacking equipment. There's a good market for such things in Peru where the demand always exceeds the supply. The South American Explorers Club will sell your equipment for you, and Pyramid Adventures in Huaráz (and other trekking companies in that town and in Cuzco) is always looking for sleeping bags, day packs, and down parkas. You could certainly sell your backpack if you didn't mind carrying all your stuff home in a flour sack.

Bargaining for both goods (handicrafts) and services is normal in both countries, though huge discounts are not usually possible. This includes hotels; even the posh ones will often come down in price if they are half empty in the evening.

'Indeed, the efficiency of the Inca Government may well have been due to the fact that its records were verbal, thus eliminating quintuplicate forms and multiple signatures.'

Edward Lanning, Peru before the Incas.

Photography

Both Peru and Bolivia are wonderfully photogenic, and few visitors have the will power — or the desire — to travel without a camera. Here are a few tips on how to get the best out of photography in the Andes.

Camera and lenses If you are a serious photographer you will probably already own a 35mm SLR camera; for a backpacking or trekking trip you must cut down on weight and therefore on the variety of lenses you bring with you. For years I have carried an Olympus OM10 with a Tokina zoom lens with a range of 35mm to 105mm, and am completely happy with it. I, for one, would not like the hassle of changing lenses all the time, and I have seen weary trekkers give up lugging their camera equipment in their day packs and abandon it for the mules to carry. If you must take separate lenses, choose a wide angle (for markets) and a telephoto (for mountains and portraits).

The new compact cameras, many with automatic focusing, should be ideal for backpackers since they are so light. While most have a fixed lens, some have a telephoto, and this would be the best choice. Without one the magnificent Andes can look depressingly unspectacular.

Camera case Give some thought to this. Your camera should be easily accessible and the case or bag shockproof and waterproof. There's no telling how often you'll drop it or expose it to the rain.

Film Kodachrome 64 is the most suitable slide film, but bring a few rolls of fast film for poor light or interiors. I have been told that you can get wonderful results with Ektachrome 400 'pushed' to 1600 ASA (but you must tell the processing lab what you have done).

For prints 100 ASA will cope with bright and cloudy days.

Bring all your film from home, and bring much more than you think you could possibly need. You can always sell it. Film is either very expensive or unobtainable in Peru and Bolivia.

Miscellaneous A polarising filter brings drama to ordinary mountain scenes, and is particularly good for enhancing cloud. Bring spare camera batteries. Be careful of photographing people in bright sun — the harsh shadows of the tropics spoil what might otherwise be a good portrait; the softer light of a cloudy day will be better.

Camera courtesy Although the Indians of Peru and Bolivia are not, generally speaking, superstitious about photography, they quite reasonably resent being treated like safari lions, and surrounded by camera-clicking tourists. The natives of Cuzco and the area have shrewdly learned that their face is their fortune, and pose prettily with their llamas. They then demand, and often receive, an exhorbitant fee. 'After all, it's only a dollar', you may say, but consider that this is nearly as much as the child's father (or woman's husband) earns labouring in the fields all day. Apart from markets, when most people are too busy to curse photographers, you will not be able to take pictures of Indians in the Cuzco area unless you pay them. If you are a member of a group, have one person pay about 30 cents for all, and if you are alone or a couple, make sure you have plenty of small change before you go sightseeing.

Away from areas of mass tourism, avoid giving money or gifts for photographs (see *Minimum impact*). Often a smile or a joke will work wonders, as will the promise to send a copy of the photo. This gives great pleasure, and unlike successful begging does no harm, so do keep your promise.

In contrast to the Indians, those of mixed blood (*mestizos*) invariably love having their photos taken; though less picturesque than latter-day Incas, you can get some lovely cheeky portrait shots.

Health and safety

Health

Before you go   South America is not the hot bed of disease you may imagine, but routine inoculations should be taken: typhoid, tetanus and cholera, and a polio booster.

Most users of this book will not need malaria prophylactics since mosquitoes are not found above two and a half thousand metres. If, however, you are spending time in the jungle, you should take the appropriate preventative tablets. The Malaria Reference Laboratory in London (Tel: 01 636 8636) will give you the most up to date information on what is required.

Hepatitis is common in South America, so gamma globulin injections are strongly recommended. Although not one hundred percent effective in preventing the disease, I've yet to meet — or even hear of — someone who has caught hepatitis after being immunised with gamma globulin. The injections must be repeated every six weeks, so those on an extended trip should have it done locally. Pharmacists in Peru and Bolivia will give you a shot, but buy a new disposable needle yourself. Better still, bring some from home. With the new danger of Aids, improperly sterilised needles are a risk you shouldn't take. Talking of Aids, some travellers have been scared to have gamma globulin because it is made from blood serum, so carrying, they believed, a risk of Aids. John Hatt (*The Tropical Traveller*) reports that he has been assured, by the highest medical authorities, that there is no such risk. Hepatitis, on the other hand, is sometimes fatal.

If you do go down with hepatitis, you will receive the most up to date treatment in Peru or Bolivia where they are much more accustomed to the disease than in the west.

Fitness   Being in good physical condition is essential for all hikers, but fitness requirements are very different for independent backpackers planning a long trip, and trekkers or others on a short holiday where daily objectives must be achieved. The former will gradually get into shape on the trail, but the latter *must* make considerable efforts to achieve fitness before they go.

Backpackers have the enviable advantage of being able to camp when they choose, and fatigue in the early stages of a long trip is almost an advantage since it encourages a very slow ascent, so minimising the danger of altitude sickness. (Forget that, the weight of your pack at the start of the trail ensures that you go slowly and there's no point in letting lack of fitness add to your suffering).

Ideally, people signing up for an organised trek or expedition must start to get fit at least a couple of months before they leave. This preparation should as closely as possible resemble what they will actually be doing: hiking in the mountains. Therefore it is much better to walk briskly in hilly country than to run along level roads. Not all potential trekkers, of course, live close to suitable countryside, but everyone has access to flights of stairs, and walking, then running, up an increasing number of stairs is an excellent means of getting fit for the Andes. Walking to work in your hiking boots is a good, if embarrassing, activity, and cycling is also a great way of getting fit for trekking, since it involves the same muscles.

Experience of numerous trekking groups has made me something of a fanatic over the importance of fitness (in others. I don't extend it to myself). I've seen too many unfit people bring unhappiness and danger to themselves and spoil the enjoyment of others.

Before you go on a long trip, have a dental check-up; teeth often give problems at high altitudes. A medical check-up is advisable for anyone worried about his body's ability to cope with very high altitudes. And take out medical insurance.

Common medical problems

This list of the most common health problems and their treatment does not mean that you shouldn't visit a doctor in South America. Even if the medical setup down there isn't quite what you're accustomed to, remember that doctors in Latin America are well versed in diagnosing and treating local diseases. (Although I was a bit taken aback when a Lima doctor insisted on giving me a full — and mainly visual — chest examination when I consulted him for an ear infection.)

If you are unwilling or unable to see a doctor, pharmacists are used to treating the local population for minor complaints. But check the expiration date on any medicines they prescribe. Many drugs, available only on prescription in the U.S.A. or Britain, are available over the counter in South America, so don't worry about replacing your basic medical supplies there.

Remember that prevention is better than cure. Sterilise all water (even pure-looking mountain streams are often contaminated) by boiling, filtering, or with chlorine or iodine tablets. Do not allow bar-tenders to put ice-cubes in your drinks, and peel fruit and avoid salads and other raw vegetables.

Diarrhoea Almost everyone comes down with the trots in South America. Traveller's diarrhoea is caused by the bacteria *Escherischia* *coli* which everyone has in his intestines. The trouble is each geographical area has its own strain of *E.coli*, and these alien strains cause inflammation of the intestine and diarrhoea.

Everyone has his favourite remedy, and it is the subject of many a gringo conversation. Since most attacks of diarrhoea last only a day, it is best to wait it out and take no medication. Drink plenty of fluids (Coca-Cola is particularly good, and Coke syrup — available, so I have heard, in the USA — is even better) and eat bananas, papaya, mashed potatoes, and boiled rice. Or, if you have the will power, fast. The body's ability to absorb fluids and salts is greatly improved by taking sugar at the same time, so to counteract dehydration and loss of vital salts, sip a solution of salt (¾ teaspoon), baking soda (½ teaspoon), potassium chloride (¼ teaspoon), and sugar or dextrose (4 teaspoons). This 'electrolyte replacement' formula is effective and safe. Make up several packets before leaving home. Failing that, a flask of water containing 3 teaspoons of sugar to one of salt, can be made anywhere and will be beneficial.

If you are travelling by public transport or are in other places where a dash to the lavatory is impractical, some sort of chemical cork is required. John Hatt, who chases new information with unfailing energy, says that current medical opinion favours codeine-phosphate (available on prescription) followed by Lomotil. Don't be fooled into thinking these are a cure; they simply paralyse the gut.

Persistent diarrhoea, accompanied by a fever, should be treated with mild antibiotics. I have found Septrin and Bactrim particularly effective. Some people take antibiotics as a prophylactic against diarrhoea. However, although it may remove the diarrhoea risk from a short holiday in South America, taking antibiotics needlessly is never recommended, and a side effect of some, notably Vibromycin, is excessive sensitivity to the sun resulting in severe and very painful sunburn of the hands. I have experienced this myself with Vibramycin and have been with two other trekkers with the same symptoms. It is evidently a side-effect not known by all doctors who prescribe the drug, because most people are not subjected to sunlight of Andean intensity.

Long-term and seasoned travellers will find they gradually build up a nice collection of South American *E.coli* in their intestines. Having made an annual visit to Peru for seven years, I very rarely get diarrhoea nowadays, even when all the rest of the group come down with it.

Dysentery If, in addition to diarrhoea, you have severe stomach cramps, pass blood in your faeces and run a fever, then you probably have dysentery. A doctor or a clinical laboratory (*analsis clinico*) should confirm the diagnosis before you take medication. Flagyl is effective for amoebic dysentery, as is tetracycline, but in a very severe case when there is also vomiting, get an injection of Dehidroemetina.

Fever If you develop a fever for any reason you should rest and take aspirin. But bring a supply of ampicillin, penicillin, or tetracycline with you since you could be struck by some infection in a hopelessly inconvenient place. Under these circumstances, take an antibiotic as prescribed, but not for longer than four or five days without seeing a doctor (and note the side-effect mentioned above).

Sores and skin infections   If the infection is serious, you will need an antibiotic, taken regularly and over a period of several days, to clear it up. A slow healing sore can be speeded on its way by applications of honey or papaya.

Athletes' foot can be a problem (see page 73). Treat it before it cripples you. Tinactin in powder form is usually effective, but I needed a course of antibiotics. Gentian Violet, readily available in South America, is said to be a cheap and efficient treatment.

Colds and coughs   In my experience this is the most common ailment affecting visitors to Peru — even more than diarrhoea. I suspect the dramatic temperature changes in the Andes are largely to blame: people go sightseeing in Cuzco wearing only a tee-shirt, and return blue with cold when clouds or the sudden dusk puts an end to the hot sun.

Colds easily turn into coughs and even bronchitis in these conditions, so as well as decongestants, bring cough medicine and sore-throat lozenges.

Motion Sickness   The local people are not the only ones to suffer on the rough roads in the Andes. Dramamine or Diodoquin are effective and can be used as sleeping pills in an emergency!

Mountain Health
Paradoxically, backpacking in the Andes is both the healthiest and the most dangerous mode of travel. Fortunately the killers — hypothermia, pulmonary oedema, and cerebral oedema — can be avoided if you read this section carefully.

Hypothermia   Simply put, this means that the body loses heat faster than it can produce heat. The combination of wind and wet clothing can be lethal, even if the air temperature is well above freezing. Trekkers and those on day hikes are more likely to have problems with hypothermia than backpackers, who, by definition, carry their requirements with them. So if you are only carrying a daypack, make sure you include a wool sweater, a windbreaker, a waterproof and, if possible, a survival bag, however settled the weather looks when you set out. Your porters or pack animals may easily be delayed and you can get thoroughly chilled while waiting for them. Also, should you stray away from the group and become lost, the main danger to your life is taken care of. Backpackers should concentrate on keeping their warm clothes and sleeping bag dry (everything should be kept in plastic bags) and carry a space blanket survival bag for emergencies.

There are various ways of keeping warm without relying on heavy or expensive clothing. Wear a wool ski-hat, or *chullo*, to prevent heat loss from your head. Make sure heat can't escape from your body through the collar of your windbreaker; use a scarf or a roll neck sweater. Eat plenty of trail snacks with a high calorie content. Hot drinks have a marvellously warming effect. Have one just before going to sleep. Heat a stone in the campfire, or fill your water bottle with hot water, and treat yourself to a 'hotty' at night (the latter also gives you ice-free water in the morning). Wrap both the rock and the bottle in a towel first, though.

If a member of your party shows symptoms of hypothermia — uncontrolled shivering followed by drowsiness and confusion — he must be warmed up immediately. Exercise is exhausting and eventually results in worse hypothermia. Conserve energy, raise the blood sugar with food, give hot drinks, and put the person in a warmed dry sleeping bag under cover. If his condition is serious, climb (naked) into the sleeping bag with him and use your own body heat as a radiator.

Injury All the hikes described in this book take you well away from civilisation, but most are on good and well-frequented trails. Be careful and sensible. Remember that a badly injured person cannot easily be evacuated from the Andes, and that you may or may not be able to persuade local people to assist you.

All backpackers should be conversant in first aid, or should carry a first aid booklet. There are some excellent ones specifically for mountain medicine (see *Bibliography*). The medicine kit should contain closures for large wounds (that would normally need stitching). Butterfly closures or Steristrips are good. Zinc-oxide tape is useful for holding a dressing in place (bring a few sterile gauze dressings) and has many other uses as well.

Sunburn The combination of equatorial sun and high altitude makes sunburn a real danger to backpackers in the Andes. Protect yourself with clothing and a really good suncream made for skiers or mountaineers (with a protection factor of 10 to 15). Lipsalve is essential to prevent cracked lips. Remember how vulnerable your nose is. Wear a hat and a long-sleeved shirt, at least until you have built up a protective tan.

High altitude sickness
This may be divided into three categories: Acute Mountain Sickness (AMS), Cerebral Oedema and Pulmonary Oedema.

All three variations are brought on by a too-hasty ascent to altitudes above two thousand four hundred metres without allowing time to acclimatise. Each can be prevented by climbing slowly, not more than three hundred metres daily, or even slower if a member of the climbing party shows any signs of AMS. Youth and fitness are no advantage; children and teenagers are particularly susceptible to mountain sickness, and even Sir Edmund Hillary once had to be evacuated from a Himalayan peak!

Acute mountain sickness Known locally as *soroche*, this is the most common of the three variations. The symptoms are severe headache, nausea, and sleeplessness. If the victim is only mildly active, drinks plenty of liquids, and takes aspirin (for the headache) for a day or two, these symptoms should moderate. Irregular (Cheyne-Stokes) breathing during sleep affects some people at high altitude. It is harmless, but disturbing both to the sleeper and his companion. One Diamox tablet before bed should help (see below).

Some very useful studies have been made on the use of Acetazolamide (Diamox) for preventing AMS. Southampton University tested the drug in the Andes and made the following report: 'Slow release acetazolamide 500mg daily or placebo were taken by a mixed sex group ascending rapidly to three thousand six hundred metres. Those taking Acetazolamide had fewer symptoms of AMS than those on placebo.' Reports that Diamox causes drowsiness and mental impairment were not borne out by the tests. This drug is a mild diuretic, so an irritating side effect is a frequent need to urinate.

Cerebral oedema This is a more dangerous type of altitude sickness. Fluid accumulates in the brain, and can cause permanent brain damage or death. The symptoms are intense headache or neckache, staggering gait, confusion, disorientation and hallucinations. Anyone showing signs of cerebral oedema should be taken down to a lower altitude immediately.

Pulmonary oedema More common than cerebral oedema and equally dangerous. Fluid collects in the lungs, literally drowning the person if his ill-health is not recognised. He must be taken to a lower altitude immediately. The symptoms are shortness of breath when at rest, coughing, frothy bloodstained sputum, and a crackling sound in the chest. Each year climbers die in the Andes from pulmonary oedema because they have not taken the time to acclimatise.

Avoid altitude sickness by giving the body a chance to adjust to the shortage of oxygen. If you have flown directly to Cuzco or La Paz, rest for the first day, avoid alcohol, and take it easy for the next few days. Some people find coca tea helps. Allow at least five days before starting your backpacking trip in the local *cordillera*, and then go very slowly and easily for the first couple of days. Breathe deeply and drink lots of water (more than you feel you want). Acclimatization is achieved when the heartbeat is normal at rest, you can eat and sleep well, and have no headache.

If you experience any of the symptoms of AMS while backpacking, rest for a couple of days. Then, if you don't feel better, turn back.

Medicine kit
Water purifiers, antiseptic cream, Vaseline (for cracked heels), 'moleskin' and adhesive-backed foam rubber (made by Scholl) for blisters and sore feet, butterfly closures or Steristrips, crepe (ace) bandage, Elastoplast

('dressing strip' best), Lomotil or other diarrhoea remedy, aspirins, Septrin or Bactrim, Ampicillin, thermometer, decongestants, cough and throat pills, antifungal cream and powder.

Safety

You can be put into jail fairly easily in South America. You can also be robbed. Care and common sense go a long way in avoiding such inconveniences.

Police

If you get into some sort of involvement with the police in these parts, stay cool and friendly. I know that isn't always easy, but getting hot and hostile doesn't help your case. Remember that these men are probably poorly educated and poorly paid, and having power over a rich and clever gringo is bound to have intoxicating effects. Cigarettes soften the atmosphere sometimes, and often money has a calming effect. This last resort should be discreetly handled, and only used in grave emergencies.

John Hatt advises that you shake hands with any official with whom you are about to have dealings. I have found this excellent advice; the action subtly puts you on an equal footing as well as being a universally recognised courtesy.

If you are the victim, rather than the perpetrator of the offence, the police can be extraordinarily kind and helpful. I had a meeting with the Lima Tourist Police recently when a member of my group had her necklace snatched. It took most of the morning, and we didn't get the gold chain back, but we were given a certificate for insurance purposes and the matter was handled efficiently and courteously.

Drugs Both Peru and Bolivia take drug offences seriously, with long terms of imprisonment for those caught. Whatever the temptation, it isn't worth it.

The chewing of coca leaves is a different matter; small quantities of coca can legally be bought in many highland markets.

Theft

Unfortunately theft is rife in Peru, although mostly confined to tourist areas. Bolivia is much safer (presumably because there are fewer tourists). The best defence against thieves is to know their methods and be continually on guard. Basically, theft falls into three categories:

Unguarded possessions Don't leave your luggage unless you are sure that it is properly guarded or under lock and key. A chain with a combination lock is extremely useful for this purpose. Combination locks are better than padlocks because thieves haven't yet learned how to pick them.

Airports come into the 'unguarded luggage' category, and Lima has a particularly bad record in this respect. One traveller wrote to the *Globe* magazine recently claiming it was impossible to fly to Lima without being robbed. It may seem that way to the unfortunate victim, but I have taken at least ten international flights into Lima, and never lost items from my luggage. I take the following precautions: my backpack is transported inside a strong canvas sack, tied at the neck with cord. Airport thieves are looking for easily opened luggage that looks valuable. Mine fails on both counts. If I have a duffle bag or suitcase I lock it (combination lock) and add further protection by strapping sticky tape (insulating tape is fine) around the luggage and across the opening so it would be obvious if anyone had tampered with it. Anything of great value — camera, binoculars, etc., is carried on as handluggage and once off the aircraft I never put it down for any reason.

Backpack pockets are a great temptation to a thief who has a brief encounter with your unattended luggage, perhaps on a train or bus, so have detachable pockets that can be put inside the pack when travelling, or keep only smelly socks in there.

Don't leave washing on the hotel line overnight, and try to keep an eye on it during the day.

Thefts from the person Handbag snatching, slashing and pickpocketing are very common. Attach a thin chain to your purse and secure it to your trousers or belt. The same method protects your penknife and handbag. In fact you shouldn't carry a handbag because they are prime targets for thieves with razors who slit the bottom or side. I just can't manage without a handbag of some sort, however, and have developed enough awareness of potentially dangerous situations to have kept it intact (in South America, at any rate). Mine is a woven bag which is considerably harder to slit than leather, it has a zip fastener, and I carry it round my neck and over one shoulder so it is always in the front of my body (one of the best-observed details in the film *Missing* is the way the heroine always carried her bag this way). One of these days I mean to make a bag with an un-cuttable inter-lining — mosquito screen netting would seem to be suitable — then I can carry all my bits and pieces my favourite way, and laugh at the kids with their razor blades.

Never hang a bag over the back of your chair in a restaurant. Always have it on your lap and, for extra security, put the strap round your chair leg.

Never wear jewellery such as gold chains, earrings, and expensive looking watches. Leave them at home.

Take the time to make an extra strap for your camera so it can be attached to your belt as well as round your neck.

Never carry a large quantity of money or passport in outside pockets. They can be slit or picked. Use a money belt or neck pouch, or a special pocket sewn *inside* your trousers. But bear in mind that retrieving this money can be embarrassing. For small amounts of money a pocket in your shirt is much less likely to be slit or picked than one in your trousers.

Be aware of the methods of pickpockets. They generally work in twos or threes, with one distracting the chosen victim while the others work him over. If you know your money is safely hidden under your clothes you can relax.

Armed robbery Fortunately this is still very rare in Peru and Bolivia, but not unknown. The most usual weapon is a knife or machete, used as a threat only. There's nothing you can do in such a situation except give them what they are after (although an elderly trekker recently beat off an armed robber on the Inca Trail with his walking stick).

Walking around lonely or slummy areas alone can be dangerous, especially at night or in the early morning. Your money and valuables are safer in a well-locked secure hotel room or in the hotel safe box, than on your person.

In any country there are high-crime and low-crime areas. All cities and tourist spots have their thieves. With its large number of tourists Cuzco has become the centre for robberies in Peru, although certain parts of Lima (Plazas San Martin and de Armas, Parque Universitario, markets and bus stations) are almost as bad. In other parts of the country, markets, trains and stations are all risky places where your handbag or money-bulging pockets are particularly vulnerable. Avoid crowds if you are carrying anything of value.

Rural Peru and Bolivia are still very safe, although unfortunately the numbers of 'rich' foreigners travelling through some of the villages have given the *campesinos* a new consumer awareness. Only a very few of the best known trails, suffer from this problem. To protect your valuables while hiking, your best bet is to keep them in a pouch at the bottom of your rucksack (see below). Provided you don't leave this unattended, no robber is going to take the time to rummage through it — they know where gringos keep their money.

Generally speaking it is best to camp out of sight from houses, and avoid attracting attention to yourself. In contrast with my city experiences, I've never been robbed, or felt in danger of being robbed, in the countryside.

Here is a summary of ways to protect your valuables:
Use a neck pouch, money belt, or inside pocket for cash and passports. All can be easily made from soft cotton (nylon is too sweaty). On a neck pouch the strap should be strong (a thin chain is suitable as it looks like jewellery) and the right length, so the pouch hangs inconspicuously under your loose clothing. A money belt is less visible (but most won't hold a British passport). Hidden under several layers of clothing, it may not even be detected in a body search. I use a zipped bag, just big enough for passport and money, with loops and press-fasteners (snaps) which allow it to be attached to a variety of places: under clothing, round a leg under trousers, or deep in a pack where loops have been sewn to secure it.

Leg pouches have recently become popular and John Hatt swears by Tubigrip, an elasticised tube of bandage, for making an instant leg pouch for holding money, etc. This is only appropriate as a place of security; with today's tight trouser bottoms it is impossible to reach your calf without undressing, so don't go shopping with all your money on your leg.

Emergency money in the form of one or two large dollar bills is totally safe carried under the inner sole of your boots; an excellent hiding place.

Rather than carry your passport around with you, keep handy some other form of identification such as a driving licence.

Before you leave home, write down the numbers of your passport, traveller's cheques, plane ticket, credit cards, and any other vital information, photocopy it, and keep a copy in a variety of places in your luggage.

The safest place for valuables is in a hotel safe. If your cheap hotel doesn't have a one, give your goodies to the manager in a large envelope (bring a few from home) that is sealed and signed by yourself across the seal. Get a receipt.

Shut and lock hotel doors and windows at night. A rubber wedge will keep the door closed if you suspect the lock or hotel staff are unreliable. When you go out during the day, if you can't leave your valuables with the management, find a safe hiding place in your room. Sticky tape enables you to attach things to places no-one would ever look. Don't forget to retrieve them yourself when you leave!

Remember, the point of all the above advice is not to make you paranoid, but to allow you to relax and enjoy the millions of Peruvians and Bolivians who wouldn't dream of robbing you.

Guerrillas

The stark facts are that since 1963 the *Sendero Luminoso* (Shining Path) terrorists have killed over nine thousand people. Although their aims remain vague, a Maoist state and restoration of the Inca Empire are said to be their goal. Their activities started in Ayacucho and have since moved north into the jungle.

I am not aware of any tourists being killed or harmed by *Senderistas* and the danger to backpackers seems minimal. Even so, it would be wise to seek local advice before trekking in the Vilcabamba region or in the mountains around Ayacucho.

Leaving luggage

Like all travellers, George and I would finish our trips with far more luggage than when we started. Maps accumulated, we bought handicrafts, collected books, and our packs became quite unpackable. So we became accustomed to finding a safe place to leave our unwanted luggage while we hiked. We always found a hotel that would keep a bag for us, usually free. Bring a lockable bag for this purpose, and make sure it is put under lock and key or somewhere safe, and get a receipt. Avoid leaving luggage in gringo hotels; unfortunately your fellow travellers are not all as honest as you are and the policy of claiming your own bag invites theft. If you must use a communal luggage dump, chain your bag to something, or at least put your passport number, name, and date on it with instructions to give it to no-one else.

Insurance

In addition to medical insurance, it's well worthwhile getting luggage insurance for your trip to Peru and Bolivia. As you will have gathered by now, robbery is a real possibility and the knowledge that you can get reimbursed for your precious possessions does something to allay the grief.

American Express and Thomas Cook both sell good travel insurance (you might as well get medical coverage from the same company), but read the fine print carefully before you buy it. We've had more claims turned down than accepted.

When buying medical insurance make sure you are covered for mountain sports (i.e. backpacking).

After several years of running the Lima office of the South American Explorers Club, Ethel Greene has written a highly informative — and nerve racking — report on *How not to get robbed in Peru*. This is available only to club members but I couldn't resist including extracts:

'Thieves work in groups and include charming little children and huggable grandmother types...They usually present a pleasant professional type of appearance...

GAMES THIEVES PLAY
'Sucio, sucio!' Shampoo is squirted on you or your backpack. A friendly, nicely dressed person approaches you and offers to help clean it off. ...In trying to wipe the stuff off they manage to separate you from your bag/ pack/suitcase... Ignore the person and go directly to your hotel.
'Fuckie, fuckie!' Men, beware of women who approach you with a sexual proposition and have their hands lovingly carress your body. They are good pickpockets.
'General Distraction' If you are watching your luggage beware of anyone who comes up to talk to you or tries to distract your attention. Fights may be staged for this purpose.

Local Transport

On (and off) the road

Transport

In terms of availability, public transport is excellent in both Peru and Bolivia. Any village served by some sort of road will have some sort of vehicle running there on some sort of regular schedule.

Buses   These come in various shapes and sizes, from luxury vehicles speeding along the intercity routes, to ramshackle affairs serving the rural villages. I'm happy to pay the extra for luxury. These buses are more reliable and comfortable, and not quite as dirty as the cheaper variety. The amount of fruit peel, paper, babies' pee, and vomit that the average South American family can dispose of during a lengthy trip has to be seen to be believed.

All buses stop for meals, but not necessarily at mealtimes. Make sure you understand how long you will be stopping, or the bus will leave without you. Better still, have your meal within sight of the driver. Plenty of snacks are available from local vendors who will pour on to the bus and crowd round the windows at every village, but fill your waterbottle before you leave.

Your luggage will be tied to the roof or, in posh buses, be stowed away in the luggage compartment. Either way, it will be inaccessible, so bring warm clothes and something to use as a pillow during night trips (those crescent-shaped inflatable pillows that fit round your neck are offered for sale in mail-order catalogues and some camping shops and are excellent for long journeys). You'll also need games or a book for entertainment during unexpected delays or breakdowns. Keep your passport on you for police checks, and watch your luggage like a hawk. Robbery is common on buses.

Trucks   Lorries/trucks form the backbone of public transport in both countries. Remote villages are served by trucks carrying cargo and a few passengers, but vehicles carrying only people ply between larger towns. They are cheaper than the buses covering the same routes, but even more uncomfortable, and of course it's very cold in the Andes. However, since the views are so much better than anything you can see through a dirty bus window, trucks should be your choice when the scenery is known to be outstanding. Although some trucks run to a schedule, most wait until they have collected enough passengers to make the trip worthwhile. Don't be misled by the driver telling you he is leaving '*ahorita*'. His and your concept of 'now' may be different.

Keep all your warm clothes (gloves, cap and even your sleeping bag) handy, and carry your foam pad to cushion those bare boards. Not all trucks have a tarpaulin, so bring protection from rain and snow.

It's a good idea to strap your pack onto the side of the truck so that it's neither trampled by other passengers, nor resting in a nice pool of oil or urine during the trip. With the same problems in mind, a sheet of plastic or newspaper to put under your pad isn't a bad idea. Bring something to eat and drink during long trips, although long-distance trucks, like buses, stop for meals.

Don't take a truck at night unless you are absolutely desperate and well prepared for freezing weather. Departure times are so flexible you should assume that an afternoon trip will become a night trip.

Colectivos These shared taxis run between major cities on regular schedules, and only cost a little more than the luxury buses.

Trains Although slower than buses, trains are a pleasant alternative — and the views are better. The train from Lima to Huancayo runs along the highest standard gauge track in the world, reaching a height of 4,780 metres. There are several other memorable trips; particularly popular is the Cuzco to Puno journey. Train seats are bookable in advance for first and special classes, but if you want to see local life, queue with the Indians for second class seats. In Peru nowadays, first class is almost pure gringo.

Bolivia has an efficient and intriguing variation, the *ferrobus*. This is a self-powered railway carriage which looks a little foolish zooming down the tracks all on its own.

Hitchhiking Relatively easy on the major roads, but hardly worth it in the mountains where there are few private cars and trucks are cheap and plentiful. If you're hitching, remember the drivers of jeeps and pick-up trucks usually expect to be paid, but car drivers don't. There's no rule about this, it depends on the affluence of the driver, but it is courteous to offer payment unless the fellow is conspicuously well off.

Aeroplanes The roads in Peru and Bolivia are still very bad, so even the most dedicated overlander should consider taking a plane from time to time. Although superficially it costs double the bus fare, a flight saves so much time that it may end up by being only a little more expensive. The gruelling Lima to Cuzco trip for example; I've done it twice by bus, using different routes. That's enough.

Although domestic flights are inexpensive, international ones cost a lot more, so it's worth taking a bus across the border.

Aeroplanes are frequently overbooked. Confirm, reconfirm, and reconfirm again if you think there's any doubt about your getting on a particular plane, especially during the peak tourist season of August.

Accommodation

There is always a wide variety of hotels to choose from in Peru and Bolivia, from cheap to luxurious. If neither of these two extremes appeal, there are an increasing number of middle price hotels. These are not up to European or American standards, but then they're half the price. In both countries, for around $15 a couple should get a room with private bathroom and hot water, clean towels and sheets, and in a fairly central location.

Really cheap hotels, such as are found in small towns and around train and bus stations in cities, cost about $1 to $2 per night, per person. You get a lumpy bed, no washbasin, no heat, little light, and often no bed linen. The communal toilet is likely to be in the yard, and rather unsavoury. The plumbing, if there is any, will be weak so don't strain it by trying to flush paper down it. There is usually a little box or basket in the corner — that's where your paper goes. And it's usually *your* paper. Few cheap hotels provide any. But, on the bright side, your dollar often buys friendly service, humorous incidents, and fellow guests who are not all foreigners.

The South American Handbook, that indispensable travel companion, has the most up to date listing of hotels in all price ranges, in every city, town and village.

In villages that have no obvious hotel, there is always a Señora with a room to let for the night. Just ask around. Or you may be happier camping. This is perfectly safe all over Bolivia, and away from the tourist centres in Peru, although, sadly, reports of theft from tents are increasing.

Food

Eating in both Peru and Bolivia is very pleasurable. There are all sorts of tasty snacks sold on street corners and cafes, and even the cheapest restaurant food is good, although starchy. Green vegetables are rarely served. You don't have to choose from the menu, even if you can interpret it. All restaurants will serve eggs, rice, and potatoes if you ask for them. But it's more fun to experiment with local food. Bring your dictionary to a restaurant, and don't be ashamed to wander around viewing other customers' plates. For beginners this is often the easiest way of selecting a meal — simply point to someone else's.

Most cheap restaurants (sometimes called *Picanterias*) — and some expensive ones — serve a set meal at lunchtime. This will include soup, and is quicker and cheaper than making your own selection, and essential during bus halts when you have limited time.

All markets have a *comedor* (eating area) which provides the cheapest and often tastiest meals in town, with the added advantage that you can see what's cooking. Always ask the price before ordering. You will see all sorts of tempting fruits and vegetables in the market; we often got together with other travellers and prepared an enormous salad — green or fruit — to share between us. If you do this remember to wash the lettuce in purified water, and to peel the appropriate vegetables and fruit.

In both Peru and Bolivia there are numerous Chinese restaurants known as *Chifas*. (Chinese labourers were brought in to build the railways all over South America, and many stayed on.) *Chifa* food is invariably good, and sometimes great.

Local Dishes — Peru

Restaurants in tourist areas have been falling over themselves trying to provide menu translations but unfortunately the same non-English speaking translator seems to have been used throughout the country so the entertainment value is greater than its usefulness. Our favourite was '*Langostin*: a small locust', with 'Bifstek with pickpocket sauce' a close second.

The classic Andean dish *cuy*, guinea pig, is rarely offered in tourist restaurants. You can sometimes buy it at street stalls during fiestas, or at restaurants with Indian clientele.

Guinea pig, served teeth and all in Cuzco

The following list should help those who are not looking for locusts or guinea pigs.

For starters you may be offered:
Palta rellena: Avocado filled with chicken salad.
Palta reina: Avocado filled with mixed salad and mayonnaise.
Papas huancaina: Cold potatoes with a rich egg and cheese sauce.
Rocoto relleno: Stuffed peppers (often very hot).
Sopa criolla: A creamy spiced soup with noodles and a little chopped meat. Usually excellent and very filling.
Chupe de mariscos: A very rich and creamy shellfish soup.

Then comes...
Cabro or *Cabrito*:   Goat meat.
Churrasco and *Lomo*:   Fillet or rump steak (beef); better quality than *Bifstek*.
Apanado: Breaded meat cutlet.
Chorrillana: Meat smothered in fried onions.
Adobo: A Cuzco speciality. Chopped marinated pork in a richly seasoned gravy. Served only in the mornings. A delicious start to an arduous day.
Piqueo: A very spicy stew with meat, onions and potatoes.
Sancochado: Meat, vegetables and garlic.
Lomo saltado: Chopped meat in a sauce containing onions, tomatoes and potatoes. A popular market dish.
Picante de...:   Something with a hot, spicy sauce.
Parrillada: Barbecued beef, pork, sausage and viscera.
Chicharrones: Chunks of pork fat, deep-fried.
Chaufa: Fried rice, Chinese style.

Sea food is excellent in Lima and along the coast. Try the Pacific Bass, *Corvina*.
A lo macho: The main fish dish comes with a shellfish sauce.
Cebiche, Ceviche: Raw fish or shellfish marinated in lemon juice with onions and red peppers.

For dessert you can have a variety of cakes or pancakes, or:
Mazamorra morada: Pudding made from purple maize and various fruits.
Flan: Creme caramel.
Picarones: Delicious rings of fried batter served with syrup or honey and usually cooked on street corners or in markets. Some restaurants have them on the menu.

Also cooked on the streets are *anticuchos*, baby-beef heart shish-kebab.

Alcoholic drinks

Pisco: Grape brandy, very popular in the form of *pisco sour*, with lemon, sugar and white of egg.

Chicha: Maize beer is an integral part of any celebration or communal work project in rural areas.

Local dishes — Bolivia

These are often *picante* (spicy) and usually incorporate *chuños*, freeze-dried Andean potatoes. I've never acquired the taste for these; indeed, it amazes me that any gringo can find them less than revolting, despite the attempts to make them more palatable with egg sauce.

In the Titicaca area, *trucha*, lake trout, is excellent.

Pejerrey: Small fresh-water fish.

Sajta de pollo: Chicken with a spicy yellow sauce and onions and *chuños*.

Chairo: A rich, spicy meat and vegetable soup.

Salteñas: The tastiest of all Bolivian goodies, combining meat, spices, olives, raisins, and vegetables in a rich sauce, which is then poured into pastry cases and baked. Served only in the mornings, usually as 'take-away' food. They're so delicious it's worth building your morning plans around them!

Api: A popular hot drink made from purple maize: a marvellous warmer on icy Altiplano mornings.

The Bolivian grape brandy is *singani*; not only is it drunk in large quantities during fiestas, but splashed around to ensure whatever good fortune the occasion dictates (see *Mother Earth* and *Cordillera Apolobamba*).

South Americans show excellent resourcefulness in recycling paper. If you make a small purchase the child vendor is likely to wrap it in last week's homework.

Natural history

The Quechua word *puna*, is still used is Peru and Bolivia to describe the windswept grasslands between the trees and snowline on the high plateau. Since puna is the ecological zone you'll become most familiar with during your stay, some knowledge of its flora and fauna will add to your enjoyment.

Flora

The non-botanist is faced with a problem here. There is no portable field guide to the flowers of South America. Classification is still far from complete, and I am most grateful to Pamela Holt, a horticulturalist with several South American expeditions to her credit, for the information below on the plants of the *sierra*.

First, though, a word on the more common or striking highland plants, including the trees and grass. Yes, even they are special in Peru!

Few trees can survive the harsh conditions of the Andes, but the native *queñoa* (*Polylepis incana*) tree flourishes at altitudes between four thousand and four and a half thousand metres. It can be recognised by its small trifoliate leaves and papery, peeling bark.

Queñoa forests give way to the puna, where coarse spiky *Ichu* grass (used for thatching houses) hides delicate flowers like the tiny sky-blue gentian (Gentiana sedifolia). Towering above the *Ichu* is a giant species of the familiar lupin, *Lupinus weberbauerii* ('taya'), which grows to nearly two metres. The seeds of lupins of a more modest size (L. mutabilis) have traditionally been used as food, but the long preparation needed to get rid of the bitter and poisonous chemical have caused them largely to be replaced by broad beans.

Andean lupins are not the monsters of the puna, however, this honour belongs to the tallest flower spike in the world, the *Puya raimondii*. Overall, this plant sometimes tops ten metres! *Puya*, confined to the Andes, is the oldest genus of the Bromeliad family, a huge group containing over sixteen hundred species. Pineapple and Spanish moss are both Bromeliaceae.

The *Puya raimondii* is said to live a hundred years and flower once before it dies. And how it flowers! An estimated eight thousand blossoms grow on one stalk and attract the hummingbirds and moths which pollinate it. Other birds nest among the spiky leaves and some stab themselves to death on their doorstep. The sharp spikes are also a danger to livestock.

Puya raimondii flower at the end of the dry season, from October onwards. The popular name for the plant is 'Junco' or 'Llakuash'. *Puya raimondii* are found only in Peru and Bolivia, where they now receive proper protection. The Cordillera Blanca is one area where they may be seen, and there are more in southern Peru (see *Chalhuanca*) and in Bolivia, west of La Paz.

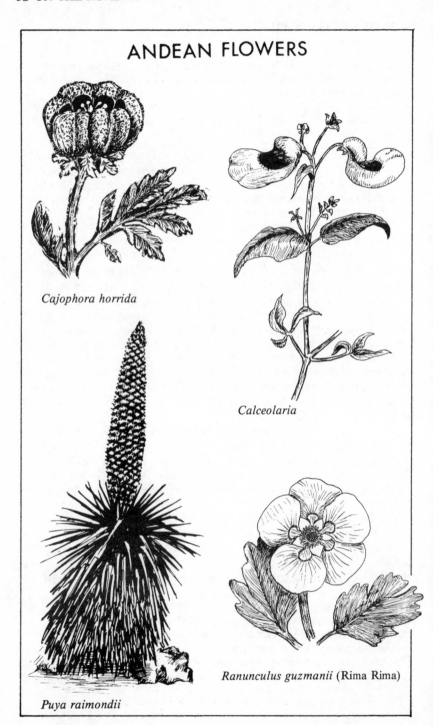

ANDEAN FLOWERS

Cajophora horrida

Calceolaria

Puya raimondii

Ranunculus guzmanii (Rima Rima)

Plants of the Sierra
By Pamela Holt

It is fortunate that the Incas used flowering plants during their religious ceremonies, for today many can be seen growing close to the famous ruins of Sacsayhuaman and Qenco.

The beautiful *Crocopsis fulgens (pax)* according to South American botanists or *Stenomesson humile* according to their British counterparts, is known locally as 'Chihuanhuai'. A small bulbous plant which only develops its narrow green leaves fully after the flower has finished. The crocus-like flower is scarlet, has six petals opening to 3cm across, and often grows at right angles to the ground. Its overall length is 9cm the lower half of the flower forming a yellow tube. A pure scarlet form was actually found growing in the crevices of Salumpunca.

Other attractive taller bulbs growing nearby are: *Stenomesson variegatum* — 30cm to 60cm long, blue-green leaves like a daffodil, with terminal clusters of striking peach/orange flowers marked with a green stripe; *Eustephia darwinii* — red tubular flowers with green tips, and *E.coccinea*, rose pink streaked with yellow at base.

Another pretty bulb is *Urceolina peruviana*, the flower being urn-shaped, orange/scarlet, with 4 to 6 nodding bells on top of a slender stem 30cm long. It has distinctive fleshy dark green leaves tapering abruptly, pale underside.

Nothoscordum andicolum grows happily among the ruins of Sacsayhuaman. A member of the lily family resembling an onion flower, but delicately scented and a white-tinted mauve. Another flower around Cuzco is *Pyrolirion aureum*. The beautiful solitary orange flower opens in November, and is 7cm across. Leaves develop from the bulb later.

Zephyranthes parvula (Peruvian botanists) *Haylockia andina* (British), is a small crocus-like white flower, its reverse streaked with violet. It grows on hills overlooking Puno, where the local name is 'Pulla Pulla'.

Bomaria species are found in many mountain valleys. Related to the Alstroemeria, with narrow, tristed blue-green leaves, some are cane-forming from 30cm to 2m tall! Others are twining climbers straggling over bushes displaying vivid yellow or orange tubular flowers in a terminal cluster. The cane type are often green or green and red flowered. All types grow from little white tubers.

Chuquiragua is a stiff leafed, erect plant with bright orange tufted flowers often making a shrub.

Berberis, some of which grace our gardens, exhibit evergreen leaves like tiny holly with spines and orange flowers. *Desfontainea spinosa* with its stiff evergreen leaves resembles holly even more, but the leaves are in pairs (holly leaves are alternate). Known as 'Tincula', its tubular red and yellow flowers are very striking.

Cantua buxifolia is the Peruvian national flower. Sometimes known as 'Cantutas', its red bell-like flowers hanging from a straggling bush are featured on the old 5 centavos coin.

Brachyotum rostratum occurs more on the eastern side of the Andes. It is a shrub with oval, deeply parallel-veined leaves in pairs and vivid purple flowers with pendulous furled petals. The local name is 'Tili Tili'.

Gaultheria erecta, a low dense bush of the heather family (Ericaceae), has leathery oval leaves, the reverse of which are covered with red hairs, and pink bell-like flowers clustered at the end of the shoot. The local name is 'Pachyla Pachyla'.

Fuchsia species vary from scarlet tubular flowers, almost bush-like, to peach-coloured downy flowers struggling to gain a foothold between ancient stone walling. The local name is 'Nonenuma', 'Uchucollgo', or 'Uchucesto'. In the same areas you will see yellow *Calceolaria* species. Their name 'Zapatilla' (slipper) is the same as the popular English name, slipperwort.

The gentians of South America are rarely seen in cultivation yet are the most spectacular, ranging from the common blue to vivid red or yellow. The flowers vary in shape, too, being crocus or cup shaped, rather than the commonly met trumpet shape. The plants range from prostrate or creeping tiny plants to upright stems of one to two metres, clothed in gorgeous pendulous bells. Many beautiful gentians occur in the mountains. In the Huancayo region grows *Gentiana flavido flamea*, a low-growing plant with alternately-striped yellow and red flowers. In contrast is *Gentiana regina* ('Challengando'), 30cm tall, with unusual pale lilac flowers arranged around the stem, seen in the mountains in Ancash Department.

Viola pigmaea with variable white flowers blotched with yellow or streaked purple is a tiny roseatte growing in the Huancayo area.

Ranunculus is the botanical name for buttercup, a very primitive family with many species in the Andes. *R.guzmanii* has large red flowers and the whole plant is covered in dense golden hairs. Many grow at very high altitudes where they feature in folk medicine. 'Lima, Lima', or 'Rima Rima' (seen in river names — Rimac) means 'speak, speak' or for the river Apurimac, 'the great speaker'. The plant is used for infants slow to begin talking.

Laccopetalum giganteum is a metre high relative of Ranunculus known as 'Pacra Pacra' and grows above four thousand metres in the department of Ancash and Cajamarca. It is now an endangered species. Being apple green with only yellow stamens in the 13cm flower and with thick textured and waxy oblong/lanceolate leaves, its appearance more closely resembles a cabbage. Highly valued for its use against coughs, lung disorders and for feeding to cattle to improve fertility, the flower heads are widely distributed on Indian markets.

Another buttercup known as 'Urco Rosa', resembles a turks head or turban with its bulging red flower. This is *Ranunculus weberbaurii*.

High on the cold windswept moorland of the puna, grow numerous tufted or cushion forming plants often with tiny white or blue gentians creeping through. In the daisy family are: *Werneria dactylophylla*, the 'Boton Boton' or 'Botoncillo' with crinkly dissected leaves and a small white daisy flower growing in felty clumps, and *Werneria nubigena* ('Llirigo') with its large white daisy flower, often tinged with pink, out of all proportion with its blue-green strap-like leaves. This daisy seems to grow directly out of the ground which it hugs closely from its long tap roots.

The hard crusty bright green 'Llareta', often seen swarming over rocks, has tiny yellow green leaves — strange to think it is of the Umbelliferae family, and relative of the cow parsley and carrot! Botanically known as *Azorella yareta* it is exploited on this treeless zone for the smokeless heat it gives when burnt. During the dry season it is a drab earth colour.

What looks like patches of thawing snow on the Puna often turn out to be *Opuntia* cacti protected by dense hair or wool. *O.floccosa*, and *O.lagopus* to name two with yellow flowers, and *OTephrocactus malayanus*, another mat-forming cactus with felt covering and greenish flowers.

Culcitum canescens, like Espletia, is a member of the daisy family with thick furry leaves with the nodding flower also covered in dense wool. It grows very high in the Andes and is valued by the Indians for easing bad coughs. 'Huila Huila' is its local name. Other Culcitium species are known as 'Vira Vira de la Sierra'.

Tiny plants known as 'Turpa', or 'Thurpa' are found growing on rock crevices over four and a half thousand metres. They belong to the mallow family and show primitive characters such as having the flower attached to the leaf. The *Nototriche* are compact roseattes of tiny grey green leaves often covered in hairs or fine wool with proportionately large flowers which may be bright yellow, white, rose or magenta, all exhibiiting stamens in a prominent globose head protruding from the centre of the flower.

The *Saxifraga magellanica* and its sub species also grows on the same terrain, with bright green compact roseattes — getting tighter the higher it grows. The flowers are usually white or a very pale pink.

The range of plants which grow on the Eastern side of the Andes is too wide to be covered here. Inca Trail trekkers will be familiar with the many species of *Orchids* and *Begonias* that abound near Machu Picchu, and the lovely *Tibouchina* with its vivid purple flowers and prominently veined downy green leaves is a commonly encountered shrub.

Finally, a warning. In the shelter of rocks high in the Bolivian *cordilleras* grows a most attractive scarlet flower that invites picking. Don't. Its scientific name *Cajophora horrida* and local name 'ortiga colorado' (red nettle) are clues. The soft looking hairs that cover the leaves and stem pack a fearful sting!

Birds

'Servants of Plants', David Attenborough calls them, and goes on to say that hummingbirds deserve all kinds of superlatives — the smallest, most brightly coloured... and I would add the most interesting of all Andean birds. The family *Trochilidae* are, of course, widespread throughout the Americas in all habitats, but more species of hummingbird live on the chilly slopes of the Andes than any other family, and these little birds show a remarkable adaptation to their habitat and food source.

Over half of the flowering plants of the puna are pollinated by hummingbirds, and these have evolved trumpet-shaped flowers, so the nectar can only be reached by the hummingbird's long bill and even longer tongue (and example is the datura flower which is pollinated by the sword bill hummingbird whose bill is actually longer than its body), and long stamens which dust the bird's forehead with pollen. Such flowers generally have little scent, because hummingbirds have no keen sense of smell. Cross pollination is ensured by providing the bird with just enough nectar to allow it to reach the next plant. Hummingbirds need to feed every 12 minutes or so — they use energy faster than any other animal. Their wings beat 70 times a second (one third of their body weight is wing muscle), and in flight their heartbeat may reach 1,200 per minute!

For the Andean hillstar, which lives just below the permanent snow-line and feeds on the flowers of the *chuquiagua* plant, special adaptation is necessary to allow it to survive the freezing nights. It saves energy by perching on, rather than hovering over, the flowers, and at night it goes into a state of torpor. Its body temperature may drop to 15°C, from its normal daytime 39.5°C, and its heart slows down to 36 beats per minute. Thus the bird is able to conserve energy. The nests of the Andean hillstar are usually built on the eastern face of rocky cliffs to catch the morning sun, and are bigger than usual as extra protection against the cold.

From the smallest to the largest. The Andean condor is the heaviest flying bird in the world. Males weigh around twelve kilogrammes and have a three metre wingspan, differing from females by their crinkly skin crest. You may be fortunate and see a condor circling below as you rest at the top of a high pass. (Once, miraculously, I saw one above the Inca Gate of the Sun in Machu Picchu). Seen from above, the broad white wing patches are unmistakable, and you'll probably pick out the neck ring of fluffy white feathers. From below, when viewed against a bright sky, it's harder to recognise the bird, but the 'fingering' at the ends of the wings is a distinctive feature. Despite their name, Andean condors are more often seen on the coast in Peru, since there's an abundance of carrion from dead sea lions and sea birds on the beaches. Compared with this feast, the pickings in the high Andes are scarce.

Another carrion eater, the Andean caracara, is very common on the puna. There's no mistaking these black and white birds with their bare red faces, and orange legs. Caracara feathers were favoured for Inca headdresses. These scavengers find roadsides profitable hunting grounds, and often follow vehicles hoping to find a delicious squashed morsel.

Puna lakes are excellent places for bird watching, especially the shallow reedy ones which support a large number of water fowl. The most conspicuous is the Andean goose (*Chloephaga melanoptera*) which feeds in pairs on marshy ground near lakes or on the open puna in bog areas. Its white head and body and black wings are instantly recognisable.

Also seen on the fringes of lakes is the Andean gull. Its black head turns white in the winter, and it usually comes down to the coast during this season.

Puna ibis also like shallow lakes, and large flocks of these dark coloured birds may be seen feeding together. On close inspection you'll see they have a green and purple sheen to their black feathers, hence the alternative name, Andean glossy ibis.

If you're lucky you may see a goose-sized black bird tiptoeing around the reeds on enormous feet. This is the giant coot. It builds a huge floating nest of weeds, nearly two metres in diameter, which is sturdy enough to support the weight of a man. More common is the Andean coot and Andean gallinule, which are much the same as their cousins in North America.

There are plenty of ducks; the Andean duck (*Oxyura ferruginea*) has a conspicuous blue bill and black head, and the Andean crested duck is larger with a distinctive brown crest. Of the smaller teal, the silver or puna teal is recognisable by its blue bill and black cap, and the speckled teal by its yellow bill and brown head.

The most interesting duck, however, is not seen on lakes but by swiftly flowing rivers. Torrent ducks spend their days diving into raging waters to feed on insects and larvae. They can swim against almost any current, helped by their small bodies, large webbed feet, and long stiff tail which is used as a rudder. You'll see these delightful little ducks feeding in pairs along any fast-flowing river up to about four thousand metres. The male is very conspicuous with his black and white patterned head and bright red bill, and the female is a more subdued reddish brown.

If you walk through clumps of ichu grass you'll probably flush a tinamou (and give yourself a hell of a fright in the process). Tinamous are typical South American birds, incorrectly called *perdiz*, partridge, by the Spaniards. Certainly they look and behave like partridges. Their speckled colouring offers perfect camouflage. Several species live in the puna; they all nest on the ground and lay olive-green or purple eggs which have a beautiful porcelain-like sheen.

Andean lapwings are unmistakable in flight, with their jazzy black and white wings and loud alarm call, but they blend surprisingly well with the puna when on the ground. Another bird which seems almost invisible until it flies is the Andean flicker, a species of woodpecker which never sees a tree in its life, but lives in holes in rocky areas. It is an attractive bird with a speckled brownish back, yellow-buff breast, and tell-tale yellow rump which shows when it flies away whistling its loud alarm call.

Andean condor

Mammals

Very few large mammals can survive the harsh puna environment, and the ones that do are secretive and nocturnal, so it's easy to get the impression that the central Andes are bereft of wild animals.

Few hikers are lucky enough to see a puma or the even rarer long-legged Andean fox, but those venturing off the beaten path may come across a herd of *teracu*, or Guemal deer. These feed on lichens and mosses near the snow line.

Smaller mammals are more common, and one you will probably see is the delightful *viscacha* which looks like a cross between a squirrel and a rabbit. Large groups of these rodents live at the foot of scree slopes where they can take shelter among the stones and boulders. If you see one you'll see twenty, bounding from rock to rock, or sitting up watching you intently, while their whistling alarm call fills the air. Viscachas are close relatives to the chinchilla, another Andean animal which has been virtually hunted to extinction in the wild for the sake of its soft, thick fur.

Wild cavies or guinea-pigs may also be seen. They are invariably a brown-olive colour (never with white) and live in colonies near rivers. Their ability to stand the harsh Andean climate enables the domestic strain to survive comfortably in Indian huts with very little care.

Vicuñas, members of the llama family sometimes seen by trekkers, are wild animals despite their long association with man. Undoubtedly the vicuña is the most beautiful animal in the Andes, with its slender neck, huge eyes, and soft golden wool. Vicuñas are at their most graceful when running, sometimes at thirty miles an hour, stretching their necks forward to increase the streamlining effect.

Viscacha

El Niño

Every year a warm current flows south along the Pacific Ocean coast. Since it arrives around Christmas, fishermen call it 'El Niño' (the Christ-child). Every four years or so, a catastrophic version of *El Niño* hits Peru and Ecuador, and the rise in water temperatures affects the entire food chain, causing the death or failure to breed of many animals and birds dependent on cold-water fish and other organisms. The last disastrous *El Niño* was in 1983.

The llama family

Llamas and their relatives were the only animals domesticated by the Incas, and have been associated with man for at least seven thousand years. Llamas, alpacas, guanacos, and vicuñas are all members of the *Camelidae* family; they are the camels of the New World. Whereas llamas, alpacas and guanacos are different species belonging to the same genus, vicuñas are generically separate.

These animals are a perfect example of adaptation to altitude. They have more red cells in their blood than lowlands mammals, thus increasing the amount of oxygen-carrying haemoglobin available, and a high respiration rate. Special water cells in the stomach rumen enable them to survive long periods without drinking.

Llamas Bred as beasts of burden and for meat, llamas are able to carry only 25 kg of cargo, so large herds are necessary for efficiency. Llamas can be distinguished from alpacas by their long ears, long legs and necks, and the cocky angle of their tails.

Alpacas These are bred for their wool, and consequently have a much heavier fleece than llamas, with a characteristic 'apron' of wool bushing out from their chests. Their noses, legs and ears are shorter than those of llamas — more sheeplike, in fact. Ideally, alpacas should be sheared every three years, but if their owner needs money, he may do it more often. Just as frequently, however, the animals are not sheared at all, but slaughtered with a full coat of wool which is sold with the hide. Certainly most of the ones I've seen looked as though they'd never seen clippers in their lives.

Both llamas and alpacas wear colourful ear tassels. These are for decoration, as marks of ownership, or sewn into the ears when the animal reaches breeding age as a symbol of fertility.

Large herds of llamas and alpacas are easily driven over the mountains since each group has a leader, so the herdsmen only need control one animal. If you meet them on the trail, stand well clear and keep still so they don't panic and scatter.

Pancho of Machu Picchu, the most photographed alpaca in Peru

Geology

The Andes are young mountains formed during the late Secondary and early Tertiary periods — at about the same time as the Alps. On the geological time scale 'young' is a relative term and before the Andes were born some fifty to sixty million years ago, the South American continent was a going concern with the Amazon flowing into the Pacific!

Continental drift, resisted by the earth's crust beneath the Pacific, created intense compression and crumpled the land's surface, releasing igneous rocks which form most of the high peaks and folding the original strata into grotesque shapes. You will see evidence of this in many of the high valleys.

The effects of glaciation, volcanic action, and water erosion have completed this process and helped form the deep gorges and sheer mountainsides that we see today.

Glaciers are still shaping the Andes. As the ice moves down a mountain, its snout forms a cutting edge and glacial debris piles up on each side, forming lateral moraines. The maximum extent of the ice is marked by a terminal moraine. This glacial footprint remains long after the glacier retreats, and can be seen far below the treeline on the eastern slopes of the Andes of Peru and Bolivia. Those flat, rock-strewn, grassy areas so commonly found at the base of mountains were once lakes, dammed by boulders or ice, into which the rocks and silt carried down from the mountains were deposited. Gradually the lakes dried up and meadows were created.

The foothills of Illimani, Bolivia

Mother Earth
by Robert Randall

For the Andean Indian the earth is his entire world — he exists as another plant in it and life apart from the land is inconceivable. The earth is called *Pachamama* (Mother Earth). She is alive, and during most of the year is passive and receptive, feeling nothing and leaving man free to cultivate her. There are days, however, when she is actively happy or sad, giving rewards or punishment, and it is prohibited to touch her. There is also a period of time (Holy Week) when she dies.

She is mother of all things, including men and women. This is meant literally, biologically. Thus offerings are made to her. At certain times there are large offerings (usually involving alcohol), and these you are more likely to witness or participate in. They are fairly simple but extremely important:

T'inka: Before drinking alcohol, one allows several drops to fall from the glass onto the soil. Thus Pachamama is served first. This is done whether outside or inside the house.

Ch'ura: Similar to the *t'inca* except the alcohol is scattered with the fingers. Often it is sprinkled this way on a house, animal or other object to be blessed.

Ch'alla: In a small glass the alcohol is thrown to the major *apus* (spirits or gods — usually the snow peaks) of the area. The *ch'alla* is done standing up, and the person doing it completes a full circle.

These rituals may vary from place to place, but they are omnipresent in the Andes. They only begin to indicate a value-system of extreme complexity and richness. From these basics, however, we should be able to glimpse the Indians' humility before, and respect for, the environment.

The Andean Indian, before first digging his *chaquitaclla* (footplough) into the soil, asks pardon and permission of Pachamama. This is an attitude which we should attempt to adopt and be constantly aware of as we walk through the Andes. The earth is alive, and we are a very small organic part of her. We should therefore approach her and her people who live with her with a profound sense of respect and humility.

We have much to learn from the Indians. Although it is impossible to generalise about so many different tribes, the people are usually honest, warm, and friendly. They have not lost the sacred connection with their environment and are aware of the spirits of the mountains, springs and rivers. If one reason we are walking through these mountains is not to re-establish some such connection, then we probably have no business there in the first place.

Indians past and present

'The origin of Peruvian man is linked to that of man in America. On one side immigrant groups came from Asia through Bering Straight [sic] distributing themselves towards the north and south of the country. On the other side, Australian and Polish [sic] immigrants arrived by means of the Pacific Ocean and they also inhabited the north and south of the country. This group is related racially and culturally to an inferior origin...'
Tourist Guide Peru (A government publication).

Well, that's one interpretation! I will concentrate on the Quechua and Aymará Indians who form the two major linguistic groups of the Andes of Peru and Bolivia. Little is known of their origin, but the two tribes probably reached the Andean highlands during roughly the same period through immigration across the Bering straits and then south. Patriotic Bolivians believe that the Aymará civilisation is very old, and the Quechua much more recent, but little evidence supports this.

The myths and way of life of the two groups are similar, but they remain two races with different physical and psychological characteristics, different dress and agriculture and, most important, a different language. A Quechuan tribesman cannot even understand an Aymará; the grammar and vocabulary of the two languages are different, although they share fundamental words in common. This inability to communicate doubtless helps keep the two tribes separate, even today. Some villages are half Quechua and half Aymará, and each half is quite different from the other. The two groups rarely intermarry.

Quechua was the language of the Incas, thus Quechua speaking Indians are found throughout the old Inca empire, from the Colombian border with Ecuador to southern Bolivia and beyond. This wide dispersal of the language is due to the Inca custom of subduing newly conquered tribes by establishing Quechua-speaking settlements within their territory. They are the linguistic majority in Peru, and the minority in Bolivia where they are found in the southern part of the Altiplano, in the department of Oruro, and around Cochabamba, Potosi and Sucre.

Aymarás live around Lake Titicaca in Peru, and on the Bolivian Altiplano within a few days' journey of the sacred lake that plays such an important part in their lives. Inca mythology had Lake Titicaca as the birth place of man, and though never subdued by the Incas, the Aymarás embraced this belief wholeheartedly. They claim that the creator, Viracocha (the name means creator in Aymará and Quechua) rose out of the lake and made a world without sun, light, or warmth, and peopled by giants. These creatures angered the god, so were destroyed by a flood, after which Viracocha appeared from an island in the lake and created the sun, moon, and stars along with men made in his own image. The Inca version held that the sun's son was Manco Capac, and that the moon's daughter, his bride, was Mama

Ojlla. They appeared on the two islands in the lake, and together journeyed to Cuzco where they founded their kingdom.

The history of the Inca empire makes fascinating reading. The best account is John Hemming's *Conquest of the Incas*, but there is an excellent short version in *Exploring Cuzco* by Peter Frost, and an even shorter one in the children's Ladybird Book series. The present theory is that the Incas conquered advanced civilisations, thus making their mark in history as organisers, not inventors. Probably the only things introduced by the Incas were mortarless masonry and trapezoid windows and doorways, but their empire still stands as one of the most perfect examples of organisation and administration in the history of man.

The Incas sought to rule by consent, not compulsion, but met with fierce resistance from the Aymarás, who did not submit to Inca rule until the end of the fifteenth century. They adopted the Inca religion, with embellishments, but kept their own language and customs.

Village life today

Since the Spanish conquest the Indians of Peru and Bolivia have developed various protective mechanisms which help them cope with present day exploitation and discrimination. Communication between Indians and Whites (be they Peruvian, Bolivian or gringo) is often difficult due to cultural differences and a seeming indifference to the modern world. Village structure and way of life are quite ritualised, and visiting backpackers will have much more empathy with the Indians if they understand something of this structure.

Village land is generally owned collectively, although private ownership still prevails in some places. Each village has its headman, who may be the governor (*gobernador*), the mayor (*alcalde* or *warayo*), or council chief (*agent municipal*). He carries a ceremonial stick (*personero*) as a symbol of his position. The headman holds office for one year, and during this time is expected to sponsor traditional fiestas, paying for the musicians, food, and drink for these occasions. So most headmen are wealthy when they first take office, and as poor as the other villagers when they leave it.

Rural Indians live virtually outside the money economy, and day to day life is organised on the basis of reciprocity or mutual help. Any big job, such as harvesting, threshing, and house building, is done with the help of neighbours who receive aid in return when they need work done. Finishing a house is an occasion for great celebration. *Safacasa*, putting the roof on, is done by a godmother or godfather who goes up onto the unfinished roof, lays the last tiles or thatch, and puts a ceramic figure or pot, or a cross, on the ridge for good luck. Ceramic bulls — to ensure fertility — are popular, as are little vessels of the alcohol *aguadiente*. He or she then throws gifts of sweets, cigarettes, and so on down to the family and neighbours below who have helped build the house.

Villages are traditionally divided into four quarters; these sections

Cuzco mother and child

may be quite separate socially, with antagonisms and rivalry between them. If you are spending some time in a village, always ask permission before visiting another part.

Indians have a strong tradition of extending hospitality to strangers. Before accepting you should decide whether this family can really afford to give some of their food to you. Yet it is considered rude to refuse hospitality. You can overcome this dilemma by offering gifts in return. This gesture is in line with the Indian system of reciprocity, and will be appreciated by your hosts.

Indians are usually very friendly and willing to help foreigners, but there are exceptions. Once we were following a trail through a valley near Cuzco when a group of *campesinos* approached us. We greeted them, but it was immediately obvious that this was no ordinary meeting. The men were all very drunk, and their leader, in a state of great agitation and sweating profusely despite the cold, was determined that we should leave the valley immediately. His scanty Spanish was sufficient to make it clear that gringos never come to that valley, that we were not welcome there, that it belonged to the *campesinos*, and we must leave — now. A few lashes from the whip he carried persuaded us that he was serious, so we left. This sort of incident is very rare but I have had similar reports from other hikers. If it happens to you, remember it is their land, and if they want you to leave, then leave. Sometimes mock threats can be turned into a joke and everyone relaxes, but if this ploy fails, simply retreat. We have heard of an incidence in the Cordillera Vilcanota where the local Indians refused to help a sick climber, despite being offered large sums of money. There is a reason for this apparent callousness. Many Indians believe that spirits dwell in the areas of perpetual snow. These *nevado* gods are called *Apu*, or *Wamani* in Peru and *Achachilas* in Bolivia, and are greatly feared. The locals believe *Wamani* will claim a certain number of lives each year so they might as well be gringos not Indians.

I must emphasise that hostility such as shown in these incidents is very unusual. One of the delights of backpacking in remote areas is the contact with the rural people. In all my years of hiking in South America, this experience near Cuzco was the first, and I hope the last, of its kind. My memories are overwhelmingly of warm, friendly, and charming people who make me dread the return to 'Civilisation'.

Fiestas

In Peru and Bolivia the rich traditions of history and religion come together in local festivals. In the larger towns and cities these are often little more than a chance to close banks and businesses and take off for a long weekend, but in small villages the population grabs this chance of escaping the rhythm of their daily lives, and explodes into an orgy of colour, music and dance.

I've been to lots of fiestas, all similar in atmosphere but different in details. Bolivian fiestas are particularly fine, and if you travel around the country at the peak of its fiesta season, September, you can hardly avoid being caught up in the action. During a six week visit George and I stumbled into six fiestas. These chance encounters were particularly delightful, but if you want to find fiestas, ask the Tourist Office for some dates or consult a Church calendar. Any village called San Pedro, San Sebastian, or San whoever will have some sort of celebration on that saint's day.

To give you an idea of what happens at a typical fiesta, I will describe four from my experience. They are only a representative selection, since each fiesta has a different character.

Chacas, Peru This village is proud of its Spanish heritage, and the principal events in its week long fiesta have a Spanish flavour. We arrived for the *carrera de caballos* (horse race). The morning was occupied by a religious procession, with the plaza full of expectant villagers as the Virgin of Chacas was carried from the church, elaborately attired for the occasion. The procession was led by the village elite with a banner-carrying horseman representing the *caballeros*. Then came the dancers, gloriously dressed and masked, some with enormous head-dresses of peacock feathers, and dancing to music from pipes, a fiddle, and an enormous harp. After the procession had wound its way round the square and the Virgin was returned to the Church, the plaza started filling up with horsemen riding magnificent Peruvian 'walking horses' (*caballo de paso*). The riders were members of top families, and their wealth was represented by the beautiful animals they rode. We'd been expecting horse races, but in fact the afternoon contest measured the skills of the riders rather than the speed of their animals. Between two posts hung a row of sashes with a ring sewn onto the lower end. The riders had to spear this ring with a short wooden pick as they galloped between the posts. The prize for the most successful was the leadership of next year's contest. There were, perhaps, more desirable prizes; the village maidens had written their names on the sashes.

The preceding day had been Pizarro's day. A horseman dressed in armour rode into town and demanded gold. He left with a weighty-looking bag. Only a very Spanish village would celebrate the rape of Peru without resorting to heavy symbolism.

The bullfight of the following day is another Spanish legacy. We missed this, but understood that the bull is not killed, nor is he in an enclosure. Yes, sometimes the villagers are hurt or killed. It sounded like a 'bull fight' we'd seen in Tarabuco, Bolivia, where the bull had money tied between its horns. A series of drunk Indians tried to retrieve the money, tripping around on their enormous handmade sandals and pausing to gain further strength and courage from the tub of *chicha* in the middle of the arena.

We went to a proper bull fight in the north of Peru. The matador was white with fear and spent his time running away from the bull, which anyway had no intention of charging.

Paucartambo, near Cuzco   This is, perhaps, the finest of all Peruvian fiestas, and deservedly popular. The dancing is continuous for three days, and performed with a tribal intensity by the Indians involved. The costumes are varied and incredible; one group reminded us of agitated birds' nests, others of animated sacks. Many were fantastically masked and dressed. There were monsters, gringos and negroes; symbolic figures that had played a part in the Indians' history or mythology.

The procession of the Virgin of Carmen was the climax of the last day. She swayed towards us, resembling a stiff white cone of lace and jewels, smothered in flowers, and with the doll face almost hidden under an elaborate crown. Preceding her came a pure white llama, beautifully decorated. On the rooftops of the houses lining her route were dancing devils, demons and winged creatures, but before the Virgin could come under their evil influence, a flight of angels conquered them, beating them out of view.

Later, at night, we heard music. Peeping in through a doorway we saw a large room with tables laden with food, and the victors and vanquished dancing together in the middle. A friendly shout went up, we were pulled into the room, filled with food and drink, and danced with until we had to beg for mercy.

Achacachi, Bolivia   Obviously it is much more fun to become involved in a fiesta, even if it's difficult to extricate yourself. Our favourite was Achacachi, near Lake Titicaca, one of our 'accidental' celebrations. We were actually heading for the neighbouring town of Sorata's fiesta when our bus was forced to stop by a large and noisy brass band blocking the road. We hastily gathered up our things, got out, and found ourselves immediately swept into the parade. The costumes here were quite incredible. The principal dancers looked like the White Queen in *Alice through the Looking Glass*. It was hard to believe they could walk, let alone dance, in such outlandish apparel.

At the fiesta, stove alcohol was the preferred drink. Fortunately the custom of returning some of each cupful to Mother Earth saved us from embarrassment. I slipped away at one point, and returned to see George dancing off down the street, arm in arm with a large white bear, and hitting bystanders on the head with a banana. Later he swore that it was part of the dance; certainly the bear and the bystanders enjoyed it enormously.

Chipaya, Bolivia   Not all Bolivian fiestas encourage gringo participation. In the isolated village of Chipaya, near the Chilean border, our presence was anything but welcome. This was a private pagan affair, and our curiosity got the better of our good judgement. We had no right to intrude, but we were invited by *mestizo* school teachers we'd befriended. We joined in the dancing and talked to some of our friends, but there was an atmosphere of tension and hostility. An old woman started pummelling me and other Indians, whom we'd never met before, joined in. We left. Later it was explained to us that this village is composed of two socially separate sections. We'd made friends with the mayor and teachers of one section but this didn't give us leave to visit the other half, where the fiesta was held.

This sort of reception is rare. Almost invariably, villagers are delighted to have gringos in their midst during a fiesta, particularly if the visitors are prepared to relax and join in. If you go to a fiesta in a rural village, be sensitive to the wishes of the people. If they invite you to join in, do so, even though it means consuming some fairly disgusting and very alcoholic drinks. Enjoy yourself. But if you feel that your presence is not welcome, you should leave. Unescorted women should also be a little wary, as the effects of alcohol liberate the male spirit. The fiesta of Santiago, held in July, is a particular chancy occasion. Rape seems to be the traditional theme.

Bolivian fiesta: Dancing in the streets

Inca roads and communications

One of the most exciting aspects of hiking in Peru and Bolivia is that the ancient trails linking village to village and mountain to valley were once the means whereby an empire was conquered and controlled.

The Inca empire was criss-crossed with roads designed to provide the fastest possible communication. Since horses and the wheel were unknown, relays of runners provided the speed and efficiency required. Roads were engineered to give the shortest and easiest route between two points. Steps were quicker to negotiate than a short steep slope, so steps were cut into the rock or laid as paving. Less precipitous slopes were made manageable by zig-zag paths, and tunnels were cut through the outcrops of rock obstructing the direct route.

From sea level to five thousand metres, and down again to Amazonia, the roads looped and curved over a distance of twenty three thousand kilometres. In particularly mountainous areas the roads may have been steep flights of steps no more than half a metre wide, but across flat, open spaces the surface was often six metres wide with a fan arrangement of shallow steps going round corners.

The Inca runners, *chasqui*, relayed verbal and numeric messages to all parts of the empire from the Sun King in Cuzco. The Incas had no written language, only one of several reasons we know so little about their culture, so the numeric messages consisted of knotted llama wool strings, *quipus*. With strings of different colours and thicknesses the Incas were able to keep detailed records. For instance a *quipucamaya*, record or account-keeper, could look at a *quipu* and learn a great deal. Gold, for example, was represented by a golden string, while the amount of gold was recorded by a series of knots along the cord. Silver was represented by white threads, while a series of red cords detailed the fighting strength of an army unit. Once the size, length and colour of a cord had been standardised throughout the empire, it was relatively easy to keep records.

The *chasqui*, sons of civil servants, were youths of great pride and physical strength. In order to fulfil their labour tax they had to run messages for two weeks in every month for about a year. Each runner was equipped with a conch-shell to blow as he approached the next *tambo*, where he would pass his message on to the next runner.

In this manner the runners could do about nine kilometres an hour, even at altitudes close to 5000 metres. No point in the empire was more than five days' run from Cuzco. The trip from Cuzco to Lima (672 kilometres) took 72 hours. The Inca was known to send down to Acari, on the coast, for seafood. In less than two days he was eating fresh fish.

Tambos, or rest houses, were built at intervals of about twenty kilometres along the roads. These also functioned as store houses, stocked with provisions from the surrounding countryside. Some also had corrals for llamas, because not only *chasqui* made use of these roads; they were crowded with traders, tax collectors, farmers, priests, soldiers, gangs of labourers, and perhaps a royal delegation off to foreign parts.

Each community was responsible for the maintenance of the road in its

Inca road near Machu Picchu

area, and for the construction of bridges over major rivers. These were made from twisted *manguey* fibre, and had to be remade every other year. The most famous bridge of this type, over the Apurimac river, was immortalised by Thornton Wilder in *The Bridge of San Luis Rey*. Nowadays only the supports can be seen.

Modern travellers rather glibly refer to any stone-paved trail as 'Inca' but we know that many of the civilizations conquered by the Incas had achieved a high standard of stone masonry and it is likely that these pre-Inca people also had an interest in well built roads to ease their passage through difficult terrain. This is particularly true of the trails connecting mountains and valleys, where tropical produce was brought to the highlands and vice versa.

Backpacking in the Andes — the experience

Backpackers from North America, where areas of wilderness are set aside for recreation, are often surprised at the lack of solitude in the Andes. They tend to forget that the indigenous people cultivate fields at extraordinarily high altitudes, and many live just below the snow line. There are villages and schools several days' walk from the nearest motorable road. The trails here are foot-roads made and maintained by the *campesinos* who use them, and a constant traffic of people and their pack animals moves along them. Only in very remote areas will you be alone in the mountains.

The reception you receive in small villages depends a lot on how popular the trail is with gringos. On some of the busier routes, the novelty of seeing foreigners has worn off, and occasionally the people are abusive. In areas seldom visited by outsiders the hospitality can be touching and a little embarassing. And if you discover your own route, chances are the women will scream and run from you.

The women may be scared of you, but you will feel the same way about their dogs. These curs rush out from houses or cultivated fields barking hysterically, but respond well to the threat of a thrown stone. You don't actually have to throw it — just stoop down and pick up an imaginary missile and most dogs will turn tail and flee. People do get bitten by dogs (and rabies is quite common), so it's as well to carry a few stones in your pocket as you approach a village.

Finding your own route

This is the most exciting sort of backpacking, and one which I hope all readers with sufficient time will adopt. Apart from the thrill of stepping into the unknown with only your map and compass to guide you, finding your own trails will help prevent over-use of the popular ones. There are thousands and thousands of footpaths in the Andes, well used and passing through beautiful scenery, and only a very few of them have been trodden by gringos.

Children of the Cordillera Huayhash

As well as the serendipity of not knowing what is over the next hill, you have the wonderful bonus of never being lost, because you never knew where you were anyway.

The methods George and I used to find the trails described in our books can be easily adopted by other fit and adventurous people. First we select an area known for its natural beauty, but with a population large enough to maintain trails between villages. No problem in the Andes. Then we try to find a topographical map covering the area, preferably 1:100,000 or 1:50,000 scale. Again, no problem with the geographical institutes in Peru and Bolivia. Even with only a road map you can pick a likely looking area above the tree line, between two towns, and be fairly confident that there'll be a trail. Then we pack enough food to last the estimated number of days, plus two more, and additional emergency rations. Then we go.

Here are a few do's and dont's for Andean explorers:

Do carry a compass and know how to use it.

Do know how to read a topographical map.

Do turn back if the route becomes dangerous.

Don't plan a jungle trip unless you know there's a trail.

Don't underestimate time, distance, or weather conditions.

Guides and pack animals

On the other end of the scale from finding your own route is to use local expertise to ensure a trouble-free trek. Guides, cooks, muleteers (*arrieros*) and their animals are a necessary part of organised trekking, and are often hired by individual hikers to take the donkey work out of backpacking.

Arrieros can be hired at most of the towns serving the main *cordilleras* described in this book. The average price for an *arriero* and his donkey is roughly $8 a day. You can (and should) give a tip or present at the end if the service has been good. Extra animals work out at about $2 per day. You will not be able to hire the donkey without its owner.

On some trails — notably the Inca Trail — porters (*portadores*) not *arrieros* are used, since animals can not squeeze through the Inca tunnels nor negotiate all those narrow steps.

If possible select an *arriero* through personal recommendation, or ask if he has written references (many collect rapturous comments from contented trekkers in a notebook). Take time to draw up a contract in writing (even if your *arriero* can't read, at least *you* will be in no doubt on what was agreed). Discuss whether cooking is part of the deal, and who will provide the food (generally that's you). *Arrieros* will have their own idea of how long a trip will take and it is almost impossible to shift them. Part of this seeming obstinacy is the necessity of camping where there is good pasture for the donkeys. Despite what may appear to us as frequent cruelty to animals, *campesinos* are very solicitous over their general welfare. They need fit, healthy animals. So ask them how many days it will be, and agree on a total price. Expect to pay a proportion of the fee in advance.

I have mixed feelings over the use of *arrieros*. Whilst it is undoubtedly a great relief not to carry your own backpack and to be sure of not getting lost, your freedom is also undoubtedly limited. Besides, there is always the gnawing feeling (not entirely unjustified) that it is not just your luggage that is being taken for a ride. Though I have had mostly good experiences with *arrieros* and welcome the chance to get to know the *campesinos* as people, not camera fodder, my personal preference is to have all the backache, headache and heartache that comes of doing it without local help, for the elation of those private views, and the satisfaction of discovering your own special campsite or private bathing spot.

Minimum impact

As backpacking and trekking become increasingly popular in Peru and Bolivia, hikers must develop an awareness of their effect on the environment. Fortunately many of the problems besetting the national parks in the developed countries, such as erosion caused by over-use, are not seen here. Environmental abuse, however, takes on a wider meaning since the foreign hiker is making his mark not just on the landscape, but on the local people. Ironically, of the two major problems, litter and begging, one is caused by imitating local customs and the other by ignoring them.

Litter The quantity of litter and rubbish left on the popular hiking trails in Peru and Bolivia is horrifying. This problem is compounded by the fact that local people are the worst culprits. Waste matter of all sorts — paper, fruit peel, plastic, etc. — is dropped in the highways and byways, and visitors soon follow suit. After all, 'when in Rome, do as the Romans', and it's frustrating to tramp around a city clutching a screwed up ball of paper, looking for a non-existent litter-bin.

Gringos drop the most litter in rural areas because the *campesinos* have so little to throw away. Cigarette packets and sardine tins are their only offerings; gringo litter is much more conspicuous: brightly coloured paper, cans, dried food packets, film cartons, and aluminium foil.

Why, oh why, must hikers blow their nose on tissues then discard them on the trail? Paper takes months to disintegrate. If your nose runs constantly while hiking (and it seems to be an occupational hazard), and you are fed up with pockets full of soggy lumps of Peruvian toilet paper, then adopt the peasant habit of blowing it through your fingers. (In the last edition I added 'disgusting' to peasant habit; Norman Croucher, a man who should be listened to in all matters mountainous, writes: 'No more disgusting than blowing it into a cloth and keeping it in your pocket! The method is what we used to call "the farmer's handkerchief" where I grew up in Cornwall...'.) I agree. Just check that no one is downwind of you when you do it!

Used toilet paper is another of the less attractive trailside decorations. One of the gallant volunteer cleaners-up of the Inca Trail said to me 'I'll pick up all manner of rubbish, but shit paper? No!'.

Even orange peel, while admittedly biodegradable, is unsightly, so as a courtesy to other hikers, dispose of it away from the trail and campsite.

Probably few readers would dream of littering a trail, but to preserve the beauty of these hikes, you must leave the trails and campsites *cleaner* than when you arrived. Carry several roomy plastic bags and collect rubbish as you walk. It's tedious and tiring, but you'll feel noble (and if you do stoop to shit-paper you'll feel hypernoble) and will be doing something positive. Later you can burn or bury your collection. People are much more likely to throw rubbish in an area that's already littered.

The preservation of the beauty of Peruvian and Bolivian hiking trails is up to you. Here are a few recommendations:

★Leave the trail and campsite cleaner than you found them. If you can't carry out other people's tin cans, bury them away from the trail.

★Defaecate well away from the trail and water supply; dig a hole, or cover your faeces with a rock, and burn the paper.

★Don't make a campfire on grass. Choose a bare area which can then be returned to its previous state before you leave. *Never* build a fire near ancient stonework.

★Don't burn firewood needed by the local population.

★Don't contaminate streams. Pans and dishes can be cleaned quite adequately without soap or detergent, or use one of the biodegradable liquid soaps sold in tubes.

Begging   Another indication that a trail is a popular gringo route is that children rush up to you and demand sweets or money. Before you offer a child such presents, reflect on the consequences of your action. You are giving him a taste for sweets which he would otherwise not have acquired, and which he can only satisfy by begging. You are teaching him that begging is rewarding and that he can, after all, get something for nothing. The child that appears so endearing to you will seem like a damn nuisance to the gringos following you. His increasingly insistent demands for *caramelos*, *dulce*, or *plata*, will irritate future trekkers and help widen the gap between gringo and *campesino*.

There are so many ways of interacting with children. I've watched a trekker sit down with a group of kids and draw pictures for them. They reciprocated with some charming illustrations in her diary. Cats cradles is a good game to teach rural children. Most can get hold of a piece of string, and the variations are endless. A frisbee also gives lots of pleasure. The idea that gringos are so rich that they can simply give valuable things away fosters deceit and perhaps robbery. Reciprocity is the foundation of village life; presents and labour are exchanged, not given. Give a smile and a greeting instead.

This seems a good place to quote from a letter by Pamela Holt describing her experiences in Bolivia, after their camp was robbed.

'We took food to a local house, explaining that we were unable to cook it and asking if we or the inhabitants could cook the food for us — then we would share it with their family... We left other food with them for the privilege of being in their home and sharing their life style. Christine, being a doctor, was able to treat one member of a household, whose brother in turn helped us after the theft. The villagers actually tracked down the culprit by the tyre marks of his bicycle! The *coregidor* (sheriff) searched the house and brought out the tent and some articles, but the bulk of our things had been carried over the mountains. Happily much of this was brought back.

I noticed that the school children — lessons suspended while the teacher helped with investigations — were kicking an improvised football, a bundle of polythene bits tied up with string. On my return to La Paz I purchased a football and sent this to the children via an English speaking miner.

While waiting for the officials to convene I spent a happy hour playing with the shop keeper's five year old daughter — identifying objects in pictures in her Quechua bible and spotting animals in her yard and imitating the noises with her telling me the Spanish name of the animal!'

A perfect example of gringo/campesino reciprocity.

Language

What kind of language is it when
sopa means soup not soap
ropa means clothes not rope, and
como no means yes?
(Anon)

In fact, Spanish is not a difficult language and backpackers should make every effort to learn the essentials. Your ignorance of the language shouldn't discourage you from making the trip, but I do advise you to learn a few greetings and a basic backpacker's vocabulary, even is you don't aspire to discussing politics and philosophy.

Both a dictionary and a phrase book are essential. The dictionary should have a Latin-American bias; avoid buying one based on the language of Spain — too many words are different.

Spanish words, given below, are incorporated into this book because their English translation is too long or doesn't convey quite the same meaning.

Campesino	Peasant, small farmer.
Cerro	Hill.
Cordillera	Mountain range.
Hacienda; estancia	Farm; estate.
Mestizo	A person of mixed Indian/European ancestry.
Pasaje, portachuelo	Pass.

Nevado .... Snow-covered mountains.
Quebrada .... Ravine; stream.
Selva .... Jungle.
Sierra.......................... Highlands.

'Gringo' is so common it's not even italicised. It means any white-skinned foreigner and is a term of convenience, not abuse.

Backpacker's Vocabulary
You must be able to recognise these questions ...

¿A donde va(n)?
(va sing. *van* plural)............. Where are you going?
¿De donde viene(n)?............. Where are you coming from?
¿De donde es (son)?............. Where are you from? (your country).

...and reply to enquiries about your purpose of travel.

Paseando...................... Passing through, on vacation.
Conociendo.................... Becoming acquainted (with the area).

Some other useful questions...

¿Podemos dejar esta bolsa aqui? ... May we leave this bag here?
¿Podemos acampar aqui? .... May we camp here?
¿Está lejos? .... Is it far?
¿Puede ayudarme? .... Can you help me?
¿Donde está el camino por...?..... Where is the path to...?
¿Hay una habitación? .... Have you a room (hotel)?
¿Qué hay a comer?.............. What is there to eat?

...and some useful general words.

Equipaje .... Baggage.
Mochila....................... Backpack.
Pueblecito (pueblito); poblado..... Settlement or small village.
Carpa......................... Tent.
Rio .... River.
Puente .... Bridge.
Derrumbe; huayco.............. Landslide.
Carro (Peru) *Mobilidad* (Bolivia)... Truck or bus.
Trámite .... Red tape; transaction.
Tienda........................ Shop.
Yurac......................... White.

Quechua and Aymará

Spanish is still the second language for many people in Peru and Bolivia. Quechua, the language of the Incas, and Aymará are still widely spoken. Place names in the *sierra* are usually Quechua, which explains the variety of spellings; the Spanish transcribed the names as best they could.

The following list of Quechua and Aymará names are to help you to understand the Inca culture, interpret place names, and ease your travel through non-Spanish speaking communities. For further information on the native language read *A Traveller's Guide to El Dorado and the Inca Empire*, by Lynn Meisch.

Inca Words
Amanta.......... Royal Inca's advisors.
Ayllu........... The basic community, or clan, of the empire.
Capac........... Lord or Chief (literally, magnificent).
Capac Raimi..... December fiesta in honour of the sun.
Condorachi ...... The annual killing of a condor to ensure good crops or banish evil spirits from a town.
Coya........... Star; wife of the ruling Inca, often his sister.
Cuntisuyu........ The Inca empire.
Huatana......... To tie, e.g. *Inti huatana*, the hitching post of the sun.
Inti.............. Sun.
Inti Raimi .... Summer solstice fiesta.
Tahuantinsuyo ... The land of the four quarters: the Inca empire.
Tambo .... Warehouses or resting places along the roads.

Origins of place names

Bamba ...... Place of
Caja .... Pass
Cota .... Lagoon
Cucho .... Corner
Jirca .... Mountain
Huanca...... Rock
Huaru .... Ford
Huaylla ..... Meadow
Lacta ...... Land
Llacta... ..... Village
Marca....... City
Yurac .... White

Machay ... Crevice
Paca...... Valley fork
Pampa .... Meadow
Pata ...... Summit, hillside
Paucar.... Flowery
Raju...... Glacier, snow peak
Rucu...... Old
Rumi ..... Stone
Tambo .... Roadside resthouse
Tingo ..... Junction of two rivers
Urcu...... Mountain

Some useful words

Quechua	English	Aymará
Maynalla	Hello	*Kamisaki*
Maypi?	Where is?	*Kaukasa*
Ari	Yes	*Jisa*
Mana.	No	*Janiwar*
Walej-pacha.	Good	*Walikiskiu*
Mana-walej	Bad.	*Janiwa Walikiti*
Mikuna	Food	*Manka*
Yaku	Water.	*Uma*
Huasi.	House	*Uta*
Mayu.	River	*Jawira*
Chaka	Bridge	*Chaka*
Cocha	Lake.	*Cota*
Chakiṅan	Footpath	*Tupu*
Yanapaway	Help.	*Yanaptita*

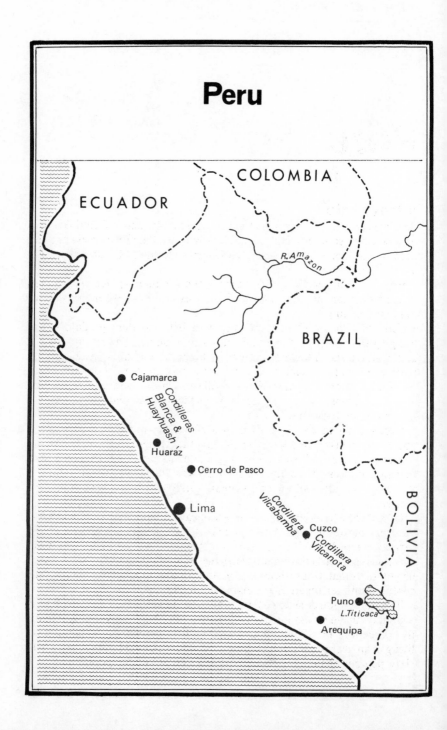

Peru

Introduction

Peru was named by Francisco Pizarro who first landed in South America on a beach in southern Colombia. Nearby flowed the Birú creek, and this became the name of his newly discovered country. Or so legend has it.

Peru is a country of dramatic scenery and weather, a place of extremes. A cross-section of the country, from west to east, would reveal the following picture.

First the Pacific Ocean, teeming with fish and their predators, and bringing the cold Humboldt Current close to shore. The strong sun and cold water create a fog, *garúa*, which blankets the entire coastal strip for part of the year. This strip is desert, some five hundred kilometres wide, but some sections are watered by run-off from the mountains. Cotton, fruit and sugar crops are grown, and most of the nation's industrial sector is located along the coast.

Crops don't really begin to grow without irrigation until a height of about two thousand metres is reached on the western slope of the Andes. Corn, potatoes and sun-loving vegetables flourish up to about four thousand metres, then cattle and general livestock take over, and mining is the only activity in the very high altitudes around five thousand metres.

Crossing the continental divide, with peaks ranging from two and a half thousand metres to over six and a half thousand metres, the descent begins to the Amazon basin. The change is noticeable immediately. Warm, moist air blowing up from the jungle makes these slopes greener and wetter. At a height of about three thousand metres dense rain forests begin, and continue uninterrupted to the Atlantic Ocean.

The population density of Peru is a story in itself, but with a few figures a great deal can be assumed. For instance, the Andes cover only twenty-five percent of Peru, but are inhabited by fifty percent of the population, living at an average altitude of three thousand metres. The jungle, covering sixty percent of Peru, contains only ten percent of the population.

Exits and entrances

Visas are not required by Western Europeans or North Americans; travellers from Australia and New Zealand *do* need one, however. All nationalities must have a tourist card to enter Peru, but this is handed out by the immigration authorities on arrival. Don't lose your copy of this card; it must be surrendered on leaving. Most nationalities are automatically given a ninety day stay, but for some reason citizens of the USA only get sixty days.

If you come overland from Ecuador, the border authorities will want to see your ticket out of the country. While a genuine air ticket is obviously the most satisfactory, you may get away with an M.C.O. (Miscellaneous Charges Order). Some people buy an air ticket and then cash it in, but delays in payment are frequent. Your best bet is a bus ticket into Chile by one of the long distance bus companies such as Tepsa. You can usually buy this at the border, but it would be safer to do so in Quito. Try to find out about the current situation from other travellers.

Australians leaving Peru for Bolivia are required to get an exit stamp in Peru before reaching the border.

Currency

The Peruvian *sol* has now given way to the *inti*. (100 *céntimos* make 1 inti). This new unit of currency was introduced in 1986 when inflation had added too many zeros to soles to be manageable. One inti is 1,000 soles, and at the time of writing (February 1987) there were 20.5 intis to a dollar. Inflation adds about .2 a week to the rate of exchange. Naturally enough, some Peruvians still talk in soles. As well as the new inti notes and coins, old sol notes and some coins are still in circulation, so check your money carefully. In a few years, however, there will only be intis and céntimos.

It is often difficult to change travellers' cheques, even in Lima. A *Casa de Cambio* may charge more commission than the Banco de la Nación (the only bank permitted to deal in foreign currency) but the savings in hassle are worth it.

Miscellaneous Peru information

Telephones   Tokens (*rins*) are needed for public phone boxes. They can be bought from news-stands etc. If you need to make an international call, it will be much cheaper to go to the local telephone company (Entel) than have your hotel connect you. Balanced against this, however, is the long wait to which Entel sometimes subjects you.

Holidays   Don't get caught out by Independence Day (July 28 & 29) which shuts all businesses down in the height of the tourist season. June 29 and August 30 are other holidays (saints' days) which catch many people unaware.

Business hours   Siesta is rigidly observed all over Peru, and in Lima, in the summer, you might as well join them since everything is closed from 12.30 - 16.00. From April to December it's a mere three hours, 12.30 - 15.30, and some shops catering to tourists even stay open all day.

Addresses   Beware Lima's system of two names for the same street (e.g. Avenida Garcilaso de la Vega, and Avenida Wilson). Beware the words *Casilla* and *Apartado* which mean P.O. Box. Beware *Avenida*, *Calle* and *Jiron* which are different words for streets.

Mail   If you want mail sent to you, American Express is more reliable than Poste Restante (here called *Lista de Correo*). Get your nearest and dearest to address your letters with your name in capitals. To ensure postal workers have a full and happy life, some post offices sort their *Lista de Correo* mail into male and female boxes.

Sending parcels home is surprisingly reliable, although it's essential to send them *certificado* (registered) which only costs a few extra soles.

Air freight   Avoid sending equipment to Peru by air. It once took me two and a half days (during which I missed my flight home) to retrieve a duffle bag sent from Bolivia. Bring equipment as accompanied baggage.

Airport surprises   Luggage allowance is complicated, but as a general rule you can expect to be permitted only a miserable 20kg when flying *from* Peru.

There's a hefty departure tax (US$10).

You may be asked to identify and open your luggage in a back room after checking in. This is a normal security procedure.

Laundry   *Lavanderias* are very cheap and plentiful in cities. You leave your washing in the morning, and it is usually ready by the evening. This is safer than doing it yourself and hanging it on the washing line of a cheap hotel.

Handicrafts   Tourist goods and handicrafts are offered for sale all over Peru and increased tourism has brought an improvement in quality. There are numerous items to choose from. Most people buy alpaca sweaters which are excellent value, and warmer than wool (although you may find yourself muttering 'If one more lady says "*es puro alpaca!*" I'll scream'). Very fine tapestry-type woollen weavings, softly coloured with vegetable dyes, are excellent in Cuzco, as are the diminishing supply of genuine antique weavings. Carved gourds (which come from the Huancayo area, so are best bought there or in Lima) are attractive, and folk or silver jewellery is a good buy. Cuzco is probably the best place to shop for handicrafts, although the quality is usually higher in Lima. So are the prices. The artisans' arcades on Av. Marina in Pueblo Libre have the best selection. Spend some time comparing prices and bargaining, but don't be fooled into thinking that handicraft markets are much cheaper than shops.

Strikes These are as popular in Peru as in industrialised countries, and certainly *¡Huelga!* (which you'll often see painted on walls) has a more defiant ring to it than 'industrial action'. Not usually well co-ordinated, nor widespread, these strikes can nonetheless cause tourists a great deal of trouble, particularly when they affect transport. I have twice been prevented from getting to Machu Picchu by strikes of railway staff.

Fortunately or unfortunately, Peruvians are no better at running their strikes on time than their buses. George's and my careful plans to be off in the mountains during a general strike came to nothing when it started a week late.

Lima

Most people arrive in Lima by air. The drive from the airport to the centre provides their first glimpse of the city, and they must wonder why on earth they came. Brown adobe slums on brown rubbish-strewn earth, and the occasional stiff body of a dead dog line this scenic drive. The relentless *garúa* provides an extra touch of gloom in the winter.

To make matters worse, this is a particularly chaotic airport. You emerge from the relative haven of the customs area to a mayhem of 'porters', taxi touts, hotel touts, and any other Limeños intent on getting an early look in on your dollars. You will need to be firm, go straight to the airport *Banco de la Nación* to change money, and take the Trans-Hotel bus the sixteen kilometres into the city. This is cheap and reliable, and the ticket office is right by the bank. For a little extra the bus will take you to your hotel or even to a private address.

Lima is a large city (a quarter of Peru's population — some eight million people — lives here), and like all large cities it has plenty to offer visitors. In the last edition I wrote 'We are quite unabashed in our love for Lima; we love the restaurants and cake shops, the cinemas, and the opulence of the plush suburbs of Miraflores and San Isdro. Perhaps we're rather indiscriminate in our admiration of the comforts of life. But we also love the museums, which are quite outstanding, the zoo full of Peruvian flora and fauna, and the colonial buildings around the Plaza de Armas.' Well, I'm afraid my love affair didn't last, and now, in common with most other visitors from the eighteenth century onwards, the best I can say is 'Lima must once have been a beautiful city'. I do still enjoy the luxuries mentioned above (you can eat superbly in Lima), and my perceptions of a dirty, uninspiring city are being changed by a preview of a just published guide to Lima by Carolyn Walton, which draws the visitor's attention to well-concealed places of interest that they'd miss in their usual sorties around Plaza San Martin.

One thing Lima excels in is museums. Even if you're not normally a museum person, I urge you to see the private collection of pottery and textiles at the Amano museum (phone 41 29 09 for an appointment), the Museum of Anthropology and Archaeology, and the Rafael Larco Herrera Museum with its wonderful Pre-Inca (Mochica) erotic pots. Most people associate ancient Peru with the Incas, but when you see the marvellous weavings and pottery of the cultures that preceded them, you will have a deeper appreciation of its rich history.

The best source of tourist information on Lima and Peru is the booklet *Where, When, How* put out by the *Lima Times* (itself an excellent source of information) and available free from the tourist office and larger hotels in Lima.

Transport   Lima has a comprehensive, though crowded, bus system, and lots of *colectivos* which, once you've mastered the system, provide an excellent service along Av. Arequipa which connects San Isidro and Miraflores with the city centre. A very useful transport map is available from news-stands showing all the bus and *colectivo* routes in the city.

Where to stay   *The South American Handbook* gives the most up to date listing on all classes of hotel. It's worth trying the large ones, such as the Bolivar, Crillon and Sheraton for bargain rates which are sometimes offered if they are having difficulty filling all their rooms. A recommended low price guesthouse in the city centre is Casa de Hospedaje Ibarra. Av Tacna 359, Piso 16, Lima (b & b in 1986 cost $5).

I prefer to stay in the suburb of Miraflores which is quieter, safer, and only ten minutes by *colectivo* from Plaza San Martin. There is a youth hostel in Miraflores; it is open to all (not just YHA members) is clean and has luggage storage facilities. The address (they have recently moved) is Av. Casmiro Ulloa 328, Miraflores. Tel: 46 54 88.

Purchasing hiking maps in Lima

The address of the Instituto Geográfico Nacionál (I.G.N.) is 1190 Av. Aramburu, San Isidro, Lima. Bus 54b from Av. Nicolas de Pierola goes there, so does the much slower no. 64 from Av. Garcilaso de la Vega. The Institute is well signposted. Not only does it admit to selling maps, but it actually encourages sales, with helpful staff and a fair degree of efficiency. There are some good departmental maps scale about 1:400,000, but the most useful are the topographical 1:100,000 ones which cover most of the Sierra. These maps are not as useful as the 1:50,000 Bolivian ones, and the trails marked can be taken as a rough guide only. They're perfectly adequate, however, and essential if you're planning your own route.

You may not be familiar with map scales. 1:100,000 means that 1 cm on the map equals 1 km on the ground; 1:50,000 is 2 cm to 1 km and 1:25,000 is 4 cm to 1 km. On smaller scale maps, 1:200,000 is ½ cm to 1 km and so on.

The hours of the I.G.N. are: Summer (October to April) 7.45 to 13.30, and Winter (May to September) 7.45 to 12.30, 13.00 to 16.00. Only in Lima can you buy I.G.N. maps.

If you are sick of straining your eyes reading by 40 watts, buy a 100 watt light bulb and use it in those dingy hotels.

The South American Explorers Club

The S.A.E.C. was founded in 1977 to encourage scientific field exploration and research, and activities such as white-water rafting, caving, mountaineering, and backpacking in South America.

The emphasis is on Peru, and the Club has much to offer; backpackers planning a trip to Peru and Bolivia are strongly advised to become members. For the annual membership fee of $25 you get the excellent 'quarterly' (they may take two years to get it out, but your $25 sub. covers those four issues) magazine *The South American Explorer*, use of the Club's information service and library, luggage storage facilities, and books and maps at reduced prices. Buying and selling used equipment is one of the Club's services, and you may have your mail sent there. The volunteer staff (usually American) are friendly and well informed. The club is open Monday to Friday, 9.30 to 17.00.

Non-members are allowed a one-time half hour visit, and may buy books, maps, and hiking equipment at the normal prices.

The Club is located on Avenida Portugal 146 (not far from the US embassy), but the postal address is: Casilla 3714, Lima 100, Peru. Tel: 31 44 80. Membership enquiries may also be addressed to the US office at 2239 East Colfax Ave, no 205, Denver, CO 80206. Tel: (303) 320 0388 or 831 7513.

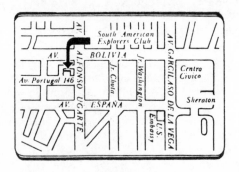

You will often be asked to show identification, so it is worth bringing something suitable for that purpose. Almost anything will do: I once got into a smart sports club by flashing my kidney donor card!

Useful Addresses in Lima

FOPTUR (Fondo de Promocion Turismo). This is the tourist agency for Peru. The main office is in Miraflores, at Av. Angamos Oeste 355, but for ordinary tourist enquiries you should go to their central office on Jirón Union 1066, just off Plaza San Martin. Hours 10.00 to 19.00; Sat 9.00 to 13.00.

Club Andino Peruano. Las Begonias 630, San Isidro, Lima 27. The main climbing club of Peru. Climbing information may also be sought from one of the country's most knowledgeable mountaineers, Cesar Morales Arnao, at Estadio Nacional, Tribuna Sur (tercero piso), Lima. Sr Morales speaks good English.

Peru Alpine Club. Shares premises with the South American Explorers Club.

Trekking and Backpacking Club Peruano. Jiron Huáscar 1152, Jesus Maria, Lima 11. Tel: 23 25 15. New, friendly. They put out a magazine called *El Trekero*. Hours Mon to Fri, 17.30 to 19.00.

The Peruvian Touring and Automobile Club. Av. César Vallejo 699, Lince, Lima. Tel: 40 32 70. Helpful to tourists with or without a car, and often have good maps.

Book Exchange. Ocoña 211. Two blocks from Plaza San Martin. A good place to buy, sell, or exchange paperbacks in any language.

In the Historical Sanctuary of Machu Picchu

The National Parks of Peru

Plans for official protection of Peru's natural resources and wildlife began in 1972, and a year later the first national park, Cutervo (North of Cajamarca) was established.

There are now at least fourteen areas (I do not have the latest figures) coming under the umbrella protection of the Sistema Nacional de Unidades de Conservación (National System of Conservation Units). The aims of the S.N.U.C. cover the full spectrum of conservation, from education and recreation to scientific study. Listed below are the names designating land use.

Parques Nacionáles   Large protected areas where recreation is permitted.

Reservas Nacionáles   Wildlife management is the aim here. A commercially valuable species is protected, but government controlled culling is allowed. The vicuña reserve at Pampa Galeras is an example.

Santuarios Nacionáles   Small national parks, stressing recreation and education.

Santuarios Históricos   Protected sites of outstanding historical or archaeological importance, such as the Inca Trail to Machu Picchu, and the ruins themselves.

Many of the parks are particularly attractive to backpackers and nature lovers. Generally speaking there are no camping restrictions in a park or a sanctuary, and no permit is required, although there are occasional exceptions.

The national reserves of Pampa Galeras and Junín deserve special mention. In the vicuña reserve there is a footpath where herds of these lovely animals can be observed. The volcanic area of Junín, near Cerro de Pasco, has a spectacular 'forest of rocks', and a lake teeming with waterfowl. There is a great variety of flowers in this reserve, and enough footpaths to satisfy a day hiker.

A most interesting park is the Reserva Nacional de Paracas. Not only is this the most developed park in terms of tourism, but it protects both the cultural and animal heritage of Peru. Established in 1975 the park contains a fascinating variety of marine and coastal wildlife, such as fur-seals, sea-lions, sea-otters, turtles, flamingoes, penguins, pelicans, boobies, and a host of other sea-birds. Surprisingly large numbers of Andean condors patrol the Paracas peninsular looking for carcasses.

The office of the S.N.U.C. is located in Lima, on the ninth floor of the Ministry of Agriculture. Edificio Plaza, Natalio Sanchez 220, just off the south block of Av Arequipa. You might get a chance to inspect a copy of *Los Parques Nacionáles del Perú* here. It's a very beautiful, full colour book covering all the national parks, and will whet your appetite.

Cajamarca and environs

If you fly to Cajamarca at the end of the dry season, as we did, you'll look down on range after range of desiccated brown hills. It seems unlikely country for good backpacking, but as you approach the city, patches of green appear and the Cajamarca valley suddenly reveals itself in a glorious expanse of flat, brilliant green, irrigated pasture land. The town itself has an unspoiled colonial charm, lovely churches, and picturesque Indian women wearing tall-crowned straw hats, who are constantly spinning as they go about their business.

Carnival is celebrated in Cajamarca with a marvellous display of costumes, music and dancing. This is one of the great Peruvian festivals, and well worth the soaking you'll get from the afternoon showers amd the efforts of water-throwers, an integral part of the Andean carnival. Water of a more pleasant variety can be enjoyed at the Baños del Inca, where thermal springs are channelled into a swimming pool and private baths. Lovely!

Cajamarca was an important area long before the Incas established themselves here. The most interesting pre-Inca sites are Cumbe Mayo and Kuntur Wasi, described later, but the town is better known as the site of one of history's great turning points, the conflict between Inca and Spaniard.

Atahualpa, victor in a bloody civil war between rival brothers, stopped in Cajamarca on his way from Quito to Cuzco. Here he met Francisco Pizarro, the Spanish conquistador, was captured and held to ransom. It was in Cajamarca that the famous room was filled once with gold, and twice with silver in an effort to pay for Atahualpa's release. But despite the efforts of his subjects, Atahualpa was murdered, and the Spanish conquest began.

These grim events are best held in the imagination. A visit to *El Cuarto de Rescate* ('the ransom room' but more likely Atahualpa's cell) is worse than uninspiring, it cancels out your own mental pictures and feelings. There are more impressive Inca ruins outside the town, the Ventanillas de Otuzco, named for the numerous trapezoid windows.

Hiking from Cumbe Mayo to Kuntur Wasi

Introduction This three-day walk connects the two pre-Inca sites in the area, allows a glimpse of the rural way of life in northern Peru, and passes through a variety of scenery.

Cumbe Mayo is an extraordinary site. Even without the pre-Inca remains, the area would be worth a visit for the 'forest of rocks' covering the bare hilltops. There are tall, thin rocks, enormous limestone faces cut deep by erosion, and isolated goblets. Local people call these eerie, almost human shapes *frailones*, or friars. Cumbe Mayo is noted for its man-made cave decorated with pictographs, and a remarkable aqueduct channelling water down to Cajamarca. These two features were probably associated with a ritual water cult, and built by people under the Chavín influence. (For more about the Chavín culture see *Cordillera Blanca*.)

The cave is part of a stone outcropping in the natural form of a giant head with the cave forming the mouth. Along with the man-made shaping, there is evidence that water trickled into the flat basin forming the floor of the cave. The pictographs on the walls show the Chavin influence. There's a feline shape, a plant, and many abstracts.

The aqueduct is carved into solid rock with geometric precision. There are many perfect right-angles, and dead straight stretches, as well as tunnels. This fine workmanship is a reminder that the Incas didn't invent the art of stone cutting. No-one knows the exact purpose of this aqueduct, but it was certainly not for purely agricultural purposes. It doesn't carry enough water, and there are numerous streams watering the valley anyway.

The destination site of Kuntur Wasi is the most important Chavín style site in the northern highlands, apart from Chavin de Huantar itself. It is the remains of a triple-terraced pyramid which once supported a temple. Set on a hill top, it is now so overgrown with bushes that it is hard to make out the original structure. The most interesting objects are the four carved stone monoliths with human/feline features, but quite different from anything found at Chavín. Gold ornaments and turquoise artefacts have been found in graves on this site.

The scenery between the two sites is often very beautiful. This is one of the few places we've seen where irrigation is extensively used. Sudden bursts of green brighten the landscape, where irrigation canals collect the water spilling down the steep *quebradas* and carry it to the dry slopes beyond.

This is a dairy farming area, and the Indian way of life is very different from that seen on the Altiplano. The Indian women wear traditional clothing: hand-woven striped skirts, and tall hats with a woven headcloth underneath. They can be seen weaving outside many of the homes along the trail.

Pre-Columbian pictographs and canal at Cumbe Mayo

'Brother can you spare some rice?'
By George Bradt

I went to Cajamarca for a vacation, Hilary went to do some hiking. I slumped around eating and sleeping while Hilary scurried about organizing a hike.

After two days of frantic activity, Hilary broke the bad news.

'George, you won't believe the wonderful hike I've plotted out for us. Out of bed, lace up your boots, put on your backpack and let's go'.

'Isn't it too late to start walking this afternoon?' I suggested hopefully.

'Isn't it too late still to be in bed?' she countered.

'Okay. Where are we going, and how long is this gem of a walk?'.

'Well, I must admit we really should have bought a map of Lima. I've tried all over town to get something but the best I could do was the library. I asked a nice man there if we could walk from Cumbe Mayo to San Pablo and he said it would only take a few hours. There's quite a big village on the way so we can stock up with more food there.'

I became suspicious.

'You have bought enough food for this trip, right?'

Hilary goes in for slimming during our walks, and doesn't mind reduced rations. I'm slim enough and the very idea of reduced rations brings on apoplexy, coupled with a feeling of weakness about the knees.

'No problem, I've already got cheese, rolls, soup and lots more.'

By this time we'd reached the outskirts of town and I'd had the chance to admire Hilary's new hiking style: she was walking on her heels like a king penguin.

'What's this, the new Bradt Ergonomic Propulsion Technique?'

'No, it's athlete's foot, and I don't want to hear any jokes about it.'

Before we could pursue the subject further we heard the welcome sound of a vehicle climbing the hill behind us. A lift to Cumbe Mayo would save us a lot of walking. Sure enough, the jeep stopped and a young archaeologist offered us a ride all the way to the site. We had plenty of time to look around the area with him before finding a campsite.

The next day in the village of Chetilla, we met the mayor, a very gracious gentleman, sitting outside a house under a *Correo* sign. A post office here? How impressive! When he saw us he bustled over and asked our business: we were missionaries perhaps? Or selling veterinary supplies? We told him about our walk and asked if we'd reach San Pablo that evening. He wasn't at all encouraging and added 'Maybe you are fast walkers'.

Hilary looked nervous, but recovered her composure and asked directions to the village shops.

'There is only one, and it's closed because the owners have gone to San Pablo'.

We thanked him and walked on. As we continued through the village Hilary kept nipping off down side streets and asking for eggs or bread. No one had any, and this was the only village along our route. At the lower end we ate our lunch. I was just reaching for a third roll when Hilary said 'George, two are plenty, why not save the rest for tomorrow?'

'Okay, just fill me in on your supper plans then; you know, kind of give me something to look forward to.'

Just as I was beginning to suspect, there would be no supper. In icy silence we put away our picnic supplies and walked down into a river valley. On the way, Hilary's search for some sort of local food became more vigorous. Braving the hysterically barking dogs, she asked at every hut we passed. The few people we saw looked very apprehensive about the two hungry gringos on their doorstep, and no one admitted to having any spare food.

We crossed the river at the bottom of the valley and had started up the other side when we met a man milking cows. We asked to buy a litre, and to our relief he agreed readily. After he had filled our water bottle with warm frothy milk he refused to accept payment.

'Why should you pay me for the milk when it has no value?' he asked. We continued in better spirits, but lunch was beginning to wear off, and after four hours of climbing our legs felt like jelly.

We climbed, slower and slower, until just before sunset. 'After all, there's nothing to cook, so there's no point in stopping early.'

Finally we found a good campsite, set up the tent, and tucked into 'supper'. Hilary, gallantly pretending that a litre of fresh milk was all she needed, swapped four peanuts for my share of the milk.

'If you're still hungry, George, you could walk over that rise and see if there's a village. I think I saw a soccer field up there from across the valley.'

'Me? Hungry? After hogging an entire roll and four peanuts? I'm full to bursting.'

'I'd go myself, but I don't think I can walk.' She'd taken off her boots and socks to reveal ten swollen, oozing toes with great raw areas where the skin had come off.

Thinking that we were lucky to have survived this far, I sped up the hill, hoping to see a road. Transport had now become our number one priority. There was no village at the top of the ridge, not even a house, and certainly no road.

It was rather depressing to wake up to no breakfast, and even more depressing to climb uphill all morning and find how quickly we were drained of the energy we had accumulated overnight. Our food-finding efforts continued unsuccessfully. We began naming specific vegetables: squash, corn, potatoes. By this time Hilary was hobbling along like an old crone, her feet wrapped in an assortment of colourful rags. Eventually we came across a woman weaving, with lots of hens scratching about in the dust.

'Have you got any eggs?' we asked as we casually waved a fair sized bank note.

'Yes, I've got two', she said.

Bliss, our salvation was at hand. The two eggs weren't much, but they'd help. We could nearly taste them. She didn't get them, however, but began weaving all the harder. Better check. Yes, we'd heard correctly, but she wasn't interested in getting them.

'You know, we're very hungry.' More weaving. 'We haven't eaten anything for three days'. Completely unmoved, even with my exaggeration. A day or two without food means nothing to these people, so obviously three didn't mean much more. Then she saw someone hurrying towards us, and unhitched her backstrap loom immediately. She lifted a sitting hen, gave us the eggs, and took the money. The youth running towards us stopped and motioned us towards him.

'Why don't I cook those for you, and give you some rice as well?' We couldn't think of any particular reason why not, so followed him to his nearby house. Very soon we were ploughing through two bowls of rice topped with a fried egg.

After watching us satisfy our initial hunger, he asked us about our trip — where we'd come from, where we were going. We told him all the details, then he asked the obvious question: 'But why didn't you bring any food with you?' We told him and he laughed long and loud. He kindly suggested we take extra rice with us in case we didn't reach San Pablo until the next day. But he assured us that even walking slowly, 'like fat ladies', we'd reach San Pablo before sundown.

We'd stuffed ourselves so full of rice we could hardly get up, let alone carry our backpacks. But we liked the stuffed feeling better than the empty feeling. And we have friends who habitually fast for days while hiking. Some people really *are* crazy!

'She began weaving all the harder.'

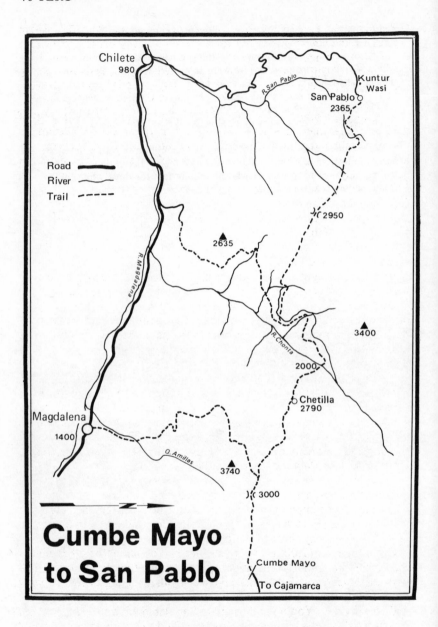

Chilete
980

R.San Pablo

Kuntur
Wasi

San Pablo
2365

Road
River
Trail

2950

▲
2635

R.Magdalena

▲
3400

R.Chonta

2000

○ Chetilla
2790

Magdalena
1400

Q. Amillas

▲
3740

3000

Cumbe Mayo
to San Pablo

Cumbe Mayo

To Cajamarca

Directions* Cumbe Mayo is 20km from Cajamarca by road, or 14km if you take the *Camino Real* which follows a more direct line. Few cars come this way since there are no villages en route, although the track does continue to Chetilla and occasionally trucks make the trip. It's best to resign yourself to walking (unless you want to bargain for a taxi), but listen for vehicles.

The road to Cumbe Mayo starts from Jiron Cajamarca, south west of the Plaza de Armas. The jeep road turns sharp left, three blocks from the plaza, but the footpath continues straight ahead over the hill. It eventually joins the road which continues upward and westward in a series of hairpin bends. There are plenty of shortcuts; just look for a well-used path. The *bosque de piedras* heralds your arrival at the Cumbe Mayo site (3,500m). Continue along the road to a narrow valley between rock-crowned hills. You will see the aqueduct from here and will have no difficulty following it along a clear path.

The carved-out rock cave is to the right of the aqueduct and can be reached on a good path.

To continue on to Chetilla and San Pablo, take the trail past the cave until it joins a broad track leading west. After about an hour you'll see the dirt road leading north. This curves round to the west again, but your direct route continues to the left of the road, passing through some rocky outcrops, and rejoins it before the top of the pass, marked by a big stone cross. The village of Chetilla lies in the valley. If you follow the road, taking short cuts, you'll arrive there in about three hours.

If you want to skip Kuntur Wasi, or take an easier way there, an alternative route presents itself shortly after the pass. Just beyond a huge conical boulder a well-used trail continues along the left side of the valley while the road bears to the right before making its descent. The trail leads to Magdalena (1,400m), on the main road to Cajamarca. The walk shouldn't take more than four or five hours. From Magdalena you can take a bus up to San Pablo, or to Cajamarca.

If you've followed the road to Chetilla (2,790m), you'll find it a very attractive little village with a green plaza adorned by a statue of Atahualpa and a charming campanile housing the church bell. Beyond the village the path drops steeply to the river. It's very muddy and rough in places, so take the easier way through the fields.

Cross the river (2,000m) via the bridge and climb up the other side of the ravine through lush vegetation until you reach the cow pastures. The path continues through the fields and over a hill, revealing a beautiful view of the Magdalena valley. Your route curves around the sides of the ravine and then divides. You'll see the path to San Pablo, *el camino blanca*, cut into the chalky hillside above the aqueduct, and a lower path which would take you to Chilete. Turn right at the fork and climb steeply until you see a curved rock cliff ahead.

---

*I have received no feedback from readers about this walk, so have reprinted the directions from the last edition. If there have been any changes I would very much like to hear about them.

Your path soon joins a stream channelled into an aqueduct. Follow this round the ravine to a bridge, cross, and climb steeply uphill again to the shoulder. It's a good three hours from here to the top of the pass. You'll follow a good trail past scattered houses and a variety of campsites if your strength is beginning to fail. You've reached the top of the pass when the path flattens out near a house, though the path seems to continue up a hill in front of you. Before you burst into tears, look left; there's a gate, a path, and San Pablo, and it's all downhill. Well, almost.

Just when you think you've arrived (there are houses and a couple of shops), you'll find the town itself (2,365m) lies 3km further on, and uphill, but it's a most rewarding walk. Perched at the top of a green valley, village streets are lined with attractive whitewashed houses; there are well stocked shops and a hotel. The monoliths of Kuntur Wasi, at La Copa, are reached in an hour. Walk down the road towards Chilete, taking shortcuts, until you reach the small village of Pueblo Nuevo. From here you can see the little guard's house on the top of the hill on the right, maybe 1km away. Take the small path leading from a flight of steps by the last house in the village and follow the path for 20 minutes or so. If you have any doubts, ask a child from the village to guide you.

A guard is supposed to stay on the site when there are visitors.

You can camp in the area, or ask for accommodation at the shop in Pueblo Nuevo. A bus leaves San Pablo for Chilete at about 6.30, a beautiful journey. There's another bus around noon. Chilete is on the main road between the coast and Cajamarca so there's no shortage of transport from here.

There's no reason why you shouldn't do this route in reverse, if you wish to. The bus leaves Chilete for San Pablo at about 11.00.

PRACTICAL INFORMATION

Time/Rating: Allow 4 days if you walk from Cajamarca to Cumbe Mayo, 3 days if you get transport to the site. This is a comparatively easy walk compared with others described in this book, but it's steeply up and down hill.

The alternative walk to Magdalena is much shorter, (one night out) but some will find the 2,200m descent very tiring.

Conditions/What to bring At this relatively low altitude, a tent is not essential, but if you camp at Cumbe Mayo be prepared for a cold night. During the rest of the trip you'll suffer from heat more than cold. Good camping places and fresh water are plentiful.

Maps The I.G.M. *Cajamarca* sheet, (15f) scale 1:100,000 covers the area. Cumbe Mayo and Kuntur Wasi are not marked on the map.

Huaráz and the Callejón de Huaylas

The Callejón de Huaylas, sometimes called 'The Switzerland of Peru', is the name given to the Rio Santa valley, separating the Cordillera Negra (west) from the Cordillera Blanca (east). Hiking is excellent in both mountain ranges, and no one should miss the wonderful drive down the Callejón de Huaylas from Yuracmarca or Caráz to Huaráz. Do it in an open truck if you can; sit on the left-hand side of the bus if you can't get a truck. I hate to tell you this, but the views of Huandoy and Huascarán are finer from this road than from many hiking trails!

This area has had more than its share of natural disasters, the most recent being the devastating earthquake of 1970 in which 20,000 people lost their lives. Huaráz was severely damaged and Yungay completely destroyed by a mudslide which buried the town and its inhabitants.

Huaráz

Huaráz was partially destroyed by floods in 1941, then an avalanche in 1958 took its toll, and the town had just been reconstructed when the 1970 earthquake left half of it in ruins. Rebuilding has been efficient, if not particularly imaginative. Perhaps the best feature of the town is the topiary along the main street.

The gringo impact on Huaráz has been considerable, and there are lots of agencies offering trekking, and many good cheap hotels and restaurants, mostly down Av Raimondi. A popular hotel is the Barcelona (no. 612) and the Cataluña next door where one of Huaráz's characters, Pepe, hires out backpacking equipment and offers advice generally. Either of these hotels are excellent for exchanging information with other walkers, and finding hiking companions.

The hotel Termas de Monterrey is more luxurious, situated 7km north of Huaráz and easily reached by bus. It is geared to mountaineers and trekkers, and surrounded by beautiful hiking country. The famous thermal pools are open to guests and visitors alike. The swimming pools are only lukewarm, but the private baths are piping hot and large enough for two people, and a whole family can frolic in the two *familia* tubs. These are two metres square and can be filled to a metre in depth. After a week in the mountains, this is bliss!

The Cordillera Blanca

This magnificent range of mountains has lured backpackers and climbers for many years and is now the most popular hiking region in South America. Along the 120km length of the Cordillera is the world's largest concentration of glaciers lying within the tropical zone, twenty peaks over 6,000m high, and Huascarán (6,768m), Peru's highest mountain.

The *campesinos*, who cultivate land up to about 4,000m and graze cattle and sheep almost to the snowline, are mainly *mestizos*. Indian culture is not strong in these parts, perhaps because the Cordillera Blanca

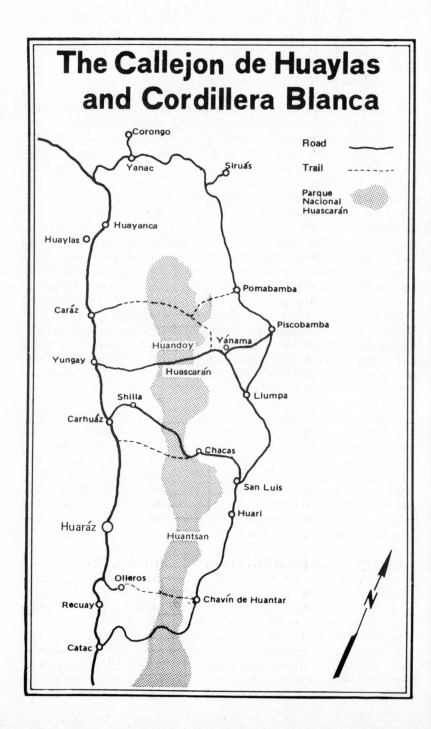

The Callejon de Huaylas and Cordillera Blanca

Corongo

Yanac

Siruás

Road

Trail

Parque
Nacional
Huascarán

Huayanca

Huaylas

Pomabamba

Caráz

Piscobamba

Huandoy

Yánama

Yungay

Huascarán

Shilla

Llumpa

Carhuáz

Chacas

San Luis

Huari

Huaráz

Huantsan

Olleros

Chavín de Huantar

Recuay

Catac

N

was never an Inca stronghold. Stephen Brush, in *Mountain, Field and Family*, suggests that the natives of the area may have been more than usually welcoming towards the Spanish because of ill-treatment by the Incas. There are no Inca ruins of any consequence in the area, which was the centre for the much earlier (and to me, even more fascinating) Recuay and Chavin cultures.

There are numerous hikes in the Cordillera Blanca, and the ones described here are only a small portion of what is available. For further ideas ask at the National Park office, or buy the excellent *Trails of the Cordilleras Blanca and Huayhuash* by Jim Bartle. The map in this book is the best available on the area. (Recommended maps for specific hikes are given after each description.)

Parque Nacional Huascarán

The Huascarán National Park was established in 1975 to protect this area of outstanding natural beauty. The park boundaries extend over the entire Cordillera, above a height of about 3,800m. The park objectives are to protect flora and fauna, and also areas of geological or archaeological interest. Scientific study of natural resources is encouraged, as is education of the public towards conservation. The park authorities also plan to 'control and develop' tourism within the park, and help raise the standard of living of the *campesinos* living in the area.

There are various regulations, two of which particularly concern hikers and trekkers: visitors should register at the park headquarters before starting their hike and pay a $3 fee, and fishing is prohibited during the trout spawning season between May and October. Both are sensible rules, which conservation-minded backpackers should obey. (To help them remember, park fees are also collected at the main entrances to the park.) The park office is located on the outskirts of Huaráz, behind the Ministry of Agriculture on Av. Centenario 912. The personnel are very pleasant and helpful, and a good source of information, maps, and if need be, equipment.

Special mention should be made of the park's most spectacular botanical exhibit, the *Puya raimondii*. These incredible plants (*not* cacti, although they look similar) grow in the Quebrada Pachacoto valley, some 57km south of Huaráz, and 26km east of the road. They flower in May. If you're around then, don't miss them.

Hiking — preparations and equipment As mentioned earlier, you will have no difficulty hiring backpacking gear in Huaráz so there is no reason to be improperly equipped. Apart from Pepe and the National Park Office, there is Andean Sport Tours and Azul Tours (both on Av. Luzuriaga) and several others.

Backpacking in this area requires the usual high-altitude equipment, although daytime temperatures can be surprisingly warm. It can rain, snow or hail at any time, even during the dry season (May to September). Carry a tent or at least a tarpaulin and warm clothing. There is little firewood, and even if you do find some you should remember that the locals need it more than you do, and the beautiful *queñoa* trees are gradually disappearing due to their use as firewood. Bring a stove. Although there are few nocturnal insects, midges and horseflies are an incessant nuisance near lakes and forests. Bring insect repellent.

Adequate maps are obtainable from the National Park Office and the Tourist Office (Pomabamba 415), but the best can only be bought in Lima.

It is easy to hire *arrieros* in Huaráz through the National Park Office. There is a non-negotiable fixed rate for their services.

Llanganuco to Santa Cruz

Introduction This is the second most popular walk in Peru, and deservedly so, although its pristine beauty has been somewhat marred by the new road that now crosses the Cordillera from Yungay to Yanama. Five days are needed to complete the loop which takes you over the Portachuelo de Llanganuco (4,767m), through the Huaripampa valley, and back over the pass of Punta Unión (4,750m). Spectacular glaciated peaks form the background of almost every view: Huascarán and Huandoy (6,768m and 6,395m), Chopicalqui (6,354m), and Taulliraja (5,830m), to name just a few.

The new road has at least shortened the backpacking route. The weak in soul and body can even start their hike at the top of the pass, if they are lucky enough to find a truck going there, but it seems a great pity to miss the chance to stand and stare at one of the loveliest views in the Cordillera Blanca.

Getting there Transport to the trail head is erratic; check at the National Parks Office in Huaráz for the latest truck schedules. Your best bet is probably to spend the night in Yungay (several cheap hotels) and from there take an early morning truck as far as you can. (My most recent feedback (1986) gave 13.00 as a truck departure time, enabling you to avoid a stayover in Yungay.) You will have no trouble getting to Laguna Orcancocha, the second of the two Llanganuco lakes and perhaps to Huiscash, 3km below the pass.

From Yungay the dirt road leaves the highway just south of the new town centre and snakes its way to the top of the pass 30km away. It climbs out of the valley, and after about 156km enters a steeply walled canyon. The lakes are another 8km further on at 3,850m. The setting is perfect, with peaks over 6,000m towering all around and there are plenty of campsites.

Directions The walk to the top of the pass takes a good 4 hours; the road makes a series of hairpin bends, but the trail follows a steeper and more direct route to the pass, el Portachuelo de Llanganuco (4,767m). As you climb, don't forget to stop and admire the spectacular views behind you. And going down the eastern side, spare a backward glance the marvellous cone of Chopicalqui.

Descending, the trail is frequently disrupted by the new road as it passes

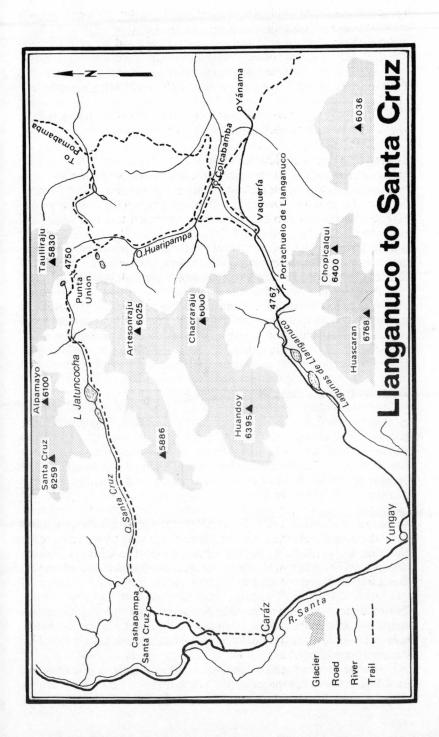

Llanganuco to Santa Cruz

To Pomabamba

Yánama

▲6036

Colcabamba

Taulliraju
▲5830

4750

Vaquería

Portachuelo de Llanganuco

Chopicalqui
6400 ▲

Q.Huaripampa

Punta
Union

4767

Chacraraju
6000 ▲

Artesonraju
▲6025

Huascaran
6768 ▲

Alpamayo
▲6100

L Jatuncocha

Lagunas de Llanganuco

Santa Cruz
6259 ▲

▲5886

Huandoy
6395 ▲

Q. Santa Cruz

Yungay

Cashapampa

Santa Cruz

Caráz

R. Santa

Glacier
Road
River
Trail

through meadows to some small lakes, then drops down through *queñoa* forests along the Quebrada Morococha until it crosses a bridge before a scatter of houses. This is Vaqueria, about 3 hours down from the pass and the last good campsite before Colcabamba, but beware of the midges.

If you want to bypass the village of Colcabamba, a short cut to Quebrada Huaripampa leads down the left bank of the stream just before the Valqueria bridge. This path follows the stream for a while and then veers north between two hills and crosses the Huaripampa river by a bridge and joins the broad trail from Colcabamba.

To visit Colcabamba — it's an attractive village with a shop and simple accommodation — take the left-hand branch of the main trail leading to Yanama. This fork is about a half hour downstream from the Vaqueria bridge, and you'll reach Colcabamba in another half hour. The Calonge family, who own the house just below the plaza, offers hikers simple accommodation and meals at reasonable prices; a welcome change from your tent.

To continue to Punta Union, leave Colcabamba via the footbridge near the village and immediately turn left, following the south west bank of the river to a footbridge less than an hour away. Cross it, and join the main trail above. At this point you'll be looking up two valleys; your trail goes up the right hand one, along the Quebrada Huaripampa which is a stunningly beautiful valley. You'll pass through lovely meadows, by some small lakes, and about 4 hours after leaving Colcabamba arrive at a flat, swampy area. The path is rather faint here, and confused by cow tracks. However, so many trekkers using pack animals take this route, that evidence of *horses* means that you are on the right trail. Keep to the extreme right hand side of the meadow by the trees.

At the end of the swamps there is a wooded area and the path re-establishes itself. Beyond the trees you'll be walking through tussocky grassland dotted with boulders, with the river on your left. Quebrada Paria, on your left, with the glaciers of Artesonraju (6,025m) as a backdrop, is a beautiful place to spend the night. There are good cow-paths up the ravine. In any case you must camp soon before the trail starts climbing up to the pass. For the adventurous, there is a possible and spectacular route that intersects the main trail via the three lakes that lie hidden above the Paría valley floor. Allow 4 hours for this (starting early in the morning if you intend to cross Punta Union). Climb the spine of the hill to the right of the cliffs (near the entrance to Quebrada Paría). The first flat area, where you would expect to find a lake, is dry, but above that (quite a scramble up the left hand side) is the most beautiful and tranquil lake imaginable (L.Tocllacocha). Cross the saddle on the far side of this lake to another lake where an outlet leads you down a rock cliff (not as dangerous as it sounds) to the trail leading to Punta Union, just below L.Morococha. This is a difficult route, and should not be attempted by inexperienced hikers.

If you are continuing along the main trail past Q.Paría, the snows of Taulliraju guide you up the valley and a massive wall of granite suporting a 'finger of God' (or something else if you're a Freudian) lies to your right.

Shortly after Q.Paría the canyon narrows and the trail crosses the river. There's a large, flat-topped boulder opposite a patch of forest on the stream's right bank; this marks the beginning of the climb up to Punta Unión, some 3 hours away. The path goes up to the left through grass and boulders, becoming more distinct as it nears the pass. The trail continues to improve, passing some lakes (Morococha, where you can camp in extremis) and brings you face to face with a granite wall. Here the path curves round to the right and veers back towards a chink in the rock face which is Punta Unión pass. The last part of the climb is up a beautifully engineered staircase, and the view that greets you at the top is stupendous. The majestic peak of Taulliraju guards the pass, its glaciers calving into a turquoise lake, Taullicocha. To the left are the snows of Chacraraju, while Huandoy and Huascarán form a mighty backdrop to the valley you've climbed up. There is even a good chance of seeing a condor from here. I have struggled up this pass five times now, and the impact of that sudden view has not diminished one jot.

The descent is easy and excellent campsites (Taullipampa) are reached in an hour. In fact you can camp almost anywhere down this valley. On your way down you might take a look at Quebrada Arteson, which leads off to the right (north) with splendid views. Good camping up here, too. Below Taullipampa the trail continues — obscured by cow paths — across flat meadows, where you will have to jump first to the right bank, then to the left side of the river, before arriving at a large swampy area. Keep to the left here until you arrive at the first of two lakes, Jatuncocha (Laguna Grande). Here the path climbs over a rock-fall and remains high above the lake on the left hand side until the far end. From this point the trail is so clear you couldn't get lost. First you pass the second of the two lakes, the reed and bird filled Laguna Ichikqocha, then the canyon narrows until there is barely rooom for the path and river to emerge into the green and lovely Santa Cruz valley. A wall and gate guard this dramatic exit (manned by National Park wardens).

Keep to the left-hand trail at a wooden cross, and you'll reach the road and a shop selling beer. This is Cashapampa. You may be lucky enough to get a truck from here (ask at the shop) at 6.00 the following morning for Caráz. Or you may find something in Santa Cruz a little further along (follow the road, then take a footpath up to the village. A punishing climb when you're tired). But, damn it all, having walked all this way, why not take the trail from Santa Cruz to Caráz, a steeper and more direct route of about 3 hours.

The descent from Punta Unión to Santa Cruz takes most people two days, although I've met hikers who've done it in one. Normal mortals should allow 6 hours from Laguna Jatuncocha to Santa Cruz.

Doing it in reverse Although the conventional route is as described above, and this certainly provides the best views, there are certain advantages of doing the circuit in reverse, the main being the ascent is gradual, over two days, so poorly acclimatised hikers can adjust to the altitude.

Here are a few pointers: If you can't get a truck from Caráz to Cashapampa, the walk takes 2 to 3 hours. Don't go into Cashapampa village, but take a right fork. The narrow steep-walled gorge of Quebrada Santa Cruz can be seen to the east and is reached in 5 or 6km. National Park fees may be collected at the gate at the foot of the Quebrada. Laguna Ichikqocha is reached 4 to 6 hours later. It's another 6 hours to Taullipampa. There may be some route-finding difficulty after skirting (to the right) the grassy plain after L.Jatuncocha. At some point you must jump to the left-hand side of the river, then back again at Taullipampa. The trail to Punta Union is now clear — 2 to 3 hours to the top. The trail from the pass to Colcabamba is straightforward and takes a total of 6 hours.

PRACTICAL INFORMATION

Time/Rating   A 5 day hike of moderate difficulty with 2 passes around 4,750m. Of these, the lower Punta Union is the more tiring.

Maps   The South American Explorers Club publishes a good map of this trail, and the I.G.N. *Corongo* (18h) and *Carhuaz* (19h) sheets cover the hike, but these are more useful for identifying surrounding mountains than for route finding.

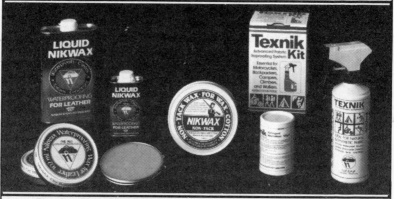

Quebrada Ulta to Colcabamba

Introduction   This is my favourite trek in the Cordillera Blanca. It's longer (6 to 8 days if you link up with the trail to Santa Cruz) and tougher than the Llanganuco loop, but there's no road to mar the feeling of isolation, and the views are a constant delight.

Getting there   Quebrada Ulta is followed up the valley by a dirt road which branches to the right off the main road from Huaráz just after Carhuaz. There are occasional trucks to the last village on the road, Llipta, and a reasonably frequent service to Shilla, a few kilometres further back. Sunday is the best day for transport because of the Shilla market. Trucks leave from Carhuaz plaza. There is now a road all the way to Chacas, passing through a tunnel beneath the Pasaje de Ulta. Whether this is actually carrying traffic, I have been unable to find out.

Directions   If you only get as far as Shilla, ask directions to Llipta — the road forks several times. At Llipta continue on the same road out of town, veering left over a bridge and you will soon enter Quebrada Ulta high above the river on its right. From here the route is clear enough along the new road and you'll have some marvellous views of Huascarán on your left. Keep following the road until you reach a stream and a path to your left. This is Quebrada Matará, and you continue along the road (or adjacent trails) for another 2 hours before starting the ascent to Yanayacu.

The trail is not always very clear, but if you keep heading north north west, keeping the multiple peaks of Contrahierbas to your right, you should be O.K. The views are spectacular as you climb gradually to a campsite below the steep part of the ascent. This will take from 2 to 3 hours. From here to the pass (4,850m) via Lake Yanayacu and a series of switchbacks is another 2 or 3 hours. This stretch is often snow-covered, so care should be taken. Yanayacu is one of the most dramatic passes in all the Cordillera Blanca; shortly after the top you will find yourself on a nerve-rackingly narrow path cut into the side of the mountain with a rock cliff on one side and sheer drop on the other; not for the faint-hearted. You descend to a very high, very cold lake full of icebergs, below the glaciers of Contrahierbas (6,036m). If you are equipped for freezing conditions this is a marvellous campsite, with rumbling avalanches during the evening and night. Or you can continue to a lower, less chilly camping area (there is plenty of choice). From the lake to Colcabamba is 3 or 4 hours, steadily downhill. Keep to the left side of the stream, and at the junction of the new Yanama-Llanganuco road take the left fork. In less than an hour you leave the road to the right, passing through Chaulla before arriving at Colcabamba in about an hour. From here you can proceed to Punta Unión or Portachuelo de Llanganuco, as described earlier.

PRACTICAL INFORMATION

Time/Rating   From Shilla to Santa Cruz takes 6 or 7 days (but take food for 8, just in case). You can shorten the hike to 3 days by leaving at

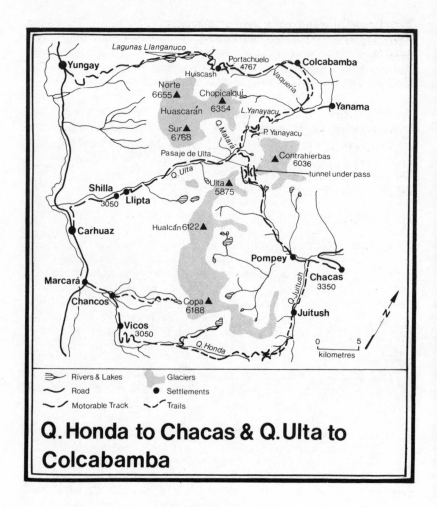

Q. Honda to Chacas & Q. Ulta to Colcabamba

Torrent duck

Yanama, or 5 if you go over the Portachuelo to Llanganuco. The pass at Punta Yanayacu is 4,850m and the path cut into the mountainside is not suitable for those with a fear of heights.

Maps   The I.G.N. *Carhuas* sheet (19h) covers most of the route.

Quebrada Honda to Chacas

Introduction   Further south there is the frequently used Quebrada Honda approach, with a 3 day hike bringing you to the village of Chacas. This is now (supposedly) connected by road to Shilla and the trek described above, so there are plenty of options.

Directions   Leave the Carhuáz-Huaráz road at Macara, a dirt road with occasional trucks running to Vicos. Although the road continues beyond this village, vehicles are rare, so you will probably have to walk. The road eventually dwindles into a trail which goes gently up the valley past lovely waterfalls, to Rinconada (3,850m), a large grassy meadow at the valley head. It takes a day to walk here from Vicos.

  The well-used path up to Portachuelo branches off to the left just before the meadow. It takes a good 4 hours to climb the steep trail to the pass (4,800m) but you are rewarded by marvellous views of the surrounding peaks — Chinchey (6,222m), Palcaraju (6,274m) and Pucaranra (6,156m). Condors are frequently seen here. Before reaching the pass the trail forks, but don't worry, they both lead to Portachuelo. The right hand one has a gentle gradient for pack animals.

  The way down from the pass is singularly beautiful as it passes through the lush Juitush valley with its many waterfalls. There's plenty of good camping in this valley before you reach the small village of Juitush. You will intercept the new road under the Pasaje de Ulta somewhere around here — I have no reports on where, but the route to Chacas should be clear enough. I would welcome any feedback on the effect of the new road on this hike.

  Chacas is a pleasant place with numerous shops, a restaurant, and two bus companies to take you to Catac, from where there is plenty of transport to Huaráz (presumably there is also transport to Shilla). Perú Andino and Cóndor de Chavin buses both leave at Latin America's favourite time — 3am.

  A fiesta is held in Chacas from August 13 to 17 each year (see *Fiestas* page 46). Horse contests are usually held on August 16 and bull-fighting the following day, but check with local people before making the trip.

PRACTICAL INFORMATION
Time/Rating   A fairly easy 3 days if you leave the trail at Chacas. The pass is 4,750m.

Maps   Most of this hike is on the I.G.N. *Huari* sheet (19i).

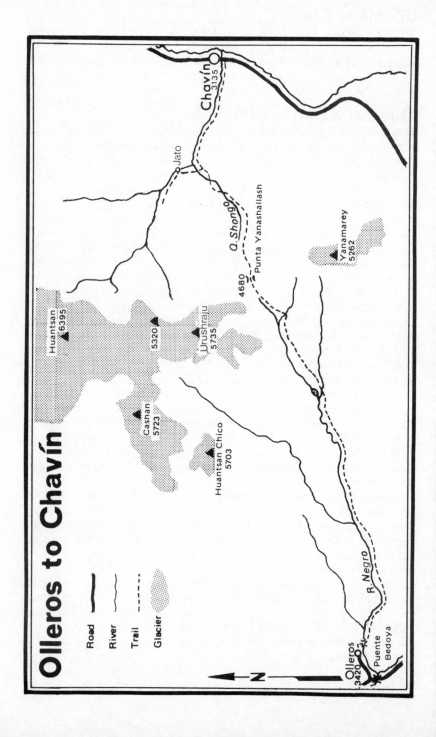

Olleros to Chavín

Road
River
Trail
Glacier

N

Olleros
3420

Puente
Bedoya

R. Negro

Huantsan Chico
5703

Cashan
5723

Urushraju
5735

5320

Huantsan
6395

Jato

Q. Shongo

4680

Punta Yanashallash

Yanamarey
5262

Chavín
3135

Olleros to Chavín

Introduction The beauty of this 35km trail is that it can be walked in 2 to 3 days, and is an ideal introduction to backpacking in Peru. It was George's and my first South American hike so I have a particular affection for it; in those days (1973) it was a big adventure since we could find no information on the route at all, but struck out with a compass and a sketch made from the 1930s map in the Hotel Monterrey. The villagers in Olleros were amazed to see us; now they are all too blasé.

Now it is an easy hike along a clear trail, and can be done by travellers with little backpacking experience, provided they are properly acclimatised (the pass is 4,700m). Best of all, it brings you to one of Peru's outstanding archaeological sites, Chavın de Huantar. Although some people attribute this trail to the Incas because of some fine stone paving, this route almost certainly pre-dates the Inca Empire.

Getting There The village of Olleros lies 2km east of the Huaráz-Recuay road. Trucks leave from the Huaráz market area for Olleros, or you can walk in from the main road at Puente Bedoya.

Directions Go through Olleros and take a clear track downhill to the right and across the river. As you cross the bridge, look for an interesting contraption on your right, a primitive kind of transporter bridge (is it still there? No-one has told me it *isn't*). The trail goes straight up the valley, keeping the RíoNegro to the left for about 16km. After passing some *estancias* and small villages, it emerges into open country where the landscape is strewn with huge boulders. These were deposited by glaciers or glacial streams at a time when the ice-caps were much more extensive than they are today. In fact the whole valley is a geomorphologist's delight, with fine ridges of morainic material deposited during temporary halts in the glacier's retreat.

The trail is clear and easy to follow almost all the way. The guide used to be the telegraph poles following the same route, but these have now been taken down. Still, you should have no problem, provided you take the left hand valley of the two that confront you about 8 hours' walk from Olleros. At the confluence of the two valleys, in a boggy stretch, the path seems to peter out, but it picks up again a short distance beyond the shepherds' huts. It seems easiest to continue walking towards the right hand valley, cross a stream, then strike across the shoulder to the left hand one.

The track now rises sharply, and spectacular views open up behind you. After some three hours you'll arrive at the top of a false pass, with a high valley beyond. Beautiful camping here, with views of pristine snow fields, jagged blue ice-falls, and black contorted strata. The trail winds up through this high altitude paradise to Punta Yanashallash (4,700m) 2 hours further on.

From the top of the pass the trail drops down for 12km to Chavín along the Quebrada Huachecsa. With a single short exception, it keeps the river

On the trail in the Cordillera Huayhuash

on its left all the way. There is a side trip up Quebrada Huantsán, recommended by Jim Bartle, and endorsed by Hessel van Hoorn who found good camping places and friendly (but inquisitive) villagers in Jato. It is possible to stay in the house by the plaza, but better to continue up the *quebrada* to camp in beautiful surroundings. Jato is reached across a bridge, shortly after the main path has crossed back right hand side of the river. Hereabouts is a small plateau which offers the last decent campsite before Chavin, 3 hours further down the valley.

The town of Chavin has several cheap restaurants and hotels, and the more expensive Albergue de Chavin. The owner of this hotel is very helpful and knowledgeable about the ruins.

Chavín de Huantar and the Chavín culture

Experts vary in their estimate of the age of this pre-Inca culture, but most agree that it flourished between 1300 and 400 BC, spreading from the coastal areas to the northern highlands, and reached its zenith around 500 BC, when the temple at Chavin de Huantar was built

Chavín appears to have been a predominantly religious culture with various animalistic deities. Highly stylised feline forms are a common feature of the sculptures and carvings, along with eagles or condors, and snakes.

I find the remains of the Chavin culture the most fascinating of ancient Peru. The enormous and enigmatic stone heads and finely carved reliefs have a strength and beauty unrivalled by the Incas, who left little in the way of representational art.

Chavin may appear a little dull at first since the finest stone work is in the seven underground chambers. There is a guide to show you round, but you should bring your own torch (flashlight) to see the carvings properly. These underground rooms are eerie places. Some people believe that the Chavin culture included a water cult, and certainly in wet weather the chambers are filled with water sounds.

Getting back   Huaráz is only about 80km from Chavin but the journey takes 7 hours. The road goes over a 4,178m pass (Abra de Cahuish), and through a dramatic tunnel before reaching its destination. If you do the trip by truck keep handy all your warmest clothes and your sleeping bag. My most miserable Peru truck journey was this one, taken at night before we learned to distrust quoted departure times. There seem to be buses every day to Huaráz (but check locally). There are others going direct to Lima (Cóndor de Chavín company).

PRACTICAL INFORMATION

Time/Rating   The easiest trek in the Cordillera Blanca, taking 2 or 3 days (with opportunities for exploration).

Maps   I.G.N. *Recuay* (21i) covers the route.

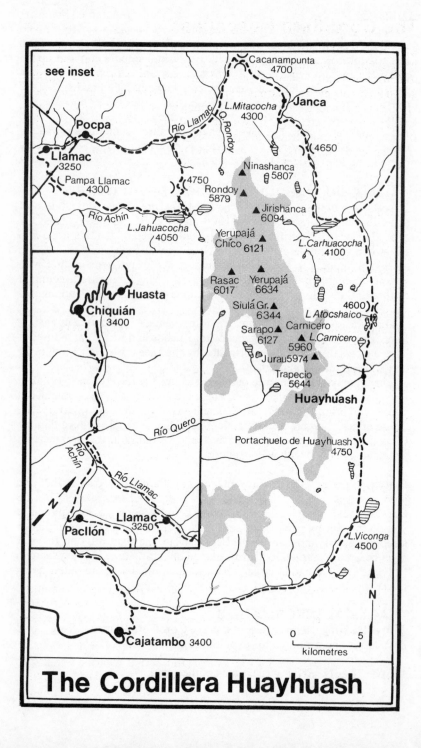

The Cordillera Huayhuash

The Cordillera Huayhuash

The Cordillera Huayhuash is a compact range (no more than 30km long) lying south of Huaráz. It claims Peru's second highest peak, Yerupajá (6,634m), and the finest mountain and lake scenery in the country, with the added bonus of year-round trout fishing. As Jim Bartle says '...it has no real highlights, just a long series of overwhelming views'. These are not earned lightly, however, and the Huayhuash is considerably tougher than the Blanca. The circuit described below should only be done by fit and experienced backpackers, who already have one or two Andean hikes under their belts (or below their boots, or wherever they care to keep them).

Chiquián to Cajatambo
Introduction   This is a 7 to 9 day hike; not a loop but a half circuit, it begins and ends at villages reasonably well served by public transport. Cajatambo, the destination, is linked by bus to Lima, so this is a suitable 'Goodbye, Huaráz' hike. The first couple of days (and the last) are at relatively low altitudes — you will be walking along cactus-lined paths and it can be very hot, but as you gain height — and views — it gets colder and colder, until heavy frosts and snow showers are common. The most dramatic scenery of the walk is around the east side of the Cordillera, where a chain of trout-filled lakes reflect the towering white peaks, but only the first and last days are without spectacular views.

Getting there   Some sort of vehicle leaves Huaráz for Chiquián on most days, shortly before noon. The journey takes 4 to 5 hours. Alternatively, take a bus or truck towards Lima, and get off at Conococha. Something will eventually take you the 30km to Chiquián. There are several small hotels in Chiquián, or you can camp below the town on the soccer pitch (watch your luggage). You must register with the police on arrival.

Directions   With a confusion of paths in the area, you will need to ask the way from time to time. Ask for Llamac (although the villagers will know where you're heading, anyway). You can go all the way to Llamac in one long 8 hour day. The first half of the trip is downhill, the second — when you're tired — is uphill.
   Half an hour after leaving the soccer pitch the path forks. Take the main, upper one. One hour after leaving the soccer pitch the trail makes a switchback to cross a stone bridge. Just across this bridge is another possible campsite. Pass a Pepsi sign and take the path by the shop (where you can buy beer, etc.). Continue on the most used path until the trail settles down and follows the Río Pativilca for a while.
   Two hours after the stone bridge, you cross the Río Quero. The river is now on your right, and is soon joined by the Río Achin. There now begins a punishingly steep and hot climb to a path fork. The right fork goes to the village of Pacllón (an alternative gateway to the lakes) and the left to Llamac. Some 4 or 5 hours after leaving Chiquián you come to an idyllic

campsite near the river. There are several more tent places in this area, and they are preferable to camping in Llamac where your large audience may get on your nerves, and which lies another 3 or 4 hours away. One to 1½ hours later you will come to the last fresh water before Llamac (2 hot hours further), so fill your water bottles. Several Señoras in Llamac offer accommodation and meals. You probably deserve a treat.

The next leg of the journey, to Laguna Jaguacocha, begins with a real slog (an altitude gain of over 1,000m) up a rocky, bare and boring hill. You will wonder why you came, but you'll know why when you get to the pass.

From Llamac, go south from the edge of the town and head left for a cleft in the mountains. If you want to break the misery of the next 5 hours, there is a perfect campsite (room for two tents) just above a mini waterfall about 1½ hours from the village. Those soldiering on will just have to grin and bear it up the eroded mountain side to a false pass, then for a further hour (enlivened somewhat by an Inca wall) to the real pass, Pampa Llamac (4,300m) which is on the right of a round loaf-shaped hill. It really *is* worth it. I experienced one of my moments of purest exhilaration here. In front lies the western face of the Cordillera: giant dragon's teeth of glistening white — Rasac, Yerupajá, Jirishjanka. As a further reward, the trail turns into a proper Andean path, and winds gently down through *queñoa* trees and lupins, past waterfalls and rocky overhangs to the valley below. In another 2 or 3 hours (if you haven't decided to camp on the way) you will arrive at Laguna Jaguacocha.

The lake is the focal point of the Cordillera Huayhuash, and sadly shows signs of base-camp litter. It's such a gorgeous spot, you will want to do your bit and clear up other people's rubbish. There are some houses in the area, and you can even sometimes buy Coca-Cola. Trout-fishing here is excellent.

The trail continues along the left (south) side of the lake, then swings to the left and begins to climb. Fill up with water before you start on the pass — there are no streams for several hours. It should take 2 or 3 hours to reach the top, but it took our group 4 hours; not because it was so difficult, but because it was so beautiful. We had to keep stopping to gaze. You seem almost on top of Rondoy's glacier, and look down into a milky blue lake full of little icebergs. The serious business starts below a long scree slope; the pass is to the right of a set of jagged grey teeth. The path goes towards the left of the teeth, then traverses across to the 4,750m pass. To descend, it is probably best to go down to a small lake at the foot of Rondoy/Ninashanka, and follow the *quebrada* to the valley floor. Or traverse the hillside on the left, but keep low. In all events, you will reach Rio Llamac, at the bottom of the valley, and turn right on a good trail. Camp anywhere.

From Rondoy (the name given to the general area — there is no village) you continue over another pass, Cacanampunta, to Laguna Mitacocha. Depending how far up the valley you camped, it will take you 5 or 6 hours.

Follow the trail by the river until it widens, with a small pyramid-shaped hill in the middle marking the confluence of two rivers. The path is clear and zig-zags up a cleft between rocks. It sometimes disappears in *ichu* grass, but goes to the right of a knob-shaped little mountain. It is about 2 hours to the first pass. and the trail drops before climbing up to the pass proper, another half hour or so further on. A vast amphitheatre of grey rocks shows no sign of an outlet but trust your trail, it will bring you through; first downhill, then up to the right and to the pass proper. From Cacanampunta (4,700m) the view is of a broad valley full of marsh and Andean geese, and rose-coloured lakes and rivers.

The descent is via switchbacks, then along the side of a long loaf-shaped hill to a couple of houses (the settlement of Janca). Veer right (along a good trail) round the end of the loaf and start climbing up above the Rio Janca. This path will lead you to Laguna Mitacocha which is reached after a long, rather boring walk across flat marshy land speckled with water fowl.

A good side trip from Mitacocha is to Laguna Ninacocha, at the foot of Jirishanka. It is a hard climb, but not difficult (go to the left of the waterfall) and well worth the effort. You can go right down to the glacial lake.

If you want to save a bit of time, omit Mitacocha and go directly from the loaf-shaped hill, across Rio Janca, to the next pass. From the lake you reach this trail by jumping across the stream and looking for the path up the first valley on your right, opposite a building (school) with a corrugated iron roof. The trail is not very clear, and there is a choice of two passes at the head of the broad valley; the easiest is to the right of the knobby mountain. This is not a pass for dramatic views, but these re-emerge as Laguna Carhuacocha comes into view — a gorgeous lake with some marvellously scenic campsites. Mitacocha to Carhuacocha takes 4 to 5 hours.

The next day you will have to find a way across the river that runs out of Carhuacocha's eastern tip. It is jumpable (just) near the lake, or there is a ford further along; a little stone wall marks the trail on the other side. Follow this path to a small bridge, then turn sharp right at a fork (the left branch goes to Queropalca) up a steep hill giving spendid views of Yerupajá and the finger of Jirishjanka. There is now a long, dull, grassy slog to a small black lake below a pass, then sudden and glorious views of the two Lagunas Atocshaico with jagged (but not glaciated) mountains behind. There are camping places near these lakes, but it's preferable to continue to Laguna Carnicero along a good path that passes between the lakes with constant changes of view. As you reach the high point by the second lake, a new range of snow peaks appear: Siulas Chico and Grande, and Nevado Sarapo. The trail descends to Laguna Carnicero, which is the nesting site for several giant coot, and offers numerous lovely campsites. This leg of the journey takes about 7 hours.

Just south of Carnicero, the maps show the village of Huayhuash. Jim Bartle says it exists, so I suppose we just missed it in the snow that had blanketed the trail. Anyway, don't get your hopes up for beer. The pass (*portachuelo*) of Huayhuash definitely does exist (4,750m) and the path there is clear enough. It is a long, slow climb (4 hours) with a very good chance of seeing vicuña on the mountain slopes to your right. From the pass there are views of the Cordillera Raura ahead. Then it's one hour to Laguna Viconga, and your first real signs of civilisation. Viconga provides part of

Lima's water supply. The path borders the lake, then goes over a hillock by workers' houses and accompanying rubbish, to a *quebrada* running down a broad valley. The trail is rather indistinct; you will need to cross to the left bank of the river eventually to reach one of the high spots of the walk. About an hour after Viconga there are hot springs! Not the best hot springs in Peru, but after 6 nights camped above 4,000m, you will not be fussy. The water is hot, and a 'tub' has been built. You will need to plug this, and it takes a long time to fill, so plan on camping nearby.

Do your hot water wallowing in the afternoon/evening because the next day is punishingly long. From the hot springs to Cajatambo is 8 knee-crunching hours as you go over one final pass, then drop 800m to the town.

Cajatambo is quite used to gringos, and some basic rooms are available as well as meals. There is a daily bus which runs on an erratic schedule (but early in the morning) to Lima. If you want to go back to Huaráz, you will need to go to Pativilca, on the coastal road, and change to a Huaráz bound bus.

PRACTICAL INFORMATION

Time/Rating   most people take 7 days, but bring food for 9 days — you may be held up by bad weather or good scenery. This is a very strenuous hike, with two passes of 4,750m and one each day (bar the first) close on that height.

Conditions/What to bring   Temperatures drop well below freezing at night, and snow storms are not uncommon. Only properly equipped backpackers should do this route. Conversely, the first and last day can be very hot, so pack accordingly. Bring binoculars for vicuña and condor spotting, and masses of film for those tremendous views!

Maps   A very beautiful topographical map is published by the German Alpine Club. This is fine for climbers looking for routes to summits, but does not show trails accurately, so is almost useless for this hike. Better are the two 1:100,000 sheets produced by the I.G.N. — *Chiquían* and *Yanahuanca*. Best of all, for walkers, is Jim Bartle's map from *Trails of the Cordilleras Blanca and Huayhuash*, a highly recommended book which gives several alternative routes in the Huayhuash.

Jirishjanka. Photo by Bill Abbott, Wilderness Travel

The Central Andes

Just south of the Huayhuash, in the departments of Huánuco and Pasco, is some fine mountain scenery, and Inca ruins far less visited than those in the Cuzco area — Huánuco Viejo. This is the most extensive of all Inca sites, and gives a very good idea of an Inca 'city'. The gateway to Huánuco Viejo is La Unión which can be reached from Huaráz or Chiquián. The central section of the Inca Road can be picked up here, or you can continue to Huánuco and Cerro de Pasco, or perhaps directly to the unusual town of Pozuzo.

Pozuzo

Travellers taking the famous train to La Oroya (a miserably cold town at 3,826m) and on to Cerro de Pasco or Huancayo, would do well to make a diversion to Oxapampa and then to Pozuzo, on the subtropical eastern flank of the Andes.

Pozuzo is to Peru what Gaiman is to Patagonia: a European settlement inhabited by descendants of the pioneers who arrived in the mid nineteenth century. In Patagonia it was the Welsh that carved out a new life for themselves in geographically hostile territory, and in Peru it was Germans and Austrians. The first colonists arrived at the behest of President Ramon Castilla (by chance his economic adviser was German) in 1857, and about a third of the town's inhabitants are still German speaking.

Even without the good hiking in the area, Pozuzo would be a fascinating place to visit (and here I make a confession. I haven't actually been there, but have talked with enough people who have that I'm confident in the recommendation). The following information has been kindly supplied by Nick Hauwert of Texas.

Getting there From Oxapampa, Nick took buses first to Tarma (1 hour), then to La Merced (4 hours), Oxapampa (4 hours), and on to Pozuzo (another 4 hours). In Pozuzo he stayed at Hostel Maldonado.

Pozuzo to Pucallpa

Introduction This sounds like a perfect trek in that it combines hiking with with river travel. The 2½ day walk takes you through beautiful jungle to Puerto Mairo, on the Río Mairo, a tributary of the Río Pozuzo. From Pto Mairo to Constitution is an 8 hour journey by cargo boat, then to Pucallpa by truck or *colectivo* for a further 8 hours. From Pucallpa you can fly, bus or truck back to Lima, or — if you're so disposed — journey down the Amazon for some 5,000km to the Atlantic!

Warnings On the second day's hike the jungle floor is filled with trails of vicious red ants, invisible and no problem until one tries camping. A real nightmare, biting holes in mosquito netting, clothes and any cloth or plastic, covering equipment by the million. Better to stay in someone's house or a school (5 hours from Pto Mairo is one) and the people are friendly. A hammock might be better than camping on the jungle floor but hard to find until Pucallpa. A rugged trail with much mud, and many river fordings some waist high with water. Few people and zero footprints. Try using a topo map though I got by without one.

Directions The trail leaves Pozuzo and follows the river. After about 1km it crosses a suspension bridge and continues on the right hand side. After about 50m you leave the main path and follow a smaller footpath leading off on the right and climbing gradually uphill. Follow a valley for about 3km, heading generally east. At the head of the valley (where there is a farm) the trail climbs up the right side of the left valley fork. Pass a cabin, and climb up through virgin jungle to a peak, about 8 hours from Pozuzo. Here is good camping with cleared space, scenic views on both sides and few insects. From here the trail descends down to the Mairo River and follows it generally towards the north east. Passing occasional houses, there is a school about 7 hours from the peak. A few kilometres from the school, the trail passes beneath a house and becomes confusing as it switches river sides from rocky beach to beach. There is no trail for the next 2 hours; follow other footprints and stay to the right side whenever possible. The trail picks up again by a side channels below a house which lies about 3 hours from Pto Mairo. Here the path leaves the river's right side, though it runs roughly parallel to it at a distance. 2½ hours later is Pto Mairo. There is a local 'hotel' (about $1 per night per bed, with no bath but the river). Every 2 or 3 days a cargo boat arrives which returns to Constitution. No one seems to know the schedule. The Pto Mairo arboretum is 30 minutes walk from the town and is supposed to be interesting.

From Constitution, trucks and *colectivos* go to Pucallpa, and a Tepsa bus leaves for Lima at 10.00 and Leon de Huánaco at 18.00. Both take 22 hours.

An alternative from Constitution, I understand, is a bus south to Larencía, then boat for 3 hours to Pto Bermudez, a *colectivo* to La Merced (6 hours), and return the same route as you came.

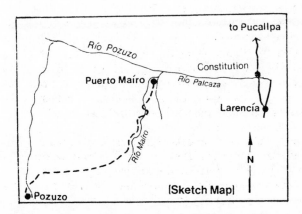

The Inca Road — Central Section
By Christopher Portway

> Accordingly the Inca constructed the grandest road that there is in the world as well as the longest, for it extends from Cuzco to Quito and was connected from Cuzco to Chile — a distance of eight hundred leagues. *Pedro Cieza de Leon, 1548.*

Perhaps the most astounding survival of Inca roads is the long stretch displaying varied constructions over different terrain, between Yanahuanca and Huari.

All the way between these two towns, for more than a hundred miles, the royal road marches northwards in a display of almost unbroken exhibitionism. This great artery, displaying its varying construction to cope with an assortment of terrain, makes no bones of the gradients it meets. Tunnelling through outcrops of rock which bar its path or changing its grass surface for stone paving or well-laid steps to mount sharp inclines it proceeds on its course where no other road dares go. Drainage was included in the construction plan, and where water threatens, systems have been provided to deal with every rivulet since, in the Andes, streams and rivers shift their banks with ease.

Sometimes behind convoys of itinerant horsemen, sometimes following a single horse carrying our heavy baggage, David and I trekked on suffering the ravages of heat and cold, hunger and fatigue, and the agonising breathlessness of altitude.

Huarautambo, Tunsacancha, the hot springs near Pilcocancha, the great complex of Huánuco Viejo, Taparaku. These are the guardians of the road to Huari. Tiny villages of adobe and thatch dot the sensational landscape housing simple Indian folk whose lives have hardly changed in five hundred years. And always, over the next escarpment, is a horizon full of straining white peaks to fill the eyes with wonder.

Travelling the remote north Peruvian Andes is a hazardous game. Hunger and exposure are very real risks. Nearing the small town of La Unión we all but succumbed to hypothermia when soaked within seconds by a prolonged downpour. In darkness we floundered across a river swollen by floodwater and were only saved from being swept away and drowned by the grace of God. We took refuge in a tiny farmhouse to spend the night in warm hay among pigs and poultry and in the morning found ourselves close to the massive fortress and temple of Huánuco Viejo. At Huarautambo, a village surrounded by pre-Inca ruins, we looked upon cave paintings and a cave-tomb full of deformed skulls only recently discovered by the local schoolmaster. It was here, too, that we first met the gold fever that grips those who live alongside the road. The region is alive with rumours of hidden treasure, but only gringos, it seems, are immune to the wrath of the gods if a search is made. David and I were involved in one such midnight tryst, but had to run the risk of earthly jealousies and village wrath. We dug all night under the directions of one who had seen the tell-tale 'money light', but we found precisely nothing.

Chris Portway's account of his trek is recorded in *Journey along the Spine of the Andes* (Oxford Illustrated Press).

The Cuzco area

Cuzco lays claim to being the oldest continuously inhabited city in the Americas. It was the religious and administrative capital of the far-flung Inca empire, and the equivalent of Mecca for the Inca's subjects; every person of importance throughout the empire tried to visit Cuzco once in his lifetime. So it is nowadays with tourists.

Cuzco is indisputably the most beautiful and interesting town in Peru, and one of the finest on the whole continent. To understand and appreciate Cuzco properly, read Peter Frost's excellent *Exploring Cuzco*. Here you'll find explanatory chapters on history and the Incas and descriptions of the major sites in the Sacred Valley and beyond.

The geographical features that made the Cuzco area so attractive to the Incas are today a magnet for backpackers. The Vilcanota and Vilcabamba valleys provide fertile land for agriculture, well watered by the many streams fed by glacial snows. The Cordilleras Vilcanota and Vilcabamba today offer some of the best hiking on the continent; not only snow covered mountains, but subtropical valleys and outstanding Inca ruins attract walkers and trekkers throughout the dry months.

Cuzco, lying at 3,540m, is an excellent place to acclimatise before tackling some serious backpacking. There are several excellent day hikes in the area introducing you to a microcosm of the pleasures and scenes awaiting you on longer trips.

Note   A ticket is available, for $10, which gives entrance to 14 major sites around Cuzco: Spanish Colonial, and Inca. It is valid for 10 days. Buy it from the tourist office, before you begin to explore the town and its surroundings.

A day hike round Cuzco

This walk takes in the ruins of Sacsayhuamán, Qenco and Salumpuncu, as well as a lovely trail through unspoilt countryside. Sacsayhuamán is a massive Inca temple-fortress overlooking Cuzco, and one of the finest ruins in the area. It's a steep half hour's walk to the site, beginning at Calle Suecia which runs from the upper corner of the Plaza de Armas by the cathedral. Keep going uphill, taking the track rather than motor road, until you reach the gigantic walls that are Sacsayhuamán.

Everything that is 'known' about the origin and purpose of Sacsayhuamán is pure speculation. Every tourist guide has a different story. Some claim that it is pre-Inca, others that it is very early Inca, and one even insists that it was built by a race of giants, hence the high doors! (However, I should add here that the quality of tour guides around Cuzco has improved noticably in recent years, and the best are well trained and knowledgeable.)

As in all matters pertaining to Cuzco, I find Peter Frost's (*Exploring Cuzco*) the best short account, though serious students of the Incas should read one of the real experts, such as John Hemming. To the casual visitor, it scarcely matters why the massive zig-zag walls (attributed to defence — in the event of an attack the enemy would expose his flank — or to the deities of lightning or the puma) were built. They are one of the wonders of Peru, and the most accessible example of massive Inca stone masonry. Climb to the top of the mound to see the recently excavated 'reservoir' or astrological structure, built in a circle with 12 radiating 'spokes'. Most likely this was the foundation of a tower, with an underground system of water channels. Opposite the giant walls, across the 'parade ground' which is now used for the spectacle of Inti Raymi on June 24, are naturally eroded rocks, some with Inca carvings. This is popularly known as the Inca's Throne, and the rocks make good slides for young Inca descendants and gringos alike.

Women bring their llamas for a highly profitable graze in the Parade Ground. They are extremely photogenic and well aware of their current worth. Bring plenty of change, and don't be conned into paying more than the equivalent of 30 cents or so.

From Sacsayhuamán you can take the road towards Pisac and visit the strange carved stone of Qenco. This lies below the road, just before it sweeps round to the left. Qenco is a huge limestone rock, naturally eroded, and skilfully carved both on top and within its caves. It is full of enigmas, too. The rock monolith in front could have had a phallic significance (unlikely, the Incas seem not too impressed with the phallus as a symbol of power), a desecrated carving of a puma... or what you will. The delicate zig-zag carvings on top of the rock were probably ceremonial channels for *chicha*, and the beautifully carved cave must surely have been associated with *Pachamama*, Mother Earth.

A path leads from Qenco through a eucalyptus grove to an open field. Another carved stone outcrop, quite as interesting and much larger than Qenco, lies to the right. Walk around the field to avoid trampling any crops that may have been planted. This rock is known as Salumpuncu. There are usually children around who'll be delighted to show you the main features: a carved cave and altar, a very eroded puma shape, and a sundial.

The old Inca road to Pisac passes near this site. Follow it in a north east direction and after about an hour it will bring you to the new Cuzco-Pisac highway, passing through well watered hills and a delightful village. You could be miles from a large town in this tranquil countryside. Look out for some strange looking buildings overlooking a cliff on the left hand side of the trail. There's a path leading up there, and you'll see that these are old kilns, used by the Spanish to make roofing tiles.

From here you can either continue up the trail to the road and hitch back to Cuzco, or walk back to the town down a path leading off to the right at the head of the valley.

You should set aside a day for this walk, to allow for getting lost, and so that you can explore the various ruins properly. Two half day trips are described in *Exploring Cuzco*, where you can also find a much more detailed description of the Inca sites mentioned here. Other walks around the Cuzco area are also described in *Apus and Incas* by Charles Brod.

Chinchero

Now the road from Cuzco to Chinchero is paved, and a new one opened across the plain to Urubamba, this once isolated and 'unspoilt' Andean village is very much on the tourist beat. And now an international airport is planned...

However, Chinchero is a perfect example of the resilience of the Andean Indian to outside influences, and the village itself has changed remarkably little since I first visited it 14 years ago. The Sunday market is still amazingly colourful, full of traditionally dressed women in the regional cartwheel hats, and geared as much to the villagers' needs as to those of the milling tourists. Women sit in groups by their produce, fry fish, or serve *chicha* from earthenware pots. Others sell handicrafts.

Chinchero is well worth visiting, even on a weekday, for the impressive Inca stone wall forming one side of the plaza, and some wonderful terracing with very fine stonework. The town used to be an important Inca centre and there are many examples of their stone carving. If you walk down the Inca stairs which start behind and below the church to the left of the terraces, you'll come to the main trail going down the valley. There are two large rocks near the path, with carved stairs, seats and water channels.

Each May 2 a fiesta is held in honour of *K'uichi* (Rainbow). The Festival of the Virgin is on September 8.

Note Chinchero is often called Chincheros in tourist literature. However, the sign in the village leaves no doubt on the spelling. Besides, there is a Chincheros on the road to Abancay.

Getting there There is plenty of transport from Cuzco to Chinchero on Sunday mornings: buses and trucks leave from 7.00 from Av Arcopata. On weekdays there are fewer, but providing you arrive early, you should find something. The trip takes around 40 minutes.

Walks from Chinchero

There are two walks from Chinchero to the Sacred Valley of the Incas, both taking about 4 hours. Although the new road has intercepted the trails in places, it is still a beautiful and interesting area. (Note: I haven't hiked these trails myself since the road was constructed, nor have I had any feedback from readers. So do let me have your comments on these walks.)

To Huayllabamba and the Sacred Valley Of the two trails described, this is the easiest to follow, but it brings you out between Calca and Urubamba so it may take a while to find transport to a night's lodging.

Take the old Inca trail described earlier, down the valley and and over the opposite ridge. As it descends towards the Urubamba valley it follows Quebrada Urquillos, passing the remains of an Inca Tambo. The path then drops very steeply down to Río Urubamba and then goes downriver to Huayllabamba (there are several villages of this name in the Cuzco area) and a bridge to the main road.

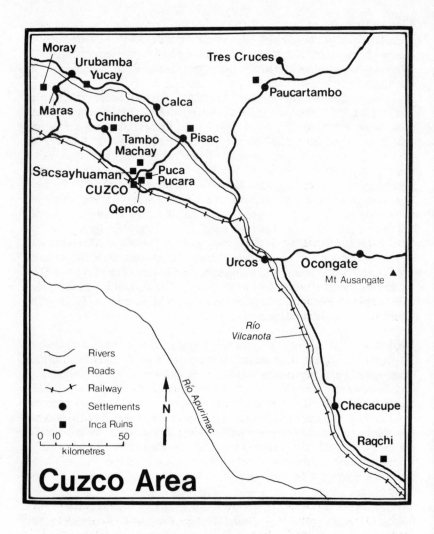

Moray
Urubamba
Yucay
Maras
Chinchero
Calca
Tambo
Machay
Pisac
Sacsayhuaman
Puca
Pucara
CUZCO
Qenco
Tres Cruces
Paucartambo
Urcos
Ocongate
Mt Ausangate
*Río
Vilcanota*
Río Apurímac
Checacupe
Raqchi

Rivers
Roads
Railway
● Settlements
■ Inca Ruins
0   10   50
kilometres
N

Cuzco Area

To Urubamba Apart from the final steep descent into Urubamba, this is a gently undulating trail, crossing a high plateau of red soil and rich farmland, and featuring splendid views of snow-capped mountains, glaciers and snowfields.

The path to Urubamba leaves Chinchero to the northwest. Standing with your back to the church, go through the archway in the far left hand corner and down the steps, then follow the jeep track across flat green pasture. Many minor paths leave this route, but you should keep to the main trail as it passes through eucalyptus groves and rich farmland. After an hour or so you'll cross under some power lines and soon descend to a village known as Comunidad Ratzky, or Cruz Pata.

The village centre is marked by a big white cross and a pond, and paths radiate in all directions. The one you want passes just to the left of the pond and through fields to a small valley. Cross the valley and continue uphill to a magnificent viewpoint. Behind you the rolling plateau is like a quilted eiderdown of fields; ahead the Urubamba River is visible far below, in its huge valley with a backdrop of snow-capped peaks. The next hour is spent in a high-level traverse of the valley side, descending gradually, but with new vistas opening up all the time. Then the town of Urubamba comes into view and you descend more steeply, finally reaching the bridge over the river by a series of zig-zags, and entering the town by turning left along the main road.

Urubamba is a pleasant place to spend the night (there are several hotels) and is a good base for exploring the Sacred Valley where there are numerous walks.

Practical information   Take plenty of warm clothes on these walks, — the weather can be very changeable. Although only about 12km long, the very steep descent make these tiring walks and tough on the knees. Don't attempt them unless you are reasonably fit. There's hardly any water along the Urubamba trail, so carry your own or buy a couple of oranges at the market. No detailed map covers the area.

Salinas
As one of the most astounding remnants of the Inca civilization this deserves a bigger heading. However, I have not had the opportunity of investigating a proper hike — although one undoubtedly exists — so will have to leave that to my adventurous readers.

Salinas, as the name suggests, is a village of salt. A salt river runs down the mountainside, and since Inca times salt has been collected here in hundreds of artificial salt pans, using a natural process of evaporation. From above, the pans look like a giant white honey-comb, with the small bee-like figures of Indians bustling around the rims harvesting their 'crop'.

From Urubamba walk or take a truck 6km towards Ollantaytambo to the village of Tarabamba. A footbridge crosses the Ri Urubamba here, and leads to an unusual small village of houses incorporated into the cliffs. This is Piychinjoto, whose inhabitants are traditionally suspicious of strangers. Their desire for privacy should be respected. Before the village there is a cemetery. Turn left here and follow the footpath that runs along the salt stream. This veers to the right, up a steep mountain path, and you will soon come to the salt pans. You may be asked to pay a small fee for entering the area.

Continue up the track until you come to a dirt road. Then you're on your own...

Intipunku. The Gate of the Sun at Machu Picchu

The Cordillera Vilcabamba

Apart from the Inca Trail, the most famous footpath in South America, there are many other equally dramatic routes through this mountain range which make the most of the opportunity of hiking from glacier to jungle in 4 or 5 days.

This is the area with the most Inca ruins. The sacred valley is overlooked by the snow-capped mountains of the Cordillera Vilcabamba, and the Incas found the mountains and richly fertile low-lying valleys ideal for the cultivation of a great variety of fruit and vegetables. Many Inca ruins remain buried in the jungle — new finds are being made all the time — and permission is needed to visit Espiritu Pampa, now credited with being the original Vilcabamba where the last Inca, Tupac Amaru, held out against the Spanish. Other important ruins are Vitcos and Choquequirau whose majestic setting is said to rival that of Machu Picchu.

Choquequirau was first discovered in the 1760s, and the first serious visit was by the French Compte de Sartiges, in 1834. There have been several subsequent expeditions, and all complain of the same discomforts: knee deep mud, and plagues of insects. Die-hard explorers wanting to reach the site should seek the help of the Delgado family (see page 119), who knows the area better than anyone.

Other sources of information on the region are Peter Frost's *Exploring Cuzco*, and William Leonard, of Leonard's Lodgings, Av.Pardo 280, Cuzco. Phone 5436. He and his wife are experts on Vilcabamba and can give you up to date information. Mr Leonard runs a guest house and sometimes organises trips to little known Inca ruins.

Warning The Sendero Luminoso are said to be active in the jungles of Vilcabamba, so check the situation before venturing deep into the area.

The Inca Trail to Machu Picchu

Not all Inca ruins are hidden in the jungle. The appeal of this particular path is the rich variety of Inca stonework: there are Inca steps, an Inca tunnel, and of course the ruins — Runkuracay, Sayacmarca, Phuyupatamarca, Huiñay Huayna (Wiñay Wayna), and Machu Picchu itself. Even without the Inca remains this trail would be breathtaking; it goes over high passes with excellent views, through cloud forest, and finally into subtropical vegetation. Over ninety species of orchid have been counted in the Parque Arqueologico Nacional de Machu Picchu, and Peter Frost recently reported seeing a pair of spectacled bears.

Note Regulations for hikers using the Inca Trail are planned and may already be in force by the time you read this (see *Conservation of the Inca Trail*). Check at the Tourist Office before making your arrangements.

It seems that you are no longer allowed to do the hike in reverse; just trying to enter Machu Picchu through the main gate carrying a backpack will cause trouble.

Conservation of the Inca Trail and its ruins

The Inca Trail has been subjected to a particularly bad litter problem for two reasons: it is very heavily used (an estimated 6,000 people a year make the trek), and for many of these hikers it is the first expedition of this kind they have ever undertaken; they don't know the rules. Compounding the problem is, ironically, the fact that this is a UNESCO World Heritage Site and maintained by the Peruvian government as part of the Historical Sanctuary of Machu Picchu. Because no development of any kind is permitted within the sanctuary, latrines, rubbish disposal bins, and designated campsites could not be built.

The first Inca Trail clean-up was done by the South American Explorers Club, along with the Peruvian Andean Club in 1980. It took years to get permission to remove the rubbish. The team collected 400 kilos of tin cans along with a mini-mountain of other trash. For purpose of analysis, the rubbish was sorted according to its country of origin: 50% had Peruvian labels, 37% were from Germany, 7% from France, and the remaining 6% divided between other gringo countries. Before you start feeling smug, however, reflect that the low U.S./British percentage is probably because we tend to go shopping locally, whilst the meticulously organised Germans bring it all with them — and leave bits of it there.

Since then, the organisation of trail clean-ups has greatly improved. Alfredo Ferreyros, one of the leading lights in Peruvian-based trekking, works with the Association of Adventure Travel Operators and the Ecology and Conservation Association (ECCO) to improve the situation. He has also been successful in getting support from various U.S. conservation agencies. One of these is the Earth Preservation Fund which has incorporated an annual Inca Trail clean-up into the adventure travel itinerary operated by Journeys International, Inc. On their first such trip, in 1985, they picked up over 700 kilos of rubbish.

If you want to hike the Inca Trail in a public spirited way, write to The Earth Preservation Fund, Inca Trail Project, PO Box 7545, Ann Arbor, MI 48107.

The Machu Picchu Sanctuary Project

This non-profit organisation has been set up by Alfredo Ferreyros and a University of California archaeologist, to study the effects of tourism on the Sanctuary, and find ways of minimizing its impact on the fragile environment. A committee has been formed at the executive level of the Peruvian government to set out a master plan. This includes printing a map of the Inca Trail showing camping spots and water sources, along with rules for low impact behaviour, and regular patrols of park guards twice a week.

In addition it is hoped that the present trend to 'improve' the ruins along the Inca Trail (which not only removes the wild beauty that you came to see, but eliminates the possibility of further scientific study) will be halted.

It is only through the Project that the Inca Trail can be preserved for future hikers. They need financial help, or at least your interest. Readers can help on site by signing up with Earthwatch, in Boston, USA (Tel. 617 926 8200). More information on the Project is available from ECCO, Vanderghen 560 2a, San Isidro, Lima, or APTA, Casilla 318, Miraflores, Lima, or from The Machu Picchu Historical Sanctuary Project, c/o Fundacion Jatari, 390 Liberty St, no. 3, San Francisco, CA 94114.

Getting there   The usual starting point for the Inca Trail is the train stop known as kilometre 88, but there are variations which I'll describe later. Trains for Machu Picchu leave from the San Pedro station near the market in Cuzco. Only the local, or 'Indian' trains stop at km 88, but you have a choice of departure times: 5.30 and 14.00. The afternoon train is less crowded, and safer since with the early one the pre-dawn darkness of the station provides excellent cover for the many thieves that make their living there. First class and 'special class' seats can be booked the day before, between 13.00 and 15.00. If you want to go second class, get there at least an hour beforehand to be sure of getting a seat.

Km 88 is the third stop after Ollantaytambo, and just after the first tunnel. If you sit on the righthand side of the train you'll see the kilmometre markers, so will know when to prepare to get out. Besides, there'll be plenty of other hikers leaving the train at the same place. If you're travelling second class remember that you'll have to make your way over the mountains of Indians, babies, and produce so start in good time; the train doesn't stop for long.

Directions   A guardian wearing one of the INC official hard hats meets the train and collects the fee for walking the trail and visiting Machu Picchu. At present this is $8. The walk then begins. Cross the new suspension bridge over the Rio Urubamba and follow the trail gently uphill through a beautiful eucalyptus grove to Llactapata and the first major ruins on the route. Vast retaining walls have converted the steeply sloping hillside into agricultural terraces: an amazing sight. There is a campsite here, and it is a suitable stop for the first night for those who have arrived on the afternoon train.

From Llactapata a clear trail crosses the Cusichaca river, a tributary of the Urubamba, and follows it upstream before crossing a tributary near Huallabamba. Before the village (the first and last on the walk, which you'll reach in 2 to 3 hours) there is a campsite.

The trail leaves the Cusichaca at Huayllabamba, and turns right (north west) up the Llullucha valley. After about half an hour you will come to the confluence of two rivers, known as The Forks. Take the left hand fork. Shortly afterwards, in a small meadow, there is a junction; take the right hand path and drop down to a log bridge across the *quebrada* and start climbing again along a clear trail. The scenery becomes increasingly spectacular and the path steeper as you walk up through mossy woods for 2 or 3 hours, and then emerge above the tree-line into a large meadow, Llullucha Pampa. This is the last campsite before the pass, Abra de Huarmihuanusca (4,198m), which you can see ahead of you. The trail is visible up the valley side on your left. This is the highest pass on the trail, so take heart — if you survive this, you'll survive the others.

At the top of the pass take time to look around you. You should be able to pick out the circular ruins of Runkuracay ahead, just below the next pass, and maybe some wildlife.

Peter Frost describes a variation of the Inca Trail here — with much impressive Inca paving and stairs. It sounds exciting but difficult, so if you

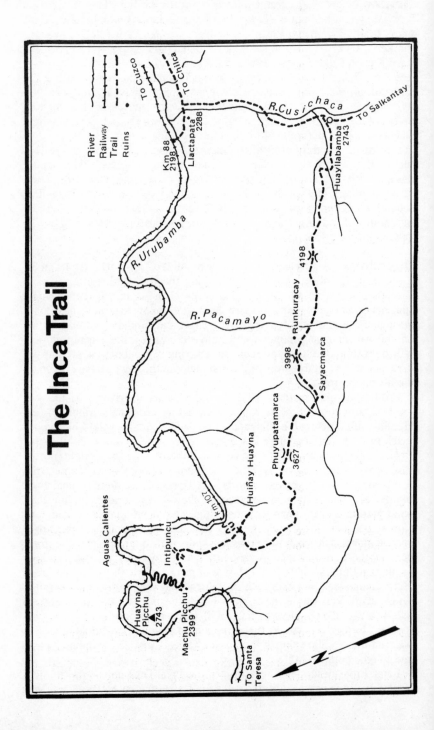

choose this route, use *Exploring Cuzco* to guide you.

The descent from the top of the pass along the normal trail is steep and difficult. Keep to the left of the stream and stay high above the woods; *don't* follow the stream down into the jungle. A good path leads to the Pacamayo campsite, about 1½ hours from the top of the pass. From the camping area you must cross the Pacamayo river which drops down from the mountains in a series of waterfalls. Resist any temptation to take a path downriver into the trees, but cross and start climbing up the left slope. The ruins of Runkuracay are about an hour away; not very impressive in themselves, but occupying a commanding position overlooking the valley, and at the end of a series of rock-hewn steps that at last give you a feeling you are on the trail of the Incas.

From Runkuracay the path is clear over the second pass (Abre de Runkuracay, 3,998m) and down the other side. You'll skirt a couple of small lakes on the way up and an incredible green one on the way down. Keeping high above the lake, you pass another cave and, rounding a corner, find yourself looking down on the ruins of Sayacmarca, the Secret City.

You'll already have noticed increasing evidence of the Inca engineers who first carved out your route; rough flights of steps will have made the going easier over the second pass but now, as you approach Sayacmarca, you'll find yourself climbing a superbly designed stone staircase. The ruins are extensive and impressive; see if you can find traces of the water supply which came by wooden aqueduct from the hillside above.

The next ruin is 2 hours further on at Phuyupatamarca. This can be a damp climb through the cloud forest — after heavy rain the ground is very sploshy — but the Inca paving on this stretch is the finest on the trail, and there's also an Inca tunnel leading to a dizzying viewpoint over the Rio Urubamba, more than a mile below. From here it's an easy half hour's walk to the third pass, which is really a grassy summit. Then you drop down to the left, and the trail soon becomes a magnificent stone staircase leading directly to Phuyupatamarca (and, perhaps more welcomely, a campsite). These ruins are fascinating. Clear water still runs through the channels cut into the rock which feed five baths, leading one from another down the hill.

An incentive to tear yourself away from this wonderful place, is the equally awe-inspiring Inca staircase that leads from the west side of the ruins and disappears into the jungle. This is a newly opened section of the trail, and much more dramatic than the old non-Inca route. There are, reportedly, over a thousand steps before you reach Huiñay Huayna, and you'll fear that your knees will never be the same again. There is also another Inca Tunnel.

Just when your imagination is ringing with the sound of Inca hammers on stone, you come to a new track, powerlines, and a series of bungalows which is the new Trekkers Hotel. Ever since I first hiked the Inca Trail in 1973, they have been building a tourist hotel near Huiñay Huayna, and its progress (lack of), and reported financial problems have been followed with keen interest and some glee by backpackers. Well, it is now finished, and considerably different from that first planned and relatively inoffensive (the area was spoiled anyway by the hydroelectric scheme). Rooms can be had from $1 (sleeping on the floor in the main lobby) to about $2.50 per person for a room and communal hot shower. They also serve food, not terribly highly priced, and will have you breakfasted and on your way in time to reach Intipunku (the Gate of the Sun) for the sunrise. (Thanks to the South American Explorers Club for this information).

First, however, you will want to explore Huiñay Huayna, the most extensive of the ruins visited so far. It has some beautiful stonework, a fantastic location, and an air of mystery often lacking in the crowded Machu Picchu ruins.

The trail from the hotel to Machu Picchu (2 hours away) is clearly marked. It contours a mountain side and disappears into cloud forest full of begonias, bromeliads and tree ferns, before coming to a steep flight of stairs leading up to the first Inca gate. On the wooded hillside below is Chaskapata, a recently excavated area of Inca remains. The path continues to the second gate, Intipunku, and suddenly the whole of Machu Picchu is spread out before you. A magical moment. After drinking in the scene, you can stroll down to the hotel, radiating smugness amongst the groups of tourists who arrived by train, and have a slap-up meal in the outdoor cafeteria. You might even take a look at the ruins!

Few backpackers stay in this hotel (it is expensive and usually fully booked) but for the incomparable experience of sleeping near the ruins (and I speak as one of the lucky ones who slept *in* the ruins during my first visit in 1969) the less impecunious might see if there has been a cancellation.

You are not permitted to camp anywhere near the hotel; the nearest possible place is the soccer pitch near the station. In fact, by this time you'll be ready for a bed and food cooked by someone else, so your best bet is to go to Aguas Calientes, 1½km back along the railway track towards Cuzco. There are several places to stay here; the favourite is 'Gringo Bill's Hostel' (Hostal Qoñi Uni), which has something of a Wild West atmosphere and (maybe) pancakes for breakfast. There is another government Youth Hostel (Albergue Juvenil).

There are thermal baths at Aguas Calientes, and although reportedly disappointing, hikers who have just completed the Inca Trail will not be too fussy. They are up a trail beginning to the right of the ticket office, about twenty minutes from the village. The police don't like gringos camping at the baths, nor do they like nude bathing. It is also prohibited to use soap in the baths, but you can wash standing below the drain in the bottom pool.

A switchback path leads from a bridge at km 107 near Aguas Calientes up to Huiñay Huayna, giving the option for a pleasant round trip via Machu Picchu. Follow the railway tracks back towards Cuzco to the dam, where you cross the river via a footbridge. Turn left, and at the last house go right. This is the trail up to the Inca Trail near Huiñay Huayna, which you'll reach in 1 to 1½ hours.

Getting back Difficult, in the peak tourist season. You may end up standing all the way. You can either catch a local train from Aguas Calientes (if you're staying there) or walk back to Machu Picchu for one of the two afternoon tourist trains (which are now very comfortable *autowagones*). The Indian train leaves at about 16.00 and the tourist train at 17.00. But check on the latest schedule before leaving Cuzco.

PRACTICAL INFORMATION

Time/Rating   The average time is 4 days; some hikers do it in 3 however, and others take 5 days. This is quite a strenuous hike. Compared with other hikes described in this book, the passes are relatively low but the gradients are very steep in places.

Conditions/What to bring   Many tourists attempting this trail are completely unprepared, mentally and physically, for a trip of this kind.

Hikers should be equipped for bad weather, a shortage of firewood, and some very persistent biting insects in the lower regions. Bring a tent or tarpaulin, a stove, and insect repellent. There is a good selection of trail food in Cuzco; the supermarket on Av Sol can supply most of your needs.

Some people prefer to do this walk in the wet season to avoid the crowds. If this is your choice, you must be prepared for lots of rain and bad trail conditions.

If you don't have your own backpacking equipment you can rent it in Cuzco from the tourist office, or from various agencies around the Plaza de Armas.

Maps and further reading   All sorts of maps have now been printed to guide people along the Inca Trail, which is just as well since the I.G.N. has no topographical map of the area. The shops renting equipment usually have maps, and the South American Explorers Club put out a good one.

Exploring Cuzco contains some very informative descriptions and maps of the ruins seen along the Inca Trail, and *Apus and Incas* is useful. This gives details of several other trails in the area not described here.

Travellers with an interest in natural history and seeking a jungle experience in relative comfort should consider the Explorers Inn in the Tambopata Reserve. This lodge is four hours by boat from Puerto Maldonado and has a resident gringo naturalist who provides expert information on the very plentiful flora and fauna. The lodge can be booked through Peruvian Safaris, Casilla 10088, Lima, or the same company has an office by Plaza San Francisco, Cuzco.

In England the Tambopata Reserve Society (TReeS) has been set up to help conserve this small but important reserve. More information from Helen Newing, 59 Redcliffe Rd, London SW10 9NQ.

The Cusichaca Project

Passengers on the train to Machu Picchu, and hikers at the start of the Inca Trail may notice an encampment up the valley from Kilometre 88. This is the Cusichaca Project, founded 1n 1968 and in action since 1978 under the direction of the British archaelogist, Dr Ann Kendall.

For ten years, teams of 60 to 80 field workers have been excavating and studying the Inca and pre-Inca remains in this valley. The purpose of the project has been twofold. First, to make a thorough archaeological study of the area, and second to implement a programme of land rehabilitation. It is this latter aim which makes the Cusichaca Project so unusual and interesting. This valley was vastly more productive in pre-Hispanic times than it is now, and by reconstructing the history of the Inca descendants who now live in the area, they are being helped to understand their past and use that knowledge to improve their present.

As the project draws to a close, the aims have been satisfyingly met. The intensive study by experts not only in archaeology, but ethnography, archaeobotany and agriculture, has produced not only a much greater understanding of the Inca presence in the area, but given impetus to the restoration of the Quishuarpata canal which will benefit the local community long after the gringos have left.

Dr Kendall and her team are now moving on to the Patacancha Valley, 30km away, near Ollantaytambo. The aims here will be the same: archaeological and ethnological programmes along with rural development. So once again by understanding the richness of their past, the local *campesinos* will be motivated to take an active role in improving their rural communities.

The Cusichaca Project Trust is an Educational Charity. The Academic Sponsors are the Institute of Archaeology at the University of London, and the Instituto Nacional de Cultura, Peru. Whilst visitors are not actively discouraged, the project workers are very busy, and too much outside interest in their work will inevitably delay them.

I am grateful to Dr Ann Kendall for permission to extract the above information from project reports.

Variations on the Inca Trail

Although most people start walking at Km 88 there are other approaches to the first part of the trail from Chilca or Ollantaytambo as well as the spendid Salkantay route described later.

Ollantaytambo or Chilca to Llactapata

This adds an extra day to the Inca Trail, but avoids the hassle of the train trip and allows a breaking-in period along more or less level ground before the steep climb to Huayllabamba and the first pass. If you start out on Saturday, you will arrive at Llactapata on Sunday, when there are no local trains so very few other hikers on the trail at the same time as you.

From Ollantaytambo, cross the road bridge (noting that the new bridge has been constructed on Inca foundations) and follow a good path along the south side of the river. You will pass some fine Inca terraces and ruins before reaching a very arid region of dry tropical vegetation. After about 7km you'll come to the Chilca bridge. (Chilca is accessible by truck or taxi from Ollantaytambo.) The trail now passes the interesting remains of a Spanish *estancia*. Note the ruined church and the beautiful courtyard on the opposite side of the trail. Both buildings are still used, but no attempt has been made to restore them to their former elegance.

Llactapata is 12km beyond Chilca. The trail is always easy to follow, and level until the hilly last section where it descends into a spectacular gorge full of tropical plants. This is a perfect camping area. The Inca Trail is less than an hour away.

Chilca to Huayllabamba

Whereas the trail just described takes you alongside the river through semi-desert conditions, this beautiful route climbs steeply to high rivers and waterfalls with some splendid views of snow-capped mountains. It adds another 2 to 3 days to the Inca Trail.

From Chilca, head due south up the river valley opposite the bridge across the Urubamba and follow the trail, which keeps close to a *quebrada*, west and north west. After about 5 hours you reach the village of Ancascocha. Turn right here, south west, and head up the valley to your right where there are camping places. The path continues towards a pass, skirting left of a small lake and reaching the top some 2 to 3 hours after Ancascocha. The two snow peaks are Nevado Salkantay Este (not to be confused with its higher cousin to the west) and Huayanay on your right. The path now drops down towards the village of Quesca, and picks up Quebrada Cusichaca, passing some Inca remains, and follows it to the Inca fortress of Paucarcancho, an almost unknown semi-circular ruin in an inspiring position at the junction of two rivers. There are several curved terraces leading up to the ruin itself.

From here you can either head for Huayllabamba and the Inca Trail by crossing to the left bank of the river and walking downstream for one hour, or turn left (south) up the *quebrada* towards Salkantay and the hike described next.

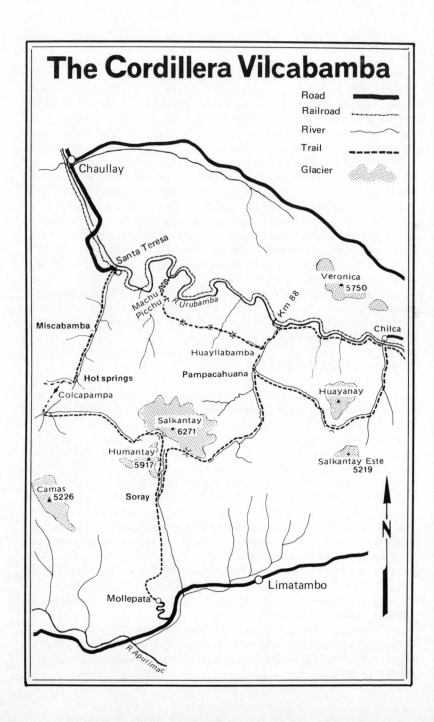

The Cordillera Vilcabamba

Road
Railroad
River
Trail
Glacier

Chaullay

Santa Teresa

Machu Picchu

R. Urubamba

Km 88

Veronica
▲ 5750

Chilca

Miscabamba

Huayllabamba

Pampacahuana

Hot springs

Colcapampa

Huayanay
▲

Salkantay
▲ 6271

Humantay
▲ 5917

Salkantay Este
5219

Camas
▲ 5226

Soray

N

Limatambo

Mollepata

R. Apurimac

Mollepata to Huayllabamba or to Santa Teresa

Introduction The link-up to the Inca Trail via Salkantay was George's and my favourite walk in Peru, and the alternative route to Santa Teresa, which I've done several times since, is now high on my list of near perfect hikes; it is also ideal for a relative new-comer to backpacking since there is only one high pass. Whether the new road which, at the time of writing had reached Soray, is going to ruin the Santa Teresa walk, remains to be seen. It is hard to greet its construction with delight.

From Mollepata, 2,803m, a village built on a mountain side overlooking a citrus producing valley, where flocks of parakeets screech in the trees, you climb steeply to the foot of the Salkantay river valley. The gradual ascent to the mountain is made through flowering shrubs buzzing with humming birds, across streams, and past isolated houses, while Nevado de Salkantay (6,240m) and its neighbour Humantay (5,917m) shine in the afternoon sun. Salkantay is an almost perfect mountain, both in shape and location, and the highest in the Cordillera Vilcabamba. It dominates the first part of both trips.

At the head of the valley, you have a choice of high passes and trails: west to Santa Teresa (3 days), past hot springs and through coffee and citrus groves, or east to Huayllabamba (2 days), hugging Salkantay's glacier and passing Inca remains. A choice of post- or pre-Columbian.

Guides and pack animals
Some hikers like to take advantage of the availability of *arrieros* for these treks. The Delgado family are well known for their reliability, honesty, and knowledge of the area. The father, Don Victor, is well into his seventies now, and does no guiding, but his two sons, Rueben and Washington, are usually available. They can be contacted by radio message (the radio station is just past the main Cuzco post office) in Limatambo. The *arrieros* will meet you at the campsite beyond Mollepata at an agreed time.

Getting there Trucks to Mollepata, or buses to Limatambo (76km from Cuzco), leave from the same place as those to Chinchero: Av Arcopata in Cuzco, between about 7.00 and 8.00. From the same place you'll find transport bound for Limatambo. There is also a Limatambo bus at 15.00; check its departure point with the tourist office (in fact, always check departure points and times with the tourist office). In a truck it's a very uncomfortable 5 hour ride to Mollepata, and you should be prepared for the heat that comes with the loss of altitude and bring some protection from the sun. There are some marvellous views of the white cone that is Salkantay, before you drop into a deep and dramatic canyon. Mollepata stands high above this, a further hour away.

Limatambo and Tarahuasi Unless you're in a great hurry I strongly recommend you spend the first night in Limatambo. It is a pleasant, low-lying little town surrounded by sub-tropical vegetation, and with a basic *albergue* and various possible camping places. Nearby, at Tarahuasi, is an Inca temple with one of the finest examples anywhere of Inca polygonal masonry in a long retaining wall. On the upper level are twenty eight tall niches, thought by John Hemming to have been for liveried attendants or for mummies. The stonework, in roseate patterns, is orange-coloured through its covering of lichen. This amazing place is rarely visited by tourists.

Tarahuasi was the site of a battle between the Spanish and Incas. Hernando de Soto and his soldiers were resting here on their way to Cuzco when they were attacked by four thousand Inca warriors; four Spaniards were killed and many injured.

Hiking directions   Mollepata has improved from the days, nearly a century ago, when George Squier described it as a 'place unsurpassed in evil repute by any in Peru'. There is an attractive green plaza, some pretty houses, and more midges than you'd believe possible.

From Mollepata either take the new road or head steeply uphill in the direction of the mountains. Both routes join in one broad trail going up the left side of the valley to the north west. After about 2½ hours you'll be nearing the top of the pass, Marcaccasa, distinguished from afar by two trees silhouetted on the horizon. There is good camping near an aqueduct. If you continue, the next (and last) possible camping place is near the cross on the hill to the right. Ask a *campesino* to show you the location of the well.

Below this cross is the beginning of a somewhat difficult to follow section of trail which bears round to the right, keeping on high ground, and heading north east through shrubs and bushes. In fact, there are many small paths through the bushes, and they all lead to the main trail, so although you may feel lost, providing you keep going in the right direction you will emerge eventually on a clear trail. This part takes about 45 minutes. Once you join the main trail the way is clear (and uphill), and you will shortly come to a stream. Fill your water bottle here — the next water is some 3 hours away. Soon you round a corner to a splendid view of Humantay at the northern head of the long Humanta river valley.

It's about a 4 hour walk from here to the small settlement of Soray. The going is gently uphill, there are lots of flowering shrubs and hummingbirds, and the views are lovely. Shortly before Soray, Salkantay comes into view. There are good campsites just above Soray before the path crosses the river (there is a bridge to the left of the pampa) and even more beautiful (but very cold) ones about an hour further on.

Soray to Huayllabamba

An hour beyond Soray is the giant V of a moraine spreading down from Salkantay. From here to the pass of Incachillasca (nearly 5,000m — just about 17,000ft!) is about 4 hours. The route is up the right side of the moraine, a none too clear path going to the north east. After some steep climbing, the terrain levels out and the path turns sharply to the right and uphill, near a big boulder, and continues along the right hand bank of a small stream. Before reaching a flat, boggy meadow, you'll see a low cliff hung with icicles formed by the dripping water.

The trail seems to disappear in this boggy stretch, but you can pick it up at the far end. In misty weather this plateau is a useful landmark. Remember that the trail continues a little to the right of it.

It's worth making a detour to the glacier. You can see the layers of ice representing annual precipitation, rather like the annual rings on a tree stump. Notice too the quality of the ice; the old compact ice is blue and almost clear, while new ice is frosty with trapped air.

Above the plateau the path zig-zags up reddish coloured scree, becoming more conspicuous as it nears the top. You are probably now higher than you have ever been (on land) in your life, so stop and gloat (and get your breath back). The path down the other side is quite clear as it traverses the right hand side of the mountain, but it becomes faint near a *campesino* shelter and some stone corrals. It will take about 2 hours to reach this point from the pass. The trail now crosses the *quebrada* and follows it down the valley. Keep to the left hand bank of the river as it turns north-east and, astonishingly, becomes a canal. The Incas frequently cut canals through valleys to increase agricultural land, and this is a fine example. The area, with its settlement, is called Pampachuana.

Shortly after the end of the canal you should cross to the right bank via a footbridge, and follow a good path down to a river junction. The Inca fortress, Paucarcancha, stands here. From the foot of the fortress you'll see the trail leading to Chilca (described earlier) and you could take this route as an alternative to doing the Inca Trail or hiking down to Km 88.

To reach Huayllabamba, cross the river and follow the left hand bank down to Rio Cusichaca. The village is one hour away, and Machu Picchu 3 days away.

Note   Don't try to attempt this trail starting at km 88 unless you want to pay the Inca Trail fee (there's no reason why the guard should believe that you are *not* hiking the Inca Trail). If you want to do it in reverse, start at Chilca.

Soray to Santa Teresa

Go up the left side of the moraine, crossing to the left bank of a stream to pick up the path leading up the side of the mountain. It goes steeply uphill for a ½ hour, then comes a series of switchbacks (*siete culebras* is the local name for this stretch). At the top of the seven switchbacks the terrain levels out under Salkantay's lateral moraine and drops gently down to a small lake, Soirococha. The pass you see above you is, alas, a false one; the main pass is a little further on, but the view of Salkantay looming above you on the right more than compensates you for the effort. The summit is marked by a cairn of stones (*apecheta*) which grows daily as each traveller adds his pebble to thank the *apus* for a safe trip. A few cattle skulls add a macabre touch. This pass is estimated to be 4,750m and is reached 3 or 4 hours after leaving the high campsite. If the weather is bad (and it often is)

Coming round Salkantay

there are caves to shelter in about 20 minutes below the pass on the other side.

The path runs down the left hand side of the valley, becoming indistinct in swampy areas. You won't get lost, however, since once the valley narrows there is only one obvious trail on the left of the river. 2 or 3 hours below the pass you'll see a small hut on your left. This is the 'summer' home of Don Victor Delgado, the patriarch of the best-known family in the area. This place is called Huayrajmachay, or 'eye of the wind', and is a popular camping area.

From here to the first major river crossing and campsite is 3 or 4 hours. You'll leave the beautiful pyramid-shaped peak of Humantay behind as you drop below the tree line (known as *ceja de selva* — the eyebrow of the jungle) and walk through groves of bamboo with many orchids and other flowers and lots of hummingbirds. Don't forget to keep looking back at the snow peaks behind you, framed by bamboo fronds. After 2 hours the trail crosses a landslide and in another 1½ hours you'll drop steeply down to the bridge across Río Chalhuay and a beautiful camping spot. But there's an even better one further on. After an hour you'll reach the tiny settlement of Colpapampa, and 20 minutes beyond this are the hot springs (turn right at the trail junction by the river) and an idyllic campsite the other side of a turf-covered bridge.

Just before the bridge a single stream of hot water is piped into a semi-natural pool on the right hand side of the trail. The water temperature is perfect if you like very hot baths.

Here is the confluence of two rivers, the Totota and the Santa Teresa, and you'll be following the Río Santa Teresa down to the town of the same name. If you follow the river bank (scramble over the rocks) a short way down from the campsite you'll come to more hot springs and beautiful mineral deposits.

There is a surprising amount of uphill walking the next day, but through such lovely surroundings you can hardly complain.

After the hot-springs bridge, the trail keeps close to the river (ignore a fork to your left) then climbs up to contour round the mountainside through bamboo groves. Soon you will come to a stream which disrupts the trail. Go up this stream for 8m to pick up the trail again. Carry on uphill to a spectacular waterfall. This cascade drops some 300m and the trail crosses it midway! There is good bathing here. More up and down and you come to a second waterfall, with more swimming in the pool above. This is an incredibly beautiful stretch, with begonias, purple and orange orchids, and strawberries lining the path. Some 4 hours after the hot springs, and 1 hour after a rather ramshackle bridge across the river (which you don't cross), you'll come to the first village of any size, Miscabamba. Large groups of trekkers usually camp on the football pitch, but — sadly — theft is sometimes a problem so you may prefer to pitch your tent above the town. There is a flat grassy area just before a very wet stretch where a stream runs along the trail; it's better to walk in the clear shallow water than chance your luck in the mud at the edges.

From Miscabamba to the houses at the start of the road (Paltachayoc, which has a beer shop!) is an up and down 2½ hours, then it's another hot 2½ hours through citrus, banana and coffee plantations to Santa Teresa. You'll notice that the houses here are more sophisticated than those in the *sierra* and the people more Spanish looking. As you approach Santa Teresa a road leading to an *hacienda* leads off to the left. Don't take this, but continue to the river and the suspension bridge leading to the station.

The train to Machu Picchu or Cuzco leaves around 13.00, and others go in the early morning and at night (there are places to stay in Santa Teresa). At Machu Picchu (the station is called Puente Ruinas), you will have to camp near the station or stay at Aguas Calientes (next stop, called Machu Picchu, just to confuse you). Mini buses start up the hill early each day to transport the workers to the ruins. Since you won't have the standard bus ticket (provided with package tours), watch out for exhorbitant charges, however.

You can also climb up to Huiñay Huayna from km 107, near Aguas Calientes, and approach Machu Picchu the athentic way, as described on page 114.

PRACTICAL INFORMATION
Time/Rating It's 4 days from Cuzco to Huayllabamba (including the truck trip) and 5 or 6 days to Santa Teresa.

Both of these are strenuous hikes, with altitude gains of around 2,000m. The Huayllabamba one is the toughest because of its 5,000m pass. But on both hikes there is only one pass, then it's downhill (almost) all the way.

Conditions/What to bring There are some rugged stretches, so good boots are essential, plus full high altitude equipment: warm clothes, hat and gloves, tent, etc. No provisions are available between Mollepata and Machu Picchu, so if you include the Inca Trail, bring at least a week's supply of food.

You'll need a swimsuit for the Santa Teresa walk, and hot-weather clothes including shorts. Insect repellent helps fight the Mollepata bugs.

Maps Unfortunately the only I.G.N. map of the region is a very inaccurate dyeline version, scale 1:200,000. There are no colour topographical maps of the Cordillera Vilcabamba.

'All these passes over the mountains are marked by piles of stones...by the contribution of a single stone from each traveller as an offering to the spirits of the mountains, as an invocation for their aid in sustaining the fatigues of travel.'

George Squier, *Travel & Exploration in the Land of the Inca, 1877.*

The Cordillera Vilcanota

Named after the Vilcanota river lying to its west, this impressive range of mountains includes the massive Nevado de Auzangate (6,372m and clearly visible from the heights of Sacsayhuaman) and three others over 6,000m.

Hiking opportunities here are excellent. The whole area lies above the treeline and is densely settled, so there are paths everywhere. This is alpaca country. Enormous herds graze in the already eroded valleys. How much grass will be left for future generations remains to be seen. The Indians here speak little Spanish, and are probably the most colourful Andean group in Peru. All women and most men wear handwoven clothes of undyed wool. Black is the most favoured, although white is frequently used for men's trousers. The woven decorative borders of the women's black skirts are intricate and very beautiful, and some have a particularly distinctive style with the front of the top skirt (all Indian women wear several skirts at once) cut back to reveal the one below. Both sexes wear black embroidered waistcoats, (vests) often decorated with rows of pearl buttons. Men's *chullos* (woollen caps) frequently have buttons sewn around the earflaps, and the women's broad hats use the same form of decoration. Old women wear an undecorated black felt pancake-shaped hat.

The finest clothes are worn on market day, so if you have the good fortune to walk along a frequented trail on this special day, you'll see freshly scrubbed young women sparkling with vitality, young men wearing flowers in their hats, and old crones with faded, carefully washed rags.

The people of the Cordillera Vilcanota hold a major fiesta, The 'ice festival' of the Virgin of Qoyoriti, in the second week in June. The costumes and dancing equal the Paucartambo fiesta, and the pilgrimage to a glacier make it a unique celebration.

The Auzangate Circuit

Introduction   This 5 or 6 day hike has everything: herds of llamas and alpacas, traditionally dressed Indians, hot springs, turquoise lakes, glaciers, ice caves, and even vicuñas. Not surprisingly, it's very popular with trekkers. It is also high, tough and cold. You are closer to snow and ice here than on any other Cuzco area hike

The route takes you right round the massif of Auzangate and over three high passes, before returning you to your starting point, the small village of Tinqui.

Getting there   There is now a nice yellow kombi (VW bus) going between Cuzco and Ocongate, taking 6 hours. It leaves Santa Domingo in Cuzco on Mondays, Wednesdays, Fridays and Sundays, and will continue on to Tinqui (the trailhead) on request. For the return journey the bus leaves Ocongate plaza at 6.00 on Tuesdays, Thursdays and Saturdays. There are also trucks. Check their departure time and place from the Tourist Office. You can stay at the Pension Josmar in

Ocongate.

Tinqui is one hour beyond Ocongate; there's a Sunday market if you need last minute supplies. Backpackers are sometimes permitted to sleep in the schoolhouse.

Guides and pack animals There are plenty of *arrieros* in Ocongate and Tinqui. Ask around. Don Faustino has my personal recommendation.

Directions (My Auzangate circuit was abbreviated; I am grateful to Rob Rachowiecki for these meticulous notes.)

Tinqui to Upis (4,400m) 5 to 7 hours
Take the broad track from the schoolhouse and cross the river via a bridge behind the school. Cross a second smaller bridge and head up to houses on the skyline to the right. Continue on a wide trail to open puna with house-sized boulders on the left. Continue on a deteriorating trail, cross a small stream and head south south east across the pampa towards Auzangate. There is no real trail here, just cattle paths.

After about two hours, cross a small stream on a stone foot bridge and ignore the track on the right immediately beyond the bridge. Instead look for a wide track on the left which climbs gently beyond a group of houses, then crosses an irrigation ditch and soon drops down through a green, boggy valley south south east to Upis.

There are hot springs at Upis; rather dirty but with room for several people at a time and with a fantastic view of Auzangate at the end of the valley. This is, naturally, a great place to camp.

Upis to Pucupata (approx. 4,800m) 5 to 7 hours
From Upis continue up the valley towards Auzangate, crossing the swampy area as soon as possible to the right of the valley where a faint narrow footpath is found. This continues to a grassy meadow. Cross the meadow and climb right to some stone corrals.

Here two passes are visible, to the left and right of a yellow hill. Both go to the same place. The low path is longer but easier, the high route more spectacular.

I headed roughly south towards Auzangate and when the trail became steep, turned right (about south south west) and climbed up and over the pass. It's about 2½ to 3½ hours to the top of the pass from Upis camp.

At the pass it is easy to scramble up a little summit to the right for beautiful all round views.

From the pass continue roughly south south west down a valley until you reach a purple moraine. From here you can see a turquoise lake with a waterfall (called Laguna Vinococha on the I.G.N. map). Head left (south east) under the jagged and obvious rocky spires of Nvdo. Sorimani. Head for the top of the waterfall cascading out of the turquoise lake (it's easiest to cross falls near the outlet of the lake) and hike over the top of a small hillock to the right of the lake and waterfall. From here hike to the right of another small hill on the far right side of the lake and continue roughly east to a campsite near the base of an obvious red mountain by a lake called Pukacocha on the map.

From the campsite you can climb the small moraine ridge north of the camp to see Lake Vinococha and perhaps a dramatic ice fall or avalanche into the lake (called Vinococha by locals because it is sometimes 'red like wine' due to glacial sediment coming down from nearby red mountains). The views of Auzangate are particularly close up and spectacular. If it's clear far off to the left (roughly north west) the pyramid of Salkantay can be seen 100km away, and behind the camp rises a sheer rock spire which has never been climbed and is reputed by some mountaineers to be 'impossible'.

Pucapata to Uchuy Finaya (4,500m) 5 to 7 hours
Ten minutes from camp reach some corrals and head right around a small rocky hill, continuing roughly east on fairly good trails below red cliffs. (The trails tend to meander from south east to north east.) After about 1½ to 2 hours you'll reach the top of a small pass with the main pass to the left (east) with turquoise Laguna Auzangatecocha below. Head down fairly steeply and for quite a long way to pasture at the right end of Laguna Auzangatecocha. (En route you suddenly come upon a small aquamarine lake with strange mineral deposits.)

When you reach Laguna Auzangatecocha, cross the small stream at the right end of the lake and then head north east on trails behind the moraine lying on the east side of the lake. It's a fairly gentle climb for a few hundred metres, then abruptly becomes steeper. You will reach this spot about 2½ hours after leaving camp; rest here for a long, steep climb ahead to the pass.

There are two choices, up a gully to the east (longer but less steep), or continue north-east up a ridge (steeper but more direct). Continue roughly north-east to the pass which is approximately where the red and black rocks meet. It is about 4 to 5 hours from the camp to the pass (nearly 5,100m — over 17,000ft!).

From the pass to the camp you can go cross-country or follow the trail roughly south east for about 1 hour through a desert-like landscape. Camp under Cerro Puca Punta (red point).

Uchuy Finaya to Lake Ticllacocha (4,800m) 4 to 5 hours
A relatively easy day compared to previous ones. From the campsite, continue east to a broad green valley (Pampa Jatunpata). Cross a stream nearby some houses and skirt the swampy green valley to the left (north east), climbing over the hill to the left rather than dropping to the bogs below. Head north east up the Río Jampa valley (which could also be called Viscacha Valley — there are dozens of these animals). It's best to stay on left of river. At the small community (six houses) of Jampa (called Campa locally) bear to the left (north and north west) around the mountain and arrive at the very small Laguna Ticllacocha which is not visible til you are there. ('Ticlla' means fierce/brave — describing

cold nights and stormy weather often encountered here.)

Lake Ticllacocha to Pacchanta (4,300m.) 5 to 6 hours
This section is the most likely for vicuña sightings, and there is also a good opportunity to explore an ice cave just before the pass.

Head approximately north west out of the high Ticllacocha camp and soon come to the 5,000m pass (1 to 1½ hours). Rough trails reach the pass on the left hand side of the 'valley' above Ticllacocha (from some points the valley appears impassable because the glacier seems to stretch all the way across — but don't worry).

There are glaciers to the right just before the pass and to the left just after. The glacier to the right has a spectacular ice cave. It's found at the rounded point of the glacier nearest the trail — be prepared to spend some time looking for it, but it's *very* worthwhile. Sometimes the cave entrance is covered by icicles and is not easily seen. Smash a hole in the icicles with rocks to get into the cave which stretches back over 100m and has several chambers; you have to crawl towards the end. Some of the chambers are three to five metres high; blue light filters through the ice pillars, stalactites, etc. A torch (flashlight) is essential. You may have difficulty in getting out of the cave — use a sharp rock to chop a couple of steps in the ice (the floor of the cave is about two foot below the entrance).

At the pass, which is covered by many cairns — an eerie place in the blowing mists — you continue in a generally north west direction.

After the pass the north west trail heads through a long scree slope (look particularly for vicuña here) and emerges above and to the left of several lakes. At the final lake (Comercocha) head past a few houses and drop down into the valley below. There's a fairly clear trail to a river where crossing appears difficult. Don't do anything drastic — the trail runs along a ridge to the right of the river (you may have to back track from the river 50 to 100 metres). Stay on top of this ridge on a narrow but obvious trail until you reach a small stone bridge which crosses the river. From here continue on a good and pleasant trail along the left bank of the river, past occasional pools and lakes, until you reach the campsite at Pacchanta. (There is a bridge over the river before the town — head to your left along the river bank until you find a bridge at the left side of Pacchanta.)

There are two hot springs here. One has had a bath of concrete built around it. Often there's green scum floating on it but most of it can easily be scooped out with a bowl.

Pacchanta to Tinqui
From the camp you have to cross the river via a bridge and then follow the obvious trail west north west to Tinqui, 3 hours away.

PRACTICAL INFORMATION
Time/Rating   5 days. A very strenuous high trek with extraordinarily high passes (two over 5,000m). It is essential to be properly acclimatised for this hike and pay particular attention to the dangers of altitude sickness (see *Health*, Chapter 2).

Conditions/What to bring Freezing cold nights and windy days mean all the warm clothes you can bring. It can also rain, snow or hail (although this is a dryer area than the Cordillera Vilcabamba). The modest will also need a swimsuit for the hot pools. Everyone needs powerful sunscreen, lipsalve, etc.

Maps The I.G.N. sell topographical maps, scale 1:100,000. The Ocongate sheet covers this hike. More useful is the excellent new Auzangate map put out by the South American Explorers Club.

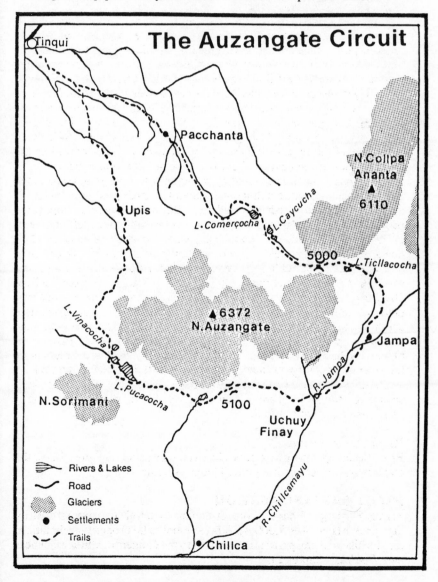

The Hovel

It was while leading a trek round Auzangate that I had the chance to indulge in some independent travel: not hiking (well, just at first) but horsing, which is certainly faster, if more painful.

I knew by the first evening that Lynn would have to leave the group. She had severe altitude sickness, and with the danger of pulmonary oedema I wasn't going to risk her continuing. She agreed to return to Cuzco. One of our two riding horses was appropriated as an equine ambulance, and an *arriero* and I started leading it and Lynn down the hillside. By the time we reached Ocongate some eight hours later, Lynn was feeling much better, and I was feeling considerably worse, not having carried my own backpack for many a moon (packed for a donkey's back, not mine, it weighed a hefty 20kg). It was decided that Lynn would return to Cuzco alone. Faustino, who was planning to return to the group, agreed to lend me a horse so I could accompany him, and to spread the journey over two days instead of his customary one. Lynn and I stayed at the best hotel in Ocongate, cleared chicken giblets out of the sink to clean our teeth, decided not to wash in the bucket outside, and spent a not uncomfortable night before I put her on the 6am bus to the Big City.

Faustino was waiting for me with Sambo, a scrawny black pony wearing the resigned expression of all Peruvian domestic animals and a Spanish saddle, with uneven stirrups, hung about with flour sacks containing my sleeping bag, etc. (my backpack travelled with Lynn). Faustino looked magnificent; now that he was master, not servant, he'd changed into a splendid multicoloured poncho, and his bearing and the respect with which he was greeted as we trotted through the town showed that in Ocongate, at least, he was a man of considerable status. We trotted through the town, we trotted out of town, and we trotted off the road and along the track towards Pacchanta. I thought I was going to die. I hadn't ridden for several years, and my bottom and knees were screaming for mercy. At the first settlement, Pacchanta, there are thermal waters, and I firmly told Faustino that we were going to stop a while so I could take a bath. He dismounted and settled down in a good position near the pool to watch.

I wondered where we were going to spend the night. It goes down to freezing at those altitudes, so I hoped we'd be under cover. Yes, said Faustino, a friend of his had a *casita* in the next valley. In a couple of hours we found the friend screaming Quechua curses at a herd of serene-looking llamas and alpacas. Or perhaps he was just conversing with them, it's hard to tell in that language. He and Faustino disappeared into a grass-thatched hovel, chattering volubly, and I decided to see if my legs still worked by climbing a nearby hill and watching the evening sun paint golden rings round the alpacas and touch the white bulk of Auzangate with pink.

It was almost dark when I returned to the hovel; the interior was lit by one guttering candle and I ducked through the low door and groped my way to a seat by the wall — a remarkably comfortable and well-sprung seat, covered with sheepskin. The hovel owner's daughter gave me a plate of tiny potatoes, and I gave them some chocolate. Then I prepared myself for sleep. Father and daughter watched entranced as I laid out my requirements. I unrolled and inflated my Thermarest, stuffed a sweater into a teeshirt as a pillow, and pulled my sleeping bag from its stuff bag. In the background I could hear incredulous squeaks from the daughter punctuating the steady drone of man-of-the-world Faustino explaining what everything was for. When I actually climbed into the blue cocoon of a sleeping bag, it was too much for her. She burst into hysterical giggles and little explosions of laughter accompanied the rest of my preparations. When the show was over, she just curled up on a pile of sheepskins and went to sleep.

The girl was up again at 4.30 to start a cooking fire (inside) with llama dung, and to round up the horses. It was bitterly cold, and dark and eye-smarting smoky in the hovel, and I buried myself in my cocoon until it was light enough to see my surroundings. I was rather surprised at what I saw. To begin with, my comfortable seat of the evening before turned out to be half a sheep carcass with a well sprung rib cage. Other bits of sheep hung from the ceiling. There was no furniture, but it would have looked bizarre anyway with the dirt floor and rough stone and adobe walls. There were no windows, but Inca-style niches made useful shelves for yet more pieces of sheep, half spun wool, burnt out candles, and a safety pin.

We reached our objective that afternoon. After labouring up the 5,000m pass, with Sambo equally breathless on the lead rope beside me (actually, one of the great advantages of trekking with horses is that out of consideration you have to stop frequently so *they* can get their breath back) we stopped at a rocky knoll overlooking Ticclacocha. Rumbling glaciers and spiky snow peaks surrounded me on all sides, with ice-cream cornices bulging over the ridges. I was well content to wait there for the group's arrival.

Alpacas and Auzangate

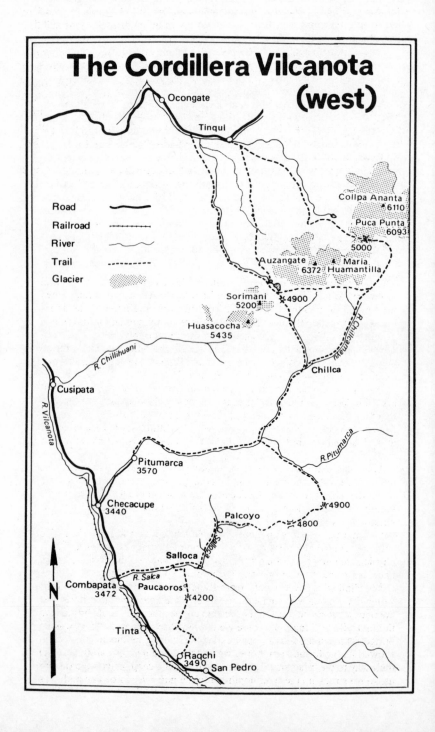

The Cordillera Vilcanota (west)

The Southern Route

Auzangate is the focus for most hikes, but we found the Inca ruins at Raqchi and the area to their north enthralling. Perhaps we needed a change from the snowy peaks that had surrounded us for the past few weeks. Not that we planned it that way, as you'll see from the account below, but the accidental discovery of 'Mars' was a wonderful stroke of luck. Since writing this account in 1980 it has inspired very few gringos to follow in our footsteps — at least according to Roger Sampson, who has updated the directions, and reported villagers being surprised to see him. So it sounds as though you can really get away from from your fellow hikers here, as well as seeing some very different scenery from the Auzangate circuit.

This is a 4 day hike, but experienced and energetic backpackers could combine it with the Auzangate circuit to make a memorable 8 to 10 day trek.

'We've landed on Mars!'
By George Bradt

The Southern route in the Cordillera Vilcanota was an accidental discovery. We were were fully committed to the Auzangate circuit when we strolled over to the Cuzco Tourist Office one afternoon to ask about buses to Ocongate the next morning. 'There's only one and it leaves this evening. You'll arrive in Ocongate at 4 in the morning.'

What, give up our lovely hotel bed for a night on a bus, and with no mental preparation? We looked at our map. Perhaps we could start from a different village. 'How about Sicuani, then?'

'No problem, buses leave every hour, and there's also the train.' That settled it. We only had a road map for our newly chosen route, but realised that Sicuani was too far to the south. It would take ages to reach Auzangate from there. So we selected Raqchi, with its little-known Inca ruins. It looked a manageable walk north to the high peaks which were our goal.

This was, perhaps, the most fascinating hike we did all summer, and different because we had no map covering our projected route. Without a map, the changes in the landscape came so unpredictably as to be breathtaking. And no map could have conveyed the many aspects of this remarkable scenery.

Our mission was to walk north from Raqchi until we found a river (Rio Pitumarca) at the bottom of a canyon running from east to west. These physical features ran along the edge of the map we did have, and we expected to be there in one day at the most. It took us three.

We climbed up over a ridge from Raqchi, and saw a river down in the valley. By the time we reached it, we'd convinced ourselves that it was just the river we were looking for. The terrain on the other side could be made to fit our 1:100,000 map, but there were a few discrepancies. There was no bridge, for instance, and the locals called the river by another name. A child showed us the fording point, and we watched two natives carefully make their way to the other side. It was much too wide, deep, and dangerous for us, so we struck up the river hoping to find a narrower ford. The path was clear and well used. [Had we walked down river we would have found an easy way to cross.]

As we went upstream, the valley closed in on us until we were walking down a deep canyon. So beguiled were we by the scenery, we almost abandoned north in favour of west up this wonderful valley. But the trail petered out and eventually we found a fording point, crossed, and walked back along the other side. A detour of, perhaps, 15km and by now we accepted the fact that this wasn't the Río Pitumarca.

As dusk approached we hurried through a village, after saying goodbye to a boy who had shown us the trail over the ridge and into the next valley to the north. Minutes later he was running towards us, shouting. 'Please come and eat supper with us,' he begged, 'then you can walk with strength and sleep deeply.'

Without giving us a chance to think about it, he herded us through a gate in an adobe wall, and we found ourselves in the small courtyard of a typical Andean house. The cooking hut was tiny and too humble for such exalted visitors, so we were motioned toward two stones covered with a blanket in the courtyard. The boy's parents came out and shyly greeted us. Father kept apologising for nothing in particular, as a counterpoint to our praising nothing in particular.

Soon two earthenware bowls of food arrived, along with more apologies; they needn't have worried, it was the most delicious meal we'd eaten since leaving Cuzco. Would you complain about small, tasty potatoes fried in pork fat with cheese? While we ate they whispered about us and we whispered about them. How could we repay them, we wondered. We decided on presents of a box of matches for father, a picture postcard of San Francisco for the son, and decorative hair grips for the mother and little daughter. That gave us an excuse to enter the kitchen and distribute the gifts.

The small stone and adobe hut had a cooking area where a fire continuously burned, a crude table with a maize grinder, and an adobe seat covered with sheep skins. The base of the seat was honeycombed with holes through which scuffled and squeaked a large number of guinea pigs.

The family were thrilled with their gifts, although they only recognised the matches. The postcard fascinated them; after we'd turned it the right way up and pointed out the high buildings and the huge bridge they gasped in amazement, but they couldn't understand the scale of it all. And how could they when their little world was made up of adobe houses, llamas, streams and footpaths? Nor did they understand us when we said how lucky they were.

We continued the next day up another valley through some of the best scenery and most interesting country life we've seen in Peru. Fantastic dark limestone formations spiked into the blue sky, little *molinos* or water-wheels crouched over the valley's stream, and we saw our first herd of pure white alpacas. As we got higher, passing small villages with grass-thatched roofs, we could see the hills had had a sprinkling of snow during the night; the slopes were bare from overgrazing, and the purple-red earth glowed in the afternoon sun. Our path snaked up a series of hills, and we always thought the pass would be just over the next one. Not until we reached an enormous valley tumbling down on our left did we realise the pass was still a long, long way off.

It was getting late, and frankly I was whacked. We'd gained 1,300m that day, and I was all for camping below the pass, but Hilary wanted to push on into the gloaming. She hoped to see our river and the Auzangate range from the top of the pass, and sleep soundly with the knowledge she was 'found' on the map at last. There was no holding her as she slogged up to the windy pass. I watched her stand motionless at the top, fling off her backpack and scamper down towards me. 'George!' she shrieked 'Guess what you see from the top!'. I stopped, got my wind and waited until she reached me. 'Cuzco?' was all I could think of that would explain such extreme behaviour. 'No, no. You simply won't believe it!' 'Lima?' 'No,' said Hilary, 'we've landed on Mars!'

When I got to the top I had to agree with her. Off to our left, at the very crest of a mountain, was a ribbon of defiant rock weathered into fantastic shapes and spikes, some as much as 30m high. Straight ahead, every hill and mountain seemed to be wearing a multi-coloured striped poncho. And the colours were amazing: lilac, green, dark yellow, and deep rich reds. There was not a living thing as far as the eye could see. As clouds swept in front of the sun, a burst of snow and hail startled us out of our bewilderment. We found a trickle of water, set up our tent and scrambled inside.

Next day we continued to hike north, though it wasn't quite as straightforward as I had hoped. There was a village, and friendly people offering *chicha*, but no trail in the direction they pointed to. We slogged on, and up, towards yet another pass, but with no comforting path to follow. Finally we got to the top, and to our relief and considerable surprise, saw Auzangate. We could even see 'our' river.

Three hours later we were walking along the river, marvelling at smartly dressed male torrent ducks as they and their mates bobbed in the swift currents and eddies. Now and again one would plunge 30m down-stream and bounce out onto a boulder as easily as 'normal' ducks dabble in a pond. The river had eroded the valley's limestone into shapes resembling swiss cheese all shot through with holes. Viscachas grazed on the green grasses, taking fright and hopping back into their rocky warrens as we approached. Crops had just been harvested, and fieldmice were busy scurrying about picking up stray grains.

During the following morning we met quite a few people coming up the valley with heavily laden animals: we assumed they were returning from market, but by our estimate it would take another day of walking before we reached Pitumarca. Naturally we were sceptical when we asked a native how far it was, and received the usual *'cerquita'* (very near) in reply, but he was right. We could hardly believe it, after all those days trying to get 'on the map'.

Getting there Both Checacupe and Raqchi lie on the Cuzco-Puno road and are easily accessible by bus or truck. These leave frequently from Av Huascar in Cuzco. The road is only paved as far as Urcos and the trip takes about 3 hours. The bus or truck will stop at Checacupe, but only on request at Raqchi which is a small village to the left, hardly visible from the road. There is a sign announcing the village and the ruins, however. You can also take the early morning train, but the station of San Pedro is 2km or so from Raqchi.

Raqchi and the Temple of Viracocha

Even without the astonishing Inca ruin this would be a remarkable village. The local people have made good use of the rubble of lava that surrounds their hillside community, and have constructed numerous walls and corrals from volcanic rock. The church is exceptionally attractive and the whole place is tranquil and spotlessly clean. The Raqchi dance fiesta, held on June 17 each year, one week before Inti Raimi, must be a splendid affair. In such a setting it could hardly fail.

The Temple of Viracocha   The bare facts do nothing to prepare you for the amazing spectacle that greets you as you pass through a little gate to the right of Raqchi church, nor for the legends surrounding the temple. A long single wall of magnificent Inca stonework is topped by an adobe extension bringing it to a height of 15m. The lower wall is nearly 1½m thick with typical trapezoid windows and doorways. The remains of a row of stone pillars run on each side of the wall, but only one has retained its adobe top. No other Inca building has pillars and no other is as tall. The adobe wall is now protected with a little tile roof, but this is a recent addition. Beyond the temple are rows of identical buildings made from rough stone, and originally topped by adobe. These are arranged round six identical squares. In another area, towards the road, are the remains of two hundred small circular constructions, arranged in lines of twelve.

These are the basic facts but what on earth was it all for? We found virtually no information in the usual guide books, so asked at the archaeological museum in Cuzco, and there we struck gold in the form of George Squier's fascinating account of his travels in Peru, published in 1877. In line with all nineteenth century explorers, Squier had a meticulous eye for detail and the patience to write it all down. I owe the following information to him, and to subsequent writings by Luis A. Pardo in the *Revista del Instituto Arqueologico del Cuzco*.

The most fascinating aspect of the Temple of Viracocha is the story of how it came to be built. Some people think it was to appease the god Viracocha, after a volcanic eruption. I suppose that's the most logical explanation but I prefer the account by the notoriously inaccurate Inca (he was *mestizo*, actually) chronicler, Garcilaso de la Vega, who described the building in all its glory.

This version is that the temple was built by Inca Viracocha, the son of Yahuar Huacac. The father was a mild, ineffectual man with little patience for his son's ambitions and impetuosity, so he sent the Prince to the village of Chita, three leagues north east of Cuzco, in honourable exile, to supervise the royal herds pastured there.

After three years the Prince returned, saying he had had a vision. During a siesta in the fields, a white-bearded, celestial being appeared before him saying 'I am the son of the sun, brother of Manco Capac. My name is Viracocha and I am sent by my father to advise the Inca that the provinces of Chinchasuya are in revolt, and that large armies are advancing thence to destroy the sacred capital. The Inca must prepare. I will protect him and his empire.' Inca Yahua Huacac was unmoved by this warning, however, and took no precautions against the coming invasion. When the attack took place, as predicted, he fled to Muyna.

The people, abandoned by their Inca, scattered in all directions, but the prince (who'd now assumed the name of Viracocha) arrived with some shepherds of Chita, and persuaded them to return and defend Cuzco. Prince Viracocha fought valiantly, though his forces were greatly outnumbered. 'The very stones rose up, armed, white-bearded men, when the weight of the battle pressed hardly on the youthful Inca.' He won, of course, and deposed his father at the request of a grateful people.

The new Inca Viracocha ordered the construction of a marvellous temple, different from any preceding it, at Cacha (de la Vega glosses over the mystery of why the temple had to be built there, rather than at Chita where the vision had appeared, or on the battlesite).

The temple was to be roofless, with an elevated second storey. It would contain a chapel with the image of the God Viracocha, as he had looked when he appeared to the prince. The floor was paved with lustrous black stones brought from afar.

De la Vega describes the temple in detail, but his descriptions don't fit with the present ruins, so it's likely that he relied on second hand reports. However, this sorrowful statement that the Spanish destroyed this magnificent temple in search of gold is certainly true. According to Squier, the churches of San Pedro and Tinta are built of stones from the temple walls, as is one of the bridges across the river Vilcanota.

Looking at the present ruins, you can see that the rows of pillars probably supported a slanting roof. The second floor could have been sustained on the columns, with beams running from them to holes in the centre wall.

De la Vega doesn't mention the other ruins, but it's probable that the identical houses were priests' dwellings, or perhaps barracks. The two hundred small circular buildings were thought by Squier to be pilgrims' lodgings, but it's more likely they were warehouses or granaries.

There is one other Inca site here, and that is the baths to the left of the temple. You will have to leave the Temple area by the gate you came in, and follow the path between stone walls. The baths have some fine water channels, and fresh running water can still be collected there. There is good camping nearby, but *please* don't litter this beautiful site.

Hiking directions   Leave the ruins by the path that runs north east past the Inca baths, and climb steeply uphill to the main trail, which snakes through the lava. Turn right, and walk between stone walls until you reach an open area, then continue in the same direction to the foot of a stone-free hill. Turn left here and follow paths up the valley, above some houses sheltered by large trees.

Go north up the valley on the right hand side of the gorge, on a good trail that crosses the stream near the top and climbs over the pass. The path becomes fainter here, but you can follow it into the valley as it zig-zags down a scree shoulder towards the village of Paucaoros. There is good camping in this area, (collect water above the houses) or you can descend to the Río Salca (3,500m) through a eucalyptus plantation on the right hand side of the stream. It takes 5 or 6 hours from Raqchi to the river.

Turn left, and follow the Salca river along a good track for approximately 2km, until you see a village on the opposite bank. Just beyond the village is a good place to camp. 1km further on there is a cable crossing to the opposite bank, with a small wooden platform suspended underneath. This is how you cross the river. Once across, walk back up the valley to the village of Salloca. Turn left here, and go up the left side of the Salloca valley. It is exceptionally beautiful, crossing and recrossing the tumbling river over well made bridges. There are flowers and flowering shrubs everywhere, and plenty of hummingbirds. You'll reach some perfect campsites about an hour after leaving the Salca valley.

About three hours from the river you'll come to a fork in the trail. The left path is the short route to Pitumarca, but you take the right hand one, and soon pass an unusually well laid out and compact village, Palcoyo. The ground levels out after this and you enter alpaca country. You will pass hundreds and hundreds of these woolly beasts during the next 12 hours or so, so don't use up all your film on the first herd.

There are several small villages built from the local red earth and, just above the highest of these and one hour from Palcoyo, you'll see the trail climbing up on the left towards the first pass. It crosses some swampy patches (some paved with stones) and skirts the right hand side of the valley. The pass never seems to get any nearer and the landscape takes on a lunar quality. Even the alpacas look extra-terrestrial. It's a steep 2 hour climb from the last village to the top of the pass (4,800m) where you 'land on Mars'. To see this at its best you arrive in the late afternoon.

Two paths lead from the pass. One runs to the right (south west) down the side of the mountain to the valley, and the other continues north east. Take this one (there's camping in a small canyon 15 minutes from the pass) and follow it to a village on the valley floor. The trail traverses a rather nasty scree slope so you may prefer to drop down to the village before that stretch.

Continue up the valley past the houses, following any handy alpaca tracks you may find. There's no trail. The pass (4,900m) is on the right hand side of the valley head. It's a hard slog and will take a discouraging 2 hours from the village. Another incredible view will greet you when you finally reach the top: Auzangate and the whole Vilcanota range stretches along the horizon. Unless you are continuing on to Auzangate, your climbing is over. It's downhill virtually all the way to Pitumarca. Just descend to the valley bottom and follow the stream until it meets the Rio Pitumarca near some houses and flat grazing land. Follow the Pitumarca west. The paths get better and better, and the going easier and easier.

There are thermal baths just below the junction of the Pitumarca and Chillca rivers. We were not tempted by the yellow scummy water and the presence of half the male population of the village waiting to see if the gringos were going to take a bath. The water is only tepid anyway.

Walk along the right hand bank of the river, and an hour before Pitumarca note the ancient millstone on the left hand side of the trail. This almost certainly dates from colonial times. You can see the rock from which these stones were cut nearby. You should reach Pitumarca a full day after that first descent to the river of the same name. Checacupe and civilization lie a further 7km down the river. Trucks leave Pitumarca in the early morning, bound for Checacupe and Cuzco, and return at dusk.

Checacupe makes a fitting end to your hike, since it contains a lovely colonial church. The building is completely unremarkable from the outside, but the interior has some marvellous paintings, a fine altar and a beautifully carved pulpit, yet retains its simplicity. It's open most early mornings for mass, but remains locked the rest of the day. Try to find the *portero* and ask him to open it for you.

There are some good restaurants at Checacupe (we ate brook trout for breakfast), and frequent (but crowded) buses and trucks to Cuzco.

Along the Southern Route

The Auzangate link I have a report, via the South American Explorers Club, from C.J. Wilson who started from Checacupe and hiked to Ocongate in 10 days total (a surprisingly long time, but he says his group had 'heavy packs and not much acclimatization time'). His route took him up Rio Pitumarca to Rio Chillcamayu, then up that river valley to Quebrada Aucatauri to Laguna Jatun Pucacocha. He continued down Quebrada Jalacocha and Rio Lauramarca to Ocongate. My preference would be to go north east at the village of Chillca to join the Auzangate circuit at its most spectacular part, Laguna Ticllacocha. It looks fine on the map, but I have no reports on the reality!

Another alternative is to go east from Chillca to the 18km long Laguna Sibinacocha, where flamingoes may be seen.

PRACTICAL INFORMATION
Time/Rating From Raqchi to Pitumarca takes 4 days, but allow at least half a day to explore the ruins. Though not as strenuous as the Auzangate circuit, this is nevertheless a tough hike with an altitude gain of 1,500m and a pass of 4,900m. The complete trek, linking with the Auzangate circuit, would be a very challenging 8 to 10 days.

Conditions/What to bring As for Auzangate. It is likely to be very cold at night, and windy on the passes.

Maps Two 1:100,000 I.G.N. maps are needed for this hike, *Sicuani* (29t), covering the area from Raqchi to 'Mars' and *Ocongate (28t)*.

THE GLOBETROTTERS CLUB

An international club which aims to share information on adventurous budget travel through monthly meetings and *Globe* magazine. Published every two months, *Globe* offers a wealth of information, from reports of members' latest adventures to recent travel bargains and tips, plus the invaluable 'Mutual Aid' column where members can swap a house, sell a camper, find a travel companion or offer information on unusual places or hospitality to visiting members.

London meetings are held monthly (Saturdays) and focus on a particular country or continent with illustrated talks.

Enquiries to: The secretary, Globetrotters Club, BCM/Roving, London WC1N 3XX.

An example of Inca stonework. John Hemming, an Inca expert, points out that the only artistic achievement of the Incas is their masonry — but what an achievement it is! The Inca stone masons' skill at making a perfect fit without mortar has never been excelled. The most famous buildings show two kinds of masonry - coursed or polygonal. Polygonal was the strongest, but coursed masonry (rectangular blocks set in straight lines) was used for most sacred buildings.

No one knows for certain how the blocks were cut and transported, but it is believed that wooden wedges were inserted into cut holes in the rock and then soaked with water. The expansion of the wood split the rock, and the rough stones were then cut to shape with a haematite stone tool. Possibly llama gut and sand were used as a saw.

The Arequipa Area

The beautiful colonial town of Arequipa (2,380m) is well worth a visit, and the perfectly shaped dormant volcano Misti, and other nearby volcanoes will be an added attraction for backpackers. I haven't hiked in this area myself, so am grateful to an Arequipa resident, Anthony Holley, and to readers Stephen Connelly, David Breen, and Robert Eckhardt for the following information. For additional information on the area's volcanoes, Robert recommends Sr G. Zárate Landoval, owner of a 'photo-shop' at Sto. Domingo 416, Arequipa, tel: 232261, who runs the Club de Andinismo de Arequipa. The guide 'Micki' has also been recommended.

Volcán Misti, 5,822m

There is no water on Misti, so enough must be carried for the whole trip. This is otherwise a fairly easy two day hike.

Chasqui buses leave Arequipa daily at 6.00 for the access point to the volcano, the Chivay road. Ask to be let off at Aguadas Blancas (the junction with El Fraile Road). Follow this road to the far side of the first dam, Aguadas Blancas. There is a hydroelectric station here, so you may experience some hassle getting through the attendant security system. From Aguadas Blancas to Monte Blanco — a flat area with corrals, so suitable for camping — is 5½ hours, but it's only about 4 hours from there to the summit of Misti (more if there's a lot of snow) so most of your gear can be left at Monte Blanco. A zig-zag path goes to the top, where there is a marvellous view. A 10m iron cross marks the summit and you can continue to the edge of the inner crater where fumeroles are occasionally seen.

The climb is easier late in the season when there's less snow.

Volcán Chachani, 6,076m

This extinct volcano is accessible from the road to the village of Chiva (4,700m) which you can reach by bus from Arequipa. The Chasqui bus company makes the trip three times a week, and there are others. Hikers should ask to get off at the dirt track leading up towards the volcano. Walk 8km to the end of this jeep track, gaining 430m and continue for another 1½ hours to a campsite in the shelter of some stone corrals, just below the saddle. Camping higher will expose you to fierce winds. On arriving at the saddle you must turn left and drop 200m before starting the final ascent which will be reached in 10 to 12 hours after leaving the corrals.

Obviously this climb is for experienced mountaineers only, who should be prepared for icy and difficult conditions.

Volcán Ubinas, 5,672m

The starting point for this walk, Laguna Salinas Borax, lies 150km from Arequipa, on the road to Puno. Robert Eckhardt recommends this climb for 'its lonely position and the saltlake with flamingoes which you pass on the way to it'.

To reach the foot of the volcano you must first go to the village of Ubinas. Take a *colectivo* at 6.00 from Sepulveda 200, Arequipa. This street is reached by the yellow-white bus 5 *de Agosto*, and it's best to book a seat the day before. It is not clear from my information whether the car goes all the way to Ubinas or if you get out at Laguna Salinas Borax so make local enquiries. In any case, going via Salinas Borax, you reach the junction of the Puno-Ubinas road in about 4 hours, and in another 1½ hours, going in the direction of Ubinas, 'You stand at the foot of the volcano (5,050m), which has been in sight all the time since Laguna Salinas Borax'. From the lake it can be seen that the volcano has three peaks. The south one, on the right side, is the highest, and the one from which you can see the crater lake.

Camp at this 5000m level and do the climb next day. The easiest route goes up the north west side, but for the highest peak and the view you must ascend by the south west route. There are many things to see here: jets of steam, fumeroles, and a turquoise lake. The lake is 270m below, so if you climb down, leave plenty of time to make the return trip or you'll be returning to the city in darkness.

Returning to the city can be a problem unless you've booked the *colectivo* in advance. 'If not, it is impossible to get a seat. The second possibility is a huge truck which travels by night and passes by between 5 and 7 o'clock in the afternoon. Extremely cold. by nightfall it is already 8 degrees below zero and the drive lasts 6 to 7 hours.'

There is no water by the volcano, so it must be carried with you.

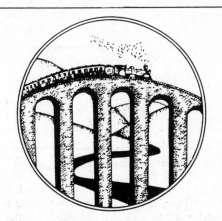

The Colca Canyon

Some 5 hours north of Arequipa by bus is Chivay, and the Colca Canyon, which in some parts is twice as deep as the Grand Canyon. This is the most exciting — and dangerous — white water rafting river in Peru (Expediciones Mayuc, Procuradores 378, Casilla 596, Cuzco, are one of the few groups who have run this river) and it is becoming increasingly popular with hikers, two of whom gave the following information to the South American Explorers Club. The Travel Information Forms filled in by Mark Lilley and Matt Cahillane and his companion Brian are available at the club to members only.

The basics Mark started from Canama, at the other end, and, with a donkey, walked to Chivay in 11 days. His route took him from Canama - Río Majes - Corrire - Huambo - Cabanaconde - Río Colca - Chivay. He reports that the walk was interesting more for the culture than for Canyon views: 'Beautiful mountain people, llamas all decked out. Lovely Inca terracing at Chivay. Only fair view of the canyon — you are never at the top of the canyon, but in the middle and the snow peaks are way above you. To get the best of the canyon you must walk to the bottom of it.'

The best base for canyon bottom excursions is Cabanaconde. Mark says: 'From Cabanaconde it takes 2 to 3 hours to go down. The path is easy to find (there are several and they all go down). There is no water on the way down in the dry season. 5 hours to come back up. Gorgeous! Tropical environment. Village across Colca. Waterfall in distance.'

Brian and Matt write: 'Catch bus from Arequipa to Cabanaconde (rough 10 hour ride). Stay in hotel (best, and probably only place to stay is right by the bus stop). Cabanaconde is a beautiful little town. Hike down Colca Canyon to suspension bridge and remember it's the only one. [The next bridge is near Yanque.] Good camping other side of bridge. Bring enough water for 5 or 6 hours of rough hiking, and fill up from river before you go back up.'

From Cabanaconde to Huambo is one long day; Cabanaconde to Chivay is 2 days (no hotels in between).

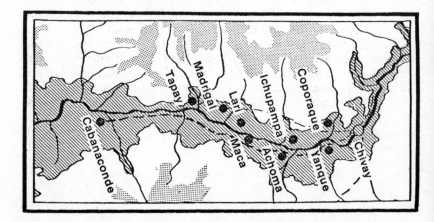

Chalhuanca area

Travellers going overland to Cuzco via Nazca should consider making a stop at Chalhuanca, which lies midway between the two towns. There are all sorts of interesting hikes in the area, bringing you to groves of *Puya raimondi*, cave paintings, and high altitude lakes. The notes below were provided by Rainer Hostnig through the South American Explorers Club. Thank you, Rainer, it sounds wonderful!

Chalhuanca There are two hotels, and supplies can be purchased here. 7km away, at Pincahuacha, there are thermal baths. There are many pre-Inca ruins in the area, very well preserved (missing only the roofs) and a lot of terracing.

Trips and hikes in the area

Cave paintings These are in three different caves near the village of Piscacococha; nearby are lakes with flamingos and other high altitude birds.

Puya raimondi forests There are three main areas where you can see these amazing plants:
1. *Totora*. From the main road it's 1½ hours by truck and then a 1 hour hike into Totora and the big *Puya raimondi* forest.
2. *Capaya*. 25km north of Chalhuanca. Walk 2 hours to Laguna Runco (very beautiful). There is a *Puya raimondi* forest that is behind Mt Apurunco (an obelisk mountain that rises 800m above the lake).
3. *Chicurune*. South of Chalhuanca by Rio Cotaruse. Walk 1 hour down the pampa to the edge of the *quebrada*. Hike down 10 minutes (500m drop) to Bosque de Puya Raimondi.

Hikes Walks in the area vary from half a day to 3 or 4 days:
1. *Cañon del Ciervo*. A deep rock-sided gorge near Palcapampa.
2. *Caraybamba*. South south east from Chalhuanca — beautiful pre-Inca terraces, 5km from the road, and funeral towers (*chullpas*).
3. *Chalhuanca to Yanaca*. A one day hike north east — a beautiful waterfall, terracing and great views. Very steep uphill.
4. *Nevado Suparaura (glacier)*. A 3 or 4 day hike. Climb from Tyaparo to Nvdo Suparaura to Santiago to Santa Rosa. Many small villages. Can buy supplies in Santa Rosa. People speak Quechua and Spanish. Ask often for directions. It's hard walking to Nvdo Suparaura — then mostly downhill. You can camp anywhere, but it's best to ask for permission. No tourists.
5. *Huanipaca*. A town in the north of Apurimac, with a mountain to climb and good trails.

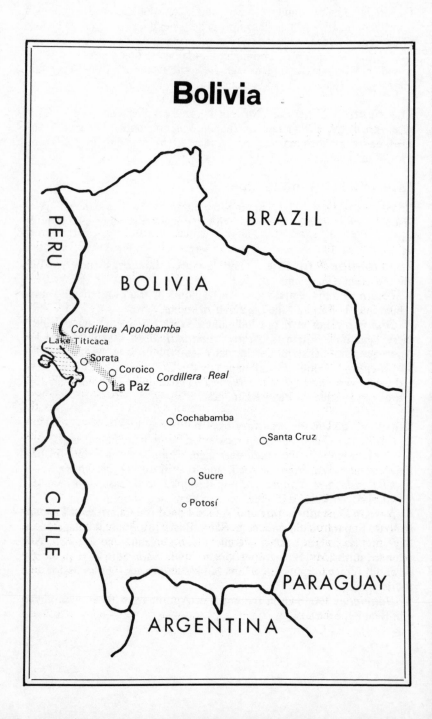

Bolivia

Introduction
Bolivia gets its name from the great Venezuelan liberator of so much of South America, Simon Bolívar, but it was probably discovered even before Pizarro first set foot in Peru. In 1520, a Portuguese explorer called Aleixo Garcia journeyed west from Brazil, but was prevented from making the first transcontinental crossing by Inca warriors and the Andes.

The population of present day Bolivia is nearly seventy percent Indian, most of whom live on the high, barren, and unproductive Altiplano, despite government efforts to encourage settlement in the more fertile lowlands. Recent studies show that the Altiplano was once forest and grassland. It seems unbelievable, looking at it now.

The Yungas refers to subtropical mountain valleys in Bolivia, the Nor Yungas and Sud Yungas, lying to the north east of La Paz. The rising moist air from the jungle is trapped by these valleys as it heads towards the Andes. Consequently the area is warm and wet for much of the year, producing large amounts of coffee, cocoa, and all sorts of fruit. This is also the main area for coca plantations, and the US government is working with the Bolivians to dissuade farmers from growing this profitable crop.

Exits and entrances
Citizens of western Europe and Canada need only a passport to enter Bolivia. Those from the U.S.A. need a tourist card. These are available at the airport and at the frontier and are valid for only 30 days, but are easily renewed at the Ministry of Immigration on Calle Gosálvez between Av Arce and Calle 6 de Agosto. At land frontiers there's no insistence on a return ticket.

Don't forget to get an exit stamp when you leave Bolivia, even if you only leave for the day (as some people do who stay at the Lake Titicaca border town of Copacabana).

Currency

When I was in Bolivia a couple of years ago I changed $200 at a *Casa de cambio*. Handing me a cubic foot of banknotes, the cashier politely said 'Shall I wrap it for you?'. I then understood the newspaper parcels and shoeboxes carried by so many Bolivians!

With the new government (1985) of Victor Paz Estensorro and subsequent stringent economic controls, this chaotic inflation (said at one time to be over 1000%) is being brought under control. With the peso now valued at around 2,000,000 to the dollar, there is talk of introducing a new currency unit, the Condor, by knocking off 6 zeros. This may be in circulation by the time you read this, and any attempt by me to give exchange rates or cost of living rates will be a waste of time — things change too fast. However, latest reports (February 1987) are that the currency has stabilised and that Bolivia is no longer ridiculously cheap (for those with dollars), but prices are comparable, or a little higher, than Peru.

Beware of Bolivians quoting prices in *mil* when they really mean *millón*. And beware of trying to change travellers' cheques outside La Paz. It may be difficult. Dollar bills can usually be changed anywhere, however.

Miscellaneous Bolivia information

Transport between La Paz and Cuzco LAB now run two planes a week (Tues and Sat) between the two cities. There are also luxury buses run by Transturin (see *Useful addresses*).

Telephones You need a 5 peso coin for these. They cost several thousand pesos from street vendors!

Holidays The ones that are likely to catch you out are Labour Day (May 1), La Paz Municipal Holiday (July 16) and Independence Day (August 5 to 7). These days are marked by military parades and closed shops and businesses.

In villages, fiestas are frequent and fabulous. The Tourist Office will give you information on when and where.

Business hours 9.00 to 12.00, 14.00 to 18.00.

Strikes and coups In a country that has had more changes of government than years of independence, strikes and coups (one often leads to the other) are a way of life — inconvenient, but usually nothing more. Coups are usually bloodless and it's very rare for ordinary people to get hurt. Strikes are more tiresome; you will just have to manage. The Bolivians do.

Mail As in Peru, letters should be sent to *Lista de Correo* or c/o American Express. When writing to businesses, always use their *casilla* number.

Parcels mailed from Bolivia are slow but quite reliable. Plan on spending most of the day at the post office (*Encomiendas Postales*, Calle Potosi 944) however. They will need to see your purchases first, and then you must pack them, wrap them, and finally sew the box into a flour sack. Bring everything you require for this operation with you (it can all be bought in the market).

Hot baths La Paz and other Altiplano towns are freezing at night, and a hotel without hot water is a real misery. If circumstances or economy force you to sleep cold, check out the public baths (*Baños Publicos*) which exist in most towns. They are usually very good value with lots of hot water.

For a real treat in La Paz, spend an afternoon in the sauna at the Plaza Hotel, and follow it up with a massage. Bliss!

Security Bolivia is a much safer country than Peru, and you are pretty safe walking and camping anywhere. For this reason it is advisable to carry your passport with you (rather than relying on a photocopy), since official checks are frequent.

Handicrafts Tourist items are about the same price in Bolivia as in Peru, and on the whole the quality is better and there is more variety. Machine knitted alpaca sweaters are a good buy, and guitar players will probably fall for a *charango*, a small twelve-stringed instrument with an armadillo shell as a sound box. If you plan to get one, buy an instruction book as well. The most beautiful weavings are undoubtedly those made in the Potosí and Sucre area. Designs on the ponchos and *mantas* woven here incorporate all sorts of mythical animals, and are unique. There is usually a good selection in La Paz although, inevitably, prices are high.

Leather goods are excellent and inexpensive, gold and silver jewellery is good value and often beautiful, and the tin cutlery and tableware sold on Calle Sagárnaga, above the church of San Francisco, is attractive and cheap, although it tarnishes easily.

La Paz

The city huddles in a bowl-like valley with the Altiplano forming the rim. Whether you arrive by air at the beautifully situated El Alto airport, or by bus, you won't forget your first sight of the city lying below you surrounded by the high peaks of the Cordillera Real. It's the highest capital city in the world, at a cool 3,632m, and you'll soon find out if you're a *soroche* sufferer. Altitude sickness hits most people flying here from a coastal town and the problem is compounded by this being one of the hilliest capitals in the world. Except for the Prado, the main street down the centre of the valley, everything of interest seems to be at the top of a steep hill. At least it's difficult to get lost in La Paz which is like a giant funnel: walk downhill and you'll arrive at the Prado.

Pachamama

In Bolivia, people of all classes make the traditional *Pago a Pachamama* or sacrifice to Mother Earth to ensure good luck (or rather to prevent bad luck) when building a new house. A Bolivian friend described an elaborate affair that she attended to inaugurate a glass factory. One llama was sacrificed for the sales department, and one for the plant itself. First a pit was dug, oriented east/west, and prepared with coca leaves, herbs and incense; a bottle of beer and a bottle of sweet wine was placed at each corner of the pit, which was then blessed by the priest. The *Brujo* was called in to 'read' the coca leaves to see what colour the sacrificial llama should be.

The beast arrived, washed and groomed and wearing a silk coat decorated with gold and silver 'coins' and paper money. The llama was made to drink three bottles of beer and one of *aguadiente* (my friend said it offered no resistance throughout the ceremony), then to kneel first towards the sun and then towards Illimani before its throat was cut. Even then it did not struggle; it did not even blink.

The blood was sprinkled around the perimeter of the factory and in the pit, which then became the llama's grave.

On a less lavish scale, but still symbolising an offering to Mother Earth, is the *Mesa con suyo*. This is what the dried llama foetuses and strange herbs and objects that are sold near Av Sagarnaga at the 'witches market' in La Paz are for. If Pachamama can't have a live llama, she'll settle for a dried foetus, rubbed with fat to simulate the real thing. This must be laid on a bed of wool (white for purity), along with candies in the shape of different animals, devils, etc., and nuts and seeds, and gold and silver trinkets. All this is by way of returning to Mother Earth what has been taken from her. The foetus may be dressed in a coat, like a real sacrificial llama, and little candy bottles take the place of the beer in the large scale sacrifice. The whole thing may be topped with a piece of cat's skin to represent the untameable, which still succumbs to the power of Pachamama.

When complete, the objects will be blessed, then parcelled up and either buried, with due ceremony, under the foundations of a new house, or (accompanied by sprinkles of alcohol and incantations) in the countryside in view of the major snow peaks and their Achachilas (mountain spirits).

Calling an Indian 'Indio' in Peru or Bolivia is akin to calling a black American 'nigger'. 'Campesino' is the correct term. A Bolivian friend told us he had watched an Indian trying to force a reluctant donkey across a bridge. 'Indio!' he cursed as he belaboured the animal with his stick.

The Prado, whose official name is Avenida 16 de Julio, is a broad street lined with modern shops and offices, but the old city, up on the hill around the government palace, is full of character. The Indian market, in the San Sebastian area of the town and above Iglesia San Francisco, is a fascinating place. Here you can buy a llama foetus to bury under the foundations of your new house for luck, or more mundane things like an aluminium saucepan for your next hike.

Purchasing hiking maps in La Paz

The availability of Bolivian maps varies. The first time I went there most things were available, but you had to go to the Bolivian equivalent of the Pentagon in order to get to the Instituto Geográfico Militar (I.G.M.). Then they opened a shop on the Prado and map-buying was a wonderfully rewarding experience with a large selection and friendly helpful staff. Then came the economic woes of the mid 80s and popular maps were not reprinted as they ran out; only poor dye-line editions were available. Now, I understand, the situation has once again improved and maps can be bought in the I.G.M. shop at Av 16 de Julio 1452. It's next to the Bank of La Paz, diagonally across the street from the Tourist Office kiosk. You may still need to go to the I.G.M. for more unusual maps. It is about a ½ hour bus journey from the centre of town (Microbus C or N) to Estadio Mayor and Av Saavedra. Bring your passport.

Bolivian maps are very good. Available in scales of 1:50,000, 1:100,000 and 1:250,000, they cover most of the Cordillera Real, though not the Cordillera Apolobamba, nor the trails down into the Yungas. Appropriate maps are given at the end of each described hike — if they exist.

Useful addresses

Tourist Office. 4th floor, Edificio Herrmann, Av 16 de Julio 1440, La Paz. They also have a kiosk on the central island of the Prado.

Club Andino Boliviano, Calle México 1638, (Casilla 1346), La Paz. Tel: 32 4682. Hours erratic.

Paititi. Calle Juan de la Riva, Edificio Alborada, oficinas 106 - 107. (Casilla 106). Tel: 329625. This company offers climbing and trekking trips. Helpful.

TAWA. Calle Rosenda Gutierrez 701, La Paz. Tel: 32 5796. A French-run tour operator with an extensive programme of treks, jeep expeditions and jungle excursions. They also operate charter flights between Paris and South America. (Peru office address: Av N. de Pierola 672, no 502. Address in France: 135 Rue Marcadet, 75018 Paris.)

Transturin Ltda. Av 16 de Julio, Edificio Alameda no 4. Two blocks below Plaza Venezuela, on the left.

The National Parks of Bolivia

Bolivia has had protected area since 1940, when the first two nature reserves were established — Cerro de Tapilla and Lagunas Alalay y Angostura. There are now eleven National Parks, nine Managed Nature Reserves, six Resource Reserves. These receive varying amounts of protection, from nil to fairly strict.

As in Peru, there are seldom any facilities for visitors, but the areas are at least safe from development, and possibilities for good wildlife viewing are enhanced.

There are several mountain National Parks: Cerro Comanche, Cerro Mirikiri, Cerro Sajama, and Tuni Condoriri among others, and the Biosphere Reserve of Ulla Ulla which protects herds of vicuña (at a recent count, some six hundred) and other fauna and flora of the altiplano.

The most recent park to be established was the Parque Nacional Amboró, in 1984, an important area of rainforest. Bolivia's President Paz has shown a keen interest in conservation, and is the president of the Bolivian Wildlife Society. In 1986 he extended a ban on the capture and export of wildlife for three years. Good news.

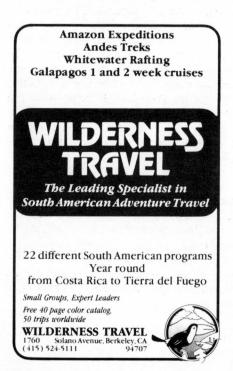
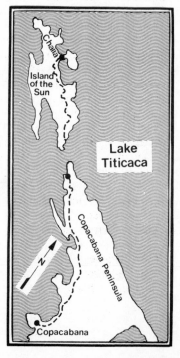

Lake Titicaca

Introduction Most people find the Bolivian side of Lake Titicaca more appealing than the Peruvian, perhaps because Copacabana is a far more rewarding town to stay in than Puno.

Copacabana has plenty of hotels (though none really first class), some good eateries (lake trout), and Religion. This has been a sacred place from earliest times. First the Tiahuanaco culture had their sacred sites near here, then the Incas, and now Bolivia's patron saint, the Dark Lady of the Lake is housed in the church. A further glimpse of Bolivia's particular brand of Catholicism is awarded to those who climb the hill behind the town. Each Sunday Bolivians make a penance ascent to the Holy Sepulchre, past the stations of the cross, clutching models of trucks, houses ... anything that they hope the good Lord will reward them with. The Copacabana fiesta is from August 5-8.

There is some excellent hiking along the lake shore, and one trip that includes the mythical birthplace of the Incas, the Island of the Sun, although you need luck in getting a boat there.

The Inca road to the Island of the Sun

Leave Copacabana at the north east side of the square near the post office. Your destination is Yampupata, 15km away. Keep to the road until just past the fish hatchery when the Inca trail leaves the road, crosses a field and a bridge, then climbs steeply over a hill. There is some Inca paving on this stretch. The trail then rejoins the road which continues to Yampupata. From here you must negotiate for a boat to take you to Pilkokaina, on the Island of the Sun.

From Pilkokaina, walk along the terraces to the the Temple of the Virgins of the Sun, which is mainly Tiahuanuco in style with early Inca influence. This is remarkable not so much for the stonework, which is simple and incorporates adobe, but for the view. Illampu, a sacred mountain, is framed by one of the windows, and George Squier, the nineteenth century exlorer, felt that the 'benches' in the temple overlooking the view showed the Inca appreciation for nature. But *nevados*, for the Incas, had more than aesthetic significance.

Beyond the Temple is a fine set of Inca baths, providing convenient drinking water. Climb the steps, turn right, and follow a good trail to the village of Challa, about 12km away. From here you may be able to get a boat to the mainland, but it's more sensible to continue to walk around the island and back to Pilkopaina or the Inca baths (from where you may be able to hitch a ride on a tour boat).

If the logistics of boats, etc. defeat you, this 'Inca pilgrimage' can be organised through TAWA. As well as transport you get the guidance of an excellent archaeologist.

The Cordillera Real

The 150 kilometres of Bolivia's Cordillera Real stretch from the Sorata valley to the Rio La Paz, providing a splendid backdrop for the world's highest capital city. There are six peaks over 6,000m, and many more above the 5,000m mark. This mountain range is perfect for backpacking, offering days of hiking above the tree-line with snow-capped mountains appearing around every bend, and steep descents to the tropical vegetation of the Yungas. Here we found two of the finest pre-Columbian highways in South America; the stone paving is even more impressive than those in Peru.

All the trails described in this section are within a day's journey of La Paz, and a couple are only a few hours away. There is no problem acclimatising for these hikes: a few days' sightseeing in La Paz will take care of that.

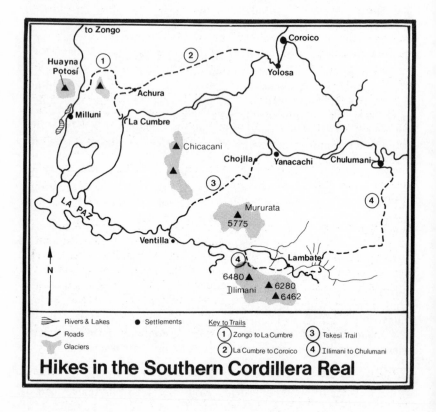

Hikes in the Southern Cordillera Real

Tingling in the fingers is a common effect of altitude, and nothing to worry about.

The Takesi Trail

This is often called the Inca Road, but was in fact almost certainly constructed before the Incas conquered the region. We don't know when it was built, or by whom, but we can admire the perfection of the work and underlying engineering principles.

The paved section covers half the trail, about 20km, and you'll see all the classic features of pre-Columbian road construction: stone paving, steps, drainage canals, and retaining walls.

The walk takes only two days, but the variety of scenery is astonishing. From the swirling snow on the 4,650m pass, you drop down to the tree line and through incredibly lush vegetation to the humid jungle below the Chojlla mine. Above the trees the colours are soft and muted; green-ochre hills, grey stones, brown llamas. In the Yungas it's steamy hot and bright with butterflies, flowers, green leaves, and sparkling blue rivers.

The two main villages along the upper section of the trail, Choquekota and Takesi, show a way of life unchanged for centuries: men herding llamas, making rope, or harvesting crops; women trampling *chuños* and preparing the next meal. Below the tree-line, however, *mestizos* mix traditional customs with new innovations. Women sit weaving outside their homes, but orlon yarn is in vogue and bright cotton dresses replace the Indian homespun.

This walk is serviced by two spectacular and contrasting bus journeys. To reach the trailhead you drive through a lunar landscape of eroded 'badlands' offering a display of brown, red, orange and yellow tones, unrelieved by any green. But the return trip from the Yungas is perhaps the most beautiful road of its kind in South America. It is cut into the mountain sides and parallels a river for much of the way. Luxuriant vegetation hangs from cliffs jutting over the road as it winds up to the bleak Altiplano.

Getting there   The access town is Ventilla. This can be reached by microbus Ñ which runs along Av Murillo in La Paz to the check point of Chasquipampa, from where you wait for a truck to Ventilla. Alternatively, the Tourist Office claims that a bus runs all the way to Ventilla from Plaza Belzu in La Paz (and they even have schedules). The ride is so spectacular that if the weather's clear and you're warmly dressed, it's worth taking a truck for the view. Ventilla is the terminus for most trucks and buses, but you may be lucky enough to get one up to Choquekota, 5km further up the road.

Directions   The walk begins at Ventilla for most people. Continue uphill from the village, taking the left fork north east up the Palca valley. This is the road to Choquekota (1½ hours away), an attractive collection of stone and adobe houses.

Keep going up the road towards the San Fransisco mine, past a charming but almost derelict church and a graveyard full of cigar shaped adobe burial mounds. The snowy flank of Cerro Mururata gradually comes into view on the right, and llamas provide a picturesque foreground.

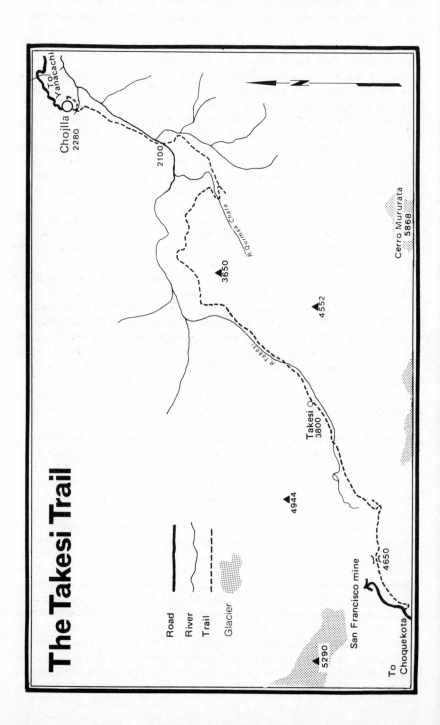

The Takesi Trail

Road

River

Trail

Glacier

To Yanacachi

Chojlla
2280

2100

R. Quimsa Chata

3650

4552

Cerro Mururata
5868

R. Takesi

Takesi
3800

4944

4650

San Francisco mine

5290

To Choquekota

Look out for a lovely example of religious folk art painted on two boulders to the right of the trail. These are not old, but have been painstakingly done in earth colours.

About 2 hours after leaving Choquekota, you'll see the termination of your road at the mine, and the 'Inca road' branching off to the right just past a small isolated house. The trail zig-zags steeply upward and soon you'll arrive at perhaps the most perfectly preserved stretches of stone paving in South America. This amazing road (one can hardly call it a trail), winds up the mountain side, easing the traveller's passing with a series of low steps. The top of the pass, 4,650m, is reached in about 1½ hours and if the weather is clear you'll have a fine view of the surrounding snowy peaks of the Cordillera Real, and the Yungas far below you. There is a mining tunnel to explore here. It goes back a long way — we never reached the end — and provides good shelter from the icy wind that blows over the pass.

The descent to Takesi village takes about 3 hours and the path, if anything, is even more perfect. Shortly before the village you pass two lakes on the left, with plenty of good campsites. For those without a tent there is a shelter for hikers in Takesi.

The village is very attractive in its isolation, and life goes on there largely unchanged since the villagers' ancestors built the road. Shortly after Takesi the moist Yungas air asserts itself; boulders are covered in bright green moss, and bushes and shrubs provide welcome relief from the stark mountain scene. Note the pre-Columbian foundations of the footbridge across the river. The trail follows the course of the Río Takesi, hugging the cliff edge. This is a dry section — in contrast to the well watered and densely forested slopes on the other side of the river — and you're advised to carry water. About 3 hours below Takesi the trail curves round Palli Palli hill and you'll see the ruins of a chapel and pass several houses surrounded by cultivated flowers. This is Kakapi, and it is very pretty. There is a well full of pure water just before these houses. The trail then drops steeply down to Río Quimsa Chata which is crossed by a footbridge, and climbs up and over a shoulder before crossing the Río Takesi again, at 2,100m. There's some lovely swimming in river pools if you can stand the cold water. From the shoulder you can see Chojlla, another 2 hours away.

The approach to this mining town (tin and wolfram) is along an aqueduct and then up a steep zig-zagging path which leaves the main trail on the left. If you've always wanted to see a slum, this is the place for you. I made further disparaging remarks in the last edition of this book, but have been taken to task by a recent hiker/correspondent who points out that the people of Chojlla are hurt that most hikers hurry through their village. Certainly, if you look beyond the rubbish and tin roofs, you will see that this is a lively, warm-hearted place. The village teacher welcomes hikers who want to sleep in the school, and appreciates a small donation. There is no restaurant in town, but vendors sell hot food.

Food and lodging are available about an hour down the road at Yanacachi (Hotel Panorama).

Getting back A daily bus leaves Chojlla early in the morning, and passes through Yanacachi on its way to Unduavi and La Paz. It was booked up days in advance when we were there. Trucks leave any time from 7.00 to mid-day. This is a very wet part of Bolivia; if it's not raining when you get on the truck, it will later, and you'll probably have snow over La Cumbre pass. However hot you feel in the Yungas, wear lots of clothes. As I've said earlier, this is one of the most stunningly beautful roads in South America, so truck transport is recommended if you can stand it. It takes about 6 hours to get to La Paz, and a stop will be made at Unduavi, so you can fill up on fried fish and other roadside goodies.

PRACTICAL INFORMATION
Time/Rating This is a very easy 2 or 3 day walk (one hiker I talked to met a Bolivian woman doing it in high heels!), but don't underestimate the wear and tear on your knees and feet. You drop down from 4,650m to 2,100m.

Conditions/What to bring The humid air rising from the Yungas often brings mist, rain and snow. Be prepared. You can probably get by without a tent by using the shelter in Takesi (sleeping bag and warm clothes needed), but a tent gives you far more flexibility. Campsites are plentiful. Bring a torch so you can explore the miners' tunnel.

Maps You really don't need a map — the path is so clear, but the I.G.M. *Chojlla* sheet (6044 1V), covers the hike from San Francisco mine to Chojlla, scale 1:50,000.

The Takesi Trail

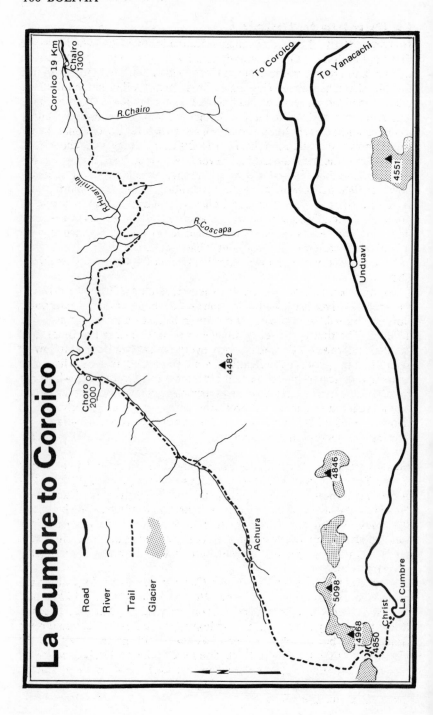

La Cumbre to Coroico

Road
River
Trail
Glacier

Coroico 19 Km
Chairo 1300
R.Chairo
R.Huarinilla
R.Coscapa
Choro 2000
4482
To Coroico
To Yanacachi
4551
Unduavi
4846
Achura
5098
4968
4850
Christ
La Cumbre
N

La Cumbre to Coroico

Introduction I have a nostalgic affection for this hike, which was the first I did in Bolivia. Our information, in 1973, was vague. An American told us that a drunk member of the Costa Rican National Orchestra had told him that if he went to a big 'Jesus Cross' near La Paz and followed the outstretched left hand, he would find an Inca trail that led into the jungle. The American hadn't tried it, but thought we should. So did we, but my sleeping bag had been stolen a couple of weeks before, and our only shelter was a shower curtain. And the Tourist Office girls giggled at the idea of walking into the Yungas and had never heard of an Inca trail — or any trail, come to that. They did know where there was a big statue of Jesus, however. We had a wonderful and serendipitous hike, and shortly after Achura (where I'd slept in a thatch and stone building on a pile of potatoes, pretending a poncho was as warm as a sleeping bag) we walked down an 'Inca' road so amazing in its engineering that we decided to write a book and share this find with other backpackers.

Now the trail is well known, and the Tourist Office used to enquiries about it.

So, the hike. It takes you from a snow-covered 4,850m pass down to sub-tropical river valleys full of parakeets, blue *morpho* butterflies, flowers and wild stawberries, and ends in hot citrus groves at just over 1,000m. The first part is easy, thanks to Inca (or rather pre-Inca) road builders, but towards the end it is very overgrown and difficult to follow. It seems that the path is periodically cleared, since readers' letters five or so years ago indicated that it was almost impassably overgrown, whilst the most recent report said it was 'kept fairly clear, widthwise, but the height of the vegetation can cause problems with a pack constantly getting tangled'. This hiker (Steve Newman) had more problems with landslips causing obstruction than vegetation.

Getting there Buses of the Flota Yungueña company leave La Paz for the Yungas region at 9.00 on weekdays (8.30 on Saturdays) from 344 Av de las Americas, Villa Fátima (microbus 'B' from Av Camacho). However, the short journey (about an hour) can easily be done by one of the trucks which leave from a little higher up Av de las Americas throughout the day. It's best to make as early a start as possible, since mist tends to start billowing over the pass early in the afternoon, obscuring the gorgeous view.

A special feature of the La Paz-La Cumbre road is the dogs which are posted like sentinels along the route. We first noticed them in 1974, and I have seen them (or their descendants) on every subsequent visit. I used to think they were just hanging around hoping for scraps (which are thrown from trucks) but a Bolivian friend has since told me that they are the Guardians of the Cordillera Real. The locals placate the *Achachilas* by feeding these dogs. Certainly when you see those patient figures, motionless but watchful in the swirling snow, it is easy to believe in the power of mountain spirits.

Directions   La Cumbre ('the Summit') is not a village, but the highest point (4,725m) on the bleak mountain road before it begins the descent to the Yungas. Here is the statue of Christ the Redeemer, facing north, his left hand helpfully pointing out the trail. Just below the statue a dirt road heads west, and after passing between two small lakes, the path veers north up a scree slope to the pass. It is well-used, and even after recent snow you should have no difficulty following foot- hoof- and llama-prints. The pass (4,850m) is the lowest point in the snowy ridge in front of you, and marked by a big *apacheta* (stone cairn). The climb takes about an hour, and you're rewarded with a spectacular view and the knowledge that it's downhill all the rest of the way.

From the pass the trail is very clear, and drops steeply down a *quebrada* canyon which broadens out after joining the river, leaving the path to continue more gently to the small village of Achura, also known as Cuchuca. There are plenty of campsites above and below the village which is reached about 5 hours after topping the pass. There have been recent reports of hostility towards hikers from the villagers of Achura, so pass through quickly and quietly.

Between Achura and the next village, Choro, the 'Inca' road really comes into its own, with some marvellous paving and low steps often arranged in a fan shape around a curve. After about 4km of paved road, you reach the treeline and the path becomes narrower. Choro is some 5 hours below the tree line, and there are no decent campsites before the village.

In 1973 Choro was a going concern, but recent hikers report that most of the houses are now empty, hence the overgrown state of the trail beyond. At least this means there is no shortage of tent places. Next day you should carry water, since from now on the supply is erratic. At Choro cross the river via a suspension bridge and climb steeply up a series of switch-backs. The path now heads east and contours along the hillside, following the Rio Huaranilla to Chairo, two hard days' bush-whacking away. The trail frequently takes you around ravines and each one contains a useful water supply, usually in the form of an icy torrent. The biggest of these side streams, the Rio Coscapa, is crossed by an exciting suspension bridge set in a magnificent gorge.

Towards the end of the first day of jungle-bashing, you will reach a new hazard — landslides. Probably by now a decent trail will have been made across the rocks and soil, but if not it can be quite exciting.

Chairo is a very small village, but it does sell beer and there are occasional trucks to Coroico. If you have to walk it is an easy 4 or 5 hour walk through coffee, citrus and banana plantations. Turn left at the first fork, ford the river, and you'll reach the main La Paz-Coroico highway. To the right is the tiny town of Yolosa and then Coroico. With luck you will get a ride.

Coroico and getting back   If you are in a hurry, you can skip Coroico altogether, and take a truck back to La Paz from Yolosa. That would be a pity, however, since Coroico is a very pretty tropical town

(1,525m) with several hotels and nothing much to do but relax after your exertions. The Flota Yungueña bus leaves for La Paz at 7.00 each morning from the street to the right of the church, but is usually booked up several days in advance, so get your ticket as soon as you arrive. If you are out of luck, there are always trucks.

The 96km road to La Paz is just as beautiful as the one from Chojlla (the two raads meet at Unduavi). It's little more than a track, really, winding under waterfalls (bring your rain gear if you are on a truck!) and above 1,000m cliffs. Its impact on impressionable travellers is heightened by the many roadside crosses commemorating those who have gone over the edge.

PRACTICAL INFORMATION
Time/Rating   A fairly easy 4 day walk with some unpleasantly overgrown stretches and one high pass.

Conditions/What to bring   The conditions have already been described. Only the first night will be cold; after that you are more likely to be too hot. Rain is frequent in the Yungas, and you'll need insect repellent. It might be sensible to bring a machete on this trip, but only if you know how to use it. Accidentally cutting off your leg on this trail would be inconvenient.

Maps   Not really necessary, but *Milluni* (5945 II) and *Unduavi* (6045 II) cover most of the route.

Note Coroico is a very popular weekend resort, so avoid arriving then.

Zongo to La Cumbre or Coroico
Introduction   This is a high altitude walk, partly along a good trail and partly cross-country, taking you parallel to the glaciers of Cerro Huayna Potosi (6,088m), past a series of lakes reflecting snow-covered mountains, and connecting with the La Cumbre-Coroico trail, thus giving you a choice of destinations. It was one of those happy hikes discovered accidentally when we were leafing through the topo maps at the I.G.M while waiting for our order. The *Milluni* sheet caught our eye, covered in evocative blue contour lines, and we soon picked out a possible trail. In fact this could only be followed part of the way, but the subsequent cross-country scramble was both exciting and beautiful.

In 1986 I was very pleased to get an update letter about this hike from Steve Newman. Until then, I had assumed that either no one else had tried it, or that they had all perished in the attempt. In fact, it seems that our original directions are still OK; it was just the *Getting there* that needed updating.

I am also throwing in directions for climbing Huayna Potosi, provided by one of my regular correspondents.

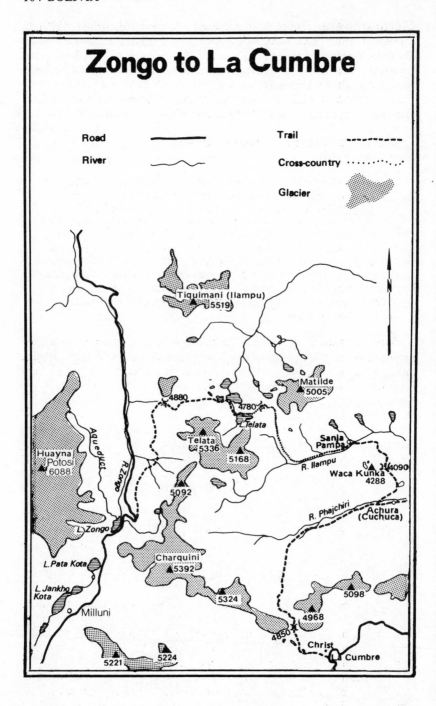

Zongo to La Cumbre

Road ——— Trail – – – – –

River ～～～ Cross-country ·········

Glacier

Tiquimani (Ilampu)
5519

Matilde
5005

4880

4780

L.Telata

Sanja
Pampa

Telata
5336

5168

R. Ilampu

Waca Kunka
4288

4090

Huayna
Potosi
6088

Aqueduct

R. Zongo

5092

R. Phajchiri

Achura
(Cuchuca)

L. Zongo

Charquini
5392

5098

L. Pata Kota

5324

4968

L. Jankho
Kota

Milluni

4850

Christ

5221

5224

La Cumbre

Getting there   When we did the trip we were able to get a lift in a CORPAC truck (CORPAC is the electricity company of Bolivia) bound for their Zongo hydroelectric station. Their office is at Av Montes and Uruguay, near the main La Paz bus station. An alternative is to get a morning bus to El Alto and then catch a truck which leaves from the Plaza Ballivian for Milluni. From that small town it is an easy walk to the dam, Laguna Zongo and Huayna Potosi, and allows for acclimatisation.

Climbing Huayna Potosi (6,094m)
by Sverre Aarseth

This is one of the easiest peaks above 6,000m in Bolivia, so popular with mountaineers. The climb for the standard route starts by crossing the dam itself, then follows the aqueduct to a small reservoir. From here the trail goes up the spine of a moraine, eventually joining a rocky ridge. It is recommended to make the summit attempt from the Campamento Argentino snow plateau at 5,500m. A well acclimatised party should make this camp in one day, after spending the night at Zongo. However, high winds can be a problem here. More than one litre of water per person should be carried for the ascent since dehydration is a real danger. Full ice climbing equipment must be carried and only experienced mountaineers should attempt this peak.

Hiking directions   Follow the Zongo road as it continues down the valley in a series of zig-zags. After 2km your trail leads off to the right, just after the second hairpin bend and across a small stream. The path is faint at times, disappearing altogether across open pasture, but you should have little difficulty in following it along the contours of the mountain, above and parallel to the valley road. The views of Huayna Potosi are splendid and soon the snowy peak of Cerro Telata (Cerro Cunatincuta) comes into view. After 1½ hours you'll pass a small lake, and 3 or 4 hours after leaving the road the path swings east round Cerro Chekapa and heads towards a pass (4,880m). Beyond the pass is a well-watered valley and a series of dammed lakes, part of another hydroelectric scheme. There's good camping all along this valley.

From the dam of the first lake, continue east to the second lake, taking a path along the south shore and uphill towards Laguna Telata, whose dam is just visible. There are marvellous views of a dramatic snow-covered mountain called Ilampu on the I.G.M. map, but better known as Tiquimani to avoid confusion with Illampu in another part of the Cordillera.

The last possible camping places for several hours are near this lake, either below the dam or at the far shore. This is where the cross-country stretch begins. Walk across the dam and make your way over the rocks and cliffs above the northern shore of the lake. This involves scrambling but no technical rock climbing. Be careful to avoid loose boulders.

On reaching the eastern point of the lake, start up the stone fall towards the lowest point on the shoulder above you on your left (north east). This climb will take about an hour and is not difficult. From the top you'll see three lakes and a shoulder to your right. From this shoulder you should make your way down to the south east, over a wall, and pick up a very faint path to the right of a stone fall. Continue steeply downhill to a swampy area studded with Andean gentians. Continue down to the valley bottom and the river. As you veer east beneath the crags of Cerro Jishka Telata you'll pass a large cave beneath some monstrous fallen boulders — an excellent shelter if the weather is bad. Continue to follow the river on its left bank until the trail at last asserts itself and you can follow it easily to an *hacienda*, Sanja Pampa, beyond which there is a bridge.

After crossing the river pass through a scatter of houses and up a steep but good trail skirting around Cerro Waca Kunca. As it levels out, the trail passes several ponds, crosses a stream, and heads downhill and south west towards the village of Achura. There's a bridge across the river and a short climb to reach the main trail just above the village.

Here you must make the decision either to go up to La Cumbre, about 6 hours away, or continue down to Coroico which will take you 2 more days.

PRACTICAL INFORMATION

Time/Rating 3 to 5 days, depending on your destination. A strenuous high altitude hike (2 passes over 4,800m) with rock scrambling and cross-country work. Not suitable for inexperienced or solo backpackers.

Conditions/What to bring It's bitterly cold for the first two nights. Bring hat, gloves, and all the warm clothes you've got. You'll need tough boots and a compass for the cross country section. Steve Newman adds: 'Don't expect too much from Achura. It took us 1½ hours to buy 2lbs of potatoes and three eggs!'

Map The I.G.M. topo map *Milluni* (5945 II), scale 1:50,000, covers the route.

'Your Majesty, encounters have become my meditation. The moment one accosts a stranger, or is accosted by him, is above all...a moment of drama. The eyes of the Indians who have crossed my trail have searched me to the very depths to estimate my power. It is true the world over - whoever we meet watches us intently at the quick strange moment of meeting, to see whether we are disposed to be friendly.'

The Marvellous Adventure of Cabeza de Vaca (1528 - 1536). Translated by Haniel Long.

Illimani to Chulumani

Introduction   This is a rugged, but wonderfully varied trek of from 3 to 7 days (it can be broken or joined half way) which takes you round the western flank of Bolivia's highest mountain, Illimani (6,480m), then, like all the other Cordillera Real hikes, down into the tropical Yungas. And like the other trails, it provides contrasts of glaciers and citrus groves, goose-pimples and sweat. I went on an organised trek with TAWA (see *Useful addresses* on page 151) and kept rather sketchy notes, so if you want to do it independently, back up this description with maps and local directions.

Getting there   The trek begins at Trés Ríos, near the mining town of Bolsa Negra, about 37km beyond Ventilla. I have been told that trucks for Tres Rios and Lambate leave every morning from a road to the left of Lower Max Paredes. The Tourist Office may be able to confirm this. Dress warmly: there is a 4,700m pass before Trés Ríos!

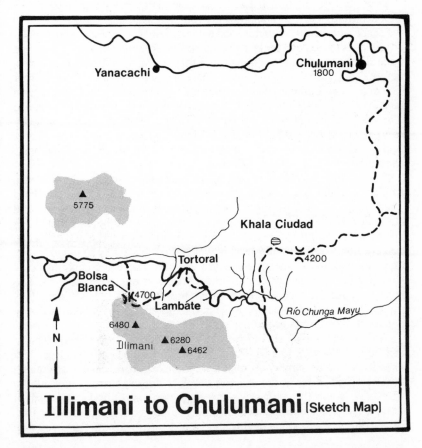

Illimani to Chulumani [Sketch Map]

Directions At Tres Rios take the old road that heads south, uphill, towards the abandoned mining camp of Bolsa Blanca. The road follows the Rio Pasto Grande to the head of the valley, becoming very faint towards the end, where cattle tracks take over. There is good camping at the end of the valley at Bolsa Blanca, and before the first high pass. There are two routes over the pass: one to the east (4,850m) and another (used by pack animals) which swings back to the north to take you round Cerro Keya Keyam. This pass is a little lower, but both are hard work and need a good 1½ to 2 hours. If the weather is clear you will be rewarded by great views of Illimani and also Mururata, and can camp the far side of the pass at a chilly 4,700m at the old mining post of Tata Condor.

Continue heading east south east to pick up the trail along the Totoral river and follow it down to the road and Totoral village (3,400m) — a very steep and tiring descent. You will find various campsites before you begin the steepest part of the descent, and you may also sleep in or by the school. From Bolsa Negra to Totoral is about 7 hours.

From here you can return to La Paz (although the road was not humming with traffic when I was there), or continue to Chulumani.

Your next destination is Lambate, which is quite a large town where supplies (and beer!) can be bought. From Totoral walk along the road to the east for about an hour (this road will also lead to Lambate) and look for a trail leaving the road to the right (try to find someone to ask). The broad path climbs up through farmland and tops a grassy hill with fine views, before dropping down to the town. You will reach here about 4 hours after Totoral. From Lambate you continue along the road, crossing a ford, and pick up a trail to the left which will take you precipitously down to the Rio Chunga Mayu which is often busy with gold prospectors. There are plenty of good campsites and bathing places along the river which is crossed by a bridge. At this point you can start asking for Chulumani, and the locals should be able to point out the trail.

Now comes the toughest part of the trek. The Chunga Mayu is at a tropical 2,300m. The next pass is 4,300m! Even taking 2 days this is hard work. The trail leads up north from the river, through a small village, and starts its relentless climb up a ridge. Carry water; once beyond the village and its water supply (a stream) there is no more for several hours and it can be very hot. Gradually the scrubby vegetation gives way to cloud forest, and you eventually emerge above the treeline. There is a camping place shortly after the first stream and others once you get above the trees. The best place for the second night's camp, however, is Khala Cuidad. This reputedly haunted spot is in a bowl in the mountains, by a lake, and very beautiful. The spirits seem peaceful.

Traversing the right side of the lake you start the climb to the final pass, at 4,200m. The view is magnificent: behind you is the Cordillera Real, and ahead lies the steamy forests of the Amazon basin, stretching uninterrupted as far as the eye can see. It is not exactly downhill all the way now, since the path skirts the mountains and climbs other small passes, but it is excitingly evident that you are now on an Inca (or Pre-Inca) trail. There is stone paving and Inca steps as the path takes you east towards the cloud forest. Once you start meeting trees and heading north, it really is downhill all the way.

The final day is one long descent, and very tough going. But it is amazingly beautiful as the morning mists roll away, and you see butterflies, flowers, birds — everything you would expect in the jungle. The trail sometimes takes you under tunnels of vegetation as it drops down to the Amazon basin. Rather suddenly you reach cultivation, and then a very pleasant *hacienda* with its own little church. There is a road here, and Chulumani is another 2 hours away. At the right time of year there are more oranges and grapefruit along the road than you can eat, streams of fresh water, and a pleasant gradient, so it is no real hardship except that you are likely to be very tired by then. There are also coffee groves, and the most important crop of the area, coca, which is grown on carefully tended terraces. Sometimes the leaves are spread out on the road to dry.

For the last hour you can see Chulumani tantalisingly just across a gorge, but you have no option but to follow the road round the head of it.

Chulumani lies at only 1,800m, and is the capital of the Sud Yungas. It is an attractive town with several hotels (which are often full). As usual, Flota Yungeña buses take you to La Paz and, as usual, you should book well in advance.

PRACTICAL INFORMATION
Time/Rating   A rugged 7 day trek with two high passes and some very steep and tiring descents. Only for the fit and experienced.

Conditions/What to bring   Mist and rain is common in the early parts, and the first two nights are very cold. After that, nights will be pleasant, but days will feel hot. Bring clothing that can be worn in layers. This is a malarial area, so anti-malaria pills should be taken. You can restock with provisions in Lambate, but don't expect a great selection.

If you quail at the thought of that 2,000m climb from the Chunga Mayu, *arrieros* can be hired in Lambate.

Maps   The first part of the trail is shown on *Palca* (no 6044 III), then, I guess, you would need 6044 II, and 6044 I, but check the maps at the I.G.M.

Sorata and the Tipuani Valley

Nestling at the foot of the Cordillera Real, Sorata has one of the finest settings in Bolivia. The second and third highest mountains in the country (Illampu, 6,362m and Ancohuma, 6,427m) overlook the town which lies at a mere 2,700m and has swanky palm trees in the plaza to prove its mild climate. After a few days of gasping and freezing in La Paz, it's a great relief to spend some time in Sorata, especially on Sunday, when the market is in full swing. Neighbouring Achacachi has an even better market.

Sorata and Achacachi hold a wonderful fiesta between September 12 and 16 each year. When we were there several years ago we were swept along by jubilant dancers until we were nearly dropping from exhaustion (see *Fiestas*, page 47). Annie Peck, the first person to climb Huascarán Peru's highest mountain, visited the fiesta in 1911. From her description it hasn't changed a bit.

This is the starting point of several long treks in the Cordillera Real, including the Gold-diggers Way here, but there are also some lovely short walks in the area. San Pedro and its cave are particularly recommended. It takes about 3½ hours to walk along the river to this cave which has a lake inside. You can camp in the area, swim (cautiously) in the chilly lake, and pay an enormous amount for the guard to turn on the lights inside.

Getting to Sorata   Buses of the Perla de Illampu company leave from the junction of Av Tumusla and Calle Isaac Tamayo in La Paz at about 7.00 on Wednesdays, Thursdays, Saturdays and Sundays. The booking office is down Calle Tamayo, just beyond Calle Graneros. On other days you can get a truck from the same area for a wonderfully scenic, but freezing cold journey which takes about 4 hours.

Vicuñas

The Gold-diggers Way
By John Pilkington

Introduction   This is a very tough walk of 6 to 8 days which takes you right across the northern Cordillera Real. From Sorata you'll climb over a 4,800m pass and then follow a roller-coaster course down the Tipuani Valley to the tropical area around Guanay (400m). During the walk you'll pass through a complete vegetational cross-section of South America, from the snows around Illampu through the Yungas to the jungle and plantations (tea, coffee, bananas) of the upper Amazon basin. You'll see grazing llamas, *morpho* butterflies 15cm from wingtip to wingtip, maybe a snake or two, and possibly even a capybara, the world's largest rodent. For much of the way you'll be treading on stones laid by Inca engineers, worn smooth and rounded by centuries of feet and hooves. You'll use spectacular (but exhausting) staircases to overcome difficult obstacles and to climb and descend seemingly sheer hillsides. [One of the most interesting features used to be an Inca tunnel but, sadly, this collapsed in 1985.] For the last three days you'll be walking through the heart of Bolivian gold-mining country, once the scene of Klondike-style activity, and now once again the centre of a feverish new gold rush.

History   The Tipuani Valley is a strange place. For nearly a thousand years this remote area north of La Paz has been a rich source of gold, and each generation of exploiters has left its mark on the landscape and on the traditions of its people. From the earliest years of the Inca Empire the inhabitants of the area had to deliver 40kg quarterly to the Sun King at Cuzco. Then during the Spanish colonial period exploitation was intensified to satisfy the greed of the *conquistadores* and new workings were opened up along the Río Tipuani and in nearby valleys as well. Later, when Bolivia regained her independence, gold production declined and today only in the Tipuani Valley is it carried out in any way seriously.

During all this time the search for gold was a haphazard affair, to say the least, and only when the Compañia Aramayo de Minas en Bolivia took over the work in 1932 were the first geological reports and maps made. By a stroke of bureaucratic genius most of these were lost when the company was nationalised in 1952, and since then many prospectors have reverted to the old wildcat methods, breaking rocks on massive slopes of wet scree in the hope of a lucky strike.

Hiking directions   [With an altitude gain of 2,100m, you may think it worthwhile to hire a jeep or truck in Sorata to take you to Ancoma.]

From Sorata to the pass you'll be walking steeply uphill for about 11 hours, so it's best to leave around midday and camp halfway up. Take the steps from the corner of the plaza past the Residencial Sorata and turn left at the top. You'll soon come to a cemetery, and here take the path leading up the hillside to the right. This leads eventually to an *estancia*, but the

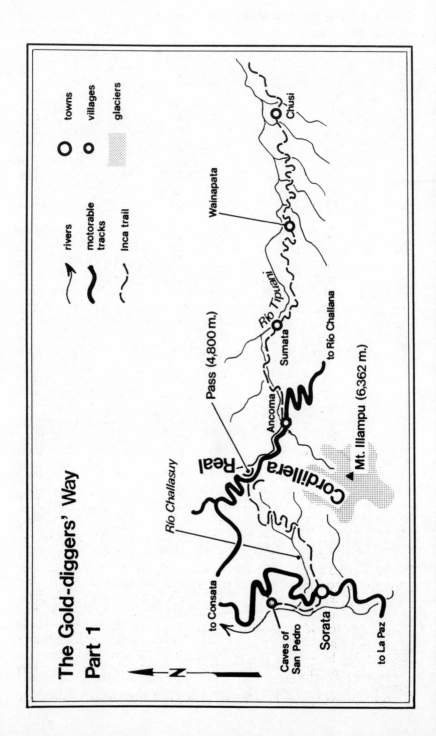

The Gold-diggers' Way
Part 1

trail to Tipuani bears off to the right in an unlikely looking spot about 100m beyond the cemetery. Scramble up the slope as best you can; whichever path you take you'll soon find yourself following a stream which drops steeply down from the hillside ahead. Keeping the stream to your left, carry on uphill until, about an hour after leaving the plaza, you meet a trail coming up from your right. This will take you right up to the pass. From here the uphill struggle is compensated for by the increasingly spectactular views of the Sorata Valley opening up behind you. The trail follows the valley of the Río Challasuy and after another three hours or so of walking up the intensively cultivated valley side you cross the river by a little footbridge. From here on there's a series of excellent campsites, but the first, about 100m beyond the bridge, is perfect. The pass is seven hours away, however, so it might be better to get a bit more distance under your belt before calling it a day. It all depends how much walking you want to do tomorrow.

The next 3 to 4 hours are steeply uphill, but at last you'll pass a small lake and beyond that a false summit, marked by a pile of stones, where a trail branches off to the left. All round here is good camping, the last before the pass. From the false summit take the right hand trail and in another half hour you'll be climbing a magnificently engineered Inca staircase. The going gets easier for a while, but soon becomes steeper again as you approach the final summit. Coming up from below you'll see the *carretera*, a jeep track built many years ago to link Sorata with the Challana valley. It's hardly used now, and trade has returned to the Inca trail.

The summit, about three hours beyond the Inca staircase, is a meeting of many ways. The one you want is the jeep track on the right, neatly short-cut by a trail which goes straight down the valley to re-join it lower down. The jeep track is followed for about 4 hours, passing excellent camping spots on the way, until it makes a wide detour and again a trail follows a shorter route, reached by a footbridge to the opposite river bank. A short distance beyond is the village of Ancoma. It is not possible to buy provisions here.

At Ancoma the jeep track bears off up the mountainside, and the trail to Guanay carries on down the river, closely following its right bank. In half an hour you'll pass a giant boulder with a cave underneath: camping possibilities here and also a large flat meadow another hour further on. Between here and Tipuani the trail makes one digression to the opposite bank, to avoid a steep cliff; otherwise the only rivers you cross are side streams. Almost the whole trail from now on is high up the valley side, with breathtaking views of the Río Tipunai tumbling through its gorge below. The mountains tower above, clad to their summits with thick jungle. And to add to the delight, many of the side streams have placid crystal-clear pools where you can strip off and splash about to her heart's content. But be warned: it is not downhill all the way. Throughout the walk, and especially on the lower part, steep uphill sections prove very tiring.

The next good campsite is in a meadow 6 or 7 hours from Ancoma, and beyond that, in 3 or 4 hours, there is some tent space (and water) just before the scatter of houses that is Sumata. About 4 hours from Sumata you pass a rather well-to-do farm on the left of the trail. This belongs to the *alcalde* of the area, a very helpful man who is responsible for the upkeep of the trail. He has a small store and can usually sell you fresh milk. In another 3 hours you'll reach Wainapata, and, if you're lucky, a supply of fresh bread. Wainapata is some 14 miles from Ancoma, and the first real village along the trail, though it is still only a few houses.

In the old days, shortly after Wainapata you dropped down to the river to what was the most spectacular part of the whole trail. Amid the orchids and flowering shrubs was a perfectly preserved and very long Inca tunnel. Hard to imagine what had caused it to collapse after so many centuries, but so it goes. Now you stay high after Wainapata for some 35 to 40 minutes, until a new 'path' descends steeply and dangerously over the rocks. On reaching the original trail, continue to the R. Cooco where there is good camping.

Cross the river on a suspension bridge and up the valley side again to those magnificent views. The village of Chusi is reached 10 hours after leaving Wainapata, and one hour before the village is a good camping place. This is a proper village — the biggest on the trail, and has two stores and a school. You can usually get permission to sleep in the school. Otherwise continue 1½ hours to an almost perfect campsite; quite suddenly, on a spur above the river, the trail opens out into a large clearing with beautiful views in three directions. I say almost perfect, because the nearest water supply is way below. There's another good place 1½ hours further on, with water nearby. It's over the Río Grande de Yavia and up a stone staircase.

From Chusi to the village of Llipi is 8 hours walking, but you won't do it in that time because of the fabulous bathing to be had in the streams along the way. It'll be hot now, the Incas having become ever more obsessional with their staircases (up and down), and even those who are decidedly not cold-water lovers will want to cool off. The best spot is where you cross the Río Ticumbaya, about five hours from Chusi. It's just beyond a little meadow on a promontory from which several paths go down the hillside in various directions — take the one leading right from the saddle, as you face the promontory.

If you can tear yourself away from this idyllic spot, it's another 3 hours to Llipi and the first of the gold deposits which have brought men to this area for centuries. A ramshackle collection of plank-and-wicket huts high on a ridge between the Ríos Tipuani and Santa Ana house the 150 souls who've come to make their fortune. [The road has now been extended to here, so your trek could end at Llipi if there is transport out. Otherwise continue to follow John's directions until you find something on wheels.]

Another 7 hours will bring you to the next mining settlement, Unutuluni. This is one of the bigger gold mining towns and boasts not only a population of 300 or more but also several *pensiones*, a pool room, and even a branch of the Banco Minero de Bolivia. A plank-and-wicket city!

From Unutuluni a jeep makes regular trips down a road of dubious safety to Gritado, Tipuani, and Guanay, so those so inclined can round off their walk here with a few glasses of beer and return to the world of motorised transport. However, if you've survived this far I've absolutely no doubt that you'll want to continue walking to Guanay — especially when you see the jeep. A magnificent walk it is too, with panoramic views almost all the way. Allow 7 hours to Tipuani — not forgetting to take the uphill branch to the left where the road forks a little beyond Unutuluni — and after availing yourself of the town's facilities (hotels, restaurants, bars, table football) it will be another 10 hours or so to Guanay the following day. This last stretch includes a long uphill climb from the Cangalli ferry but the view from the summit is so stupendous it's worth the effort. Not only will you be able to look back smugly on your route for the past few days but ahead you'll see the foothills of the Andes diminishing steadily towards the Amazon basin. Guanay lies straight ahead, at the confluence of the Mapiri, Tipuani, and Challana and Zongo rivers. It comes suddenly into view as you round a corner after passing through some villages. When you walk into the plaza you'll have hiked across the main *cordillera* of the Andes. Congratulations!

Guanay is a fair-sized town and an excellent place to relax for a few days, even though it is a little expensive. Guanay is the centre of trade for this part of the Yungas, and for a real taste of the jungle you can take canoe trips up or down the rivers. When you are ready to return to civilisation, you would do well to get a bus (book the seat as soon as you arrive). The Flota Yungueña buses leave for Carnavi, Coroico, and La Paz from 108 Calle 6 de Agosto at 5.00 daily. The 230km journey to La Paz takes about 12 hours. Trucks loaded with tropical produce also make the trip, but be warned: a hiker has just reported that he hopped on a nearly empty truck wearing his tropical clothes and hoping to reach La Paz that night, and arrived 48 hours later! Needless to say it was neither empty nor hot when he arrived. If you must get a truck, it would be sensible to break the journey in Coroico, from where, if you were mad enough, you could even hike back to La Paz up the Inca Trail.

Acknowledgement   I am very grateful to Dr Heinz Freydanck, geological consultant to the Bolivian Government, for introducing me to the Tipuani Valley and telling me about the history of gold mining there.

Another hike in the area   Dr.Freydanck also told me of an Inca trail even more impressive scenically than the one I've described, though it doesn't pass through any gold-mining areas. The trail begins at Sorata and crosses the *cordillera*, dropping down to Mapiri on the river of the same name. Colonel Fawcett used this trail in 1906. It's slightly shorter than the one to Guanay, and for much of its length follows a ridge giving spectacular views. [This trail is shown on the I.G.M. 3 sheet Department of La Paz map, scale 1:500,000.] From Mapiri you can take a canoe down

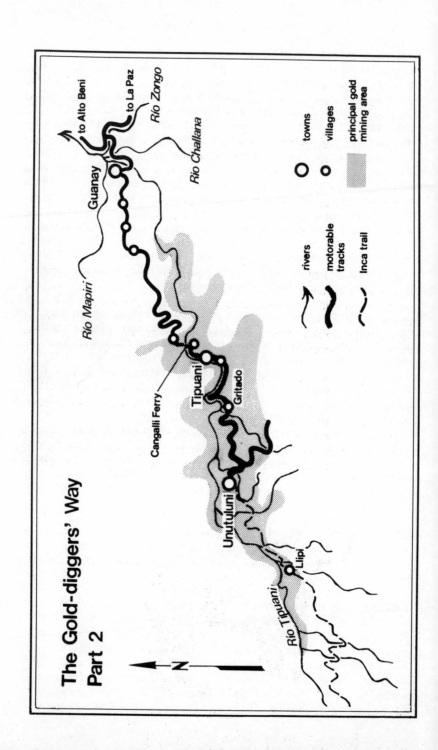

The Gold-diggers' Way
Part 2

the river to Guanay, then return to La Paz as described.

PRACTICAL INFORMATION

Time/Rating   6 to 10 very strenuous days, depending on whether you hike the entire length. Don't be fooled into thinking it's downhill all the way from Ancoma. It isn't, and the very steep Inca staircases combined with the tropical heat are exhausting.

Conditions/What to bring   Be prepared for two cold nights and several warm ones. As you drop down into the Yungas mosquitoes and other bugs become a problem, so bring a long-sleeved shirt in addition to insect repellent. In the rainy season you will get wet during the river crossings, so bring at least one change of clothing and waterproofs for the mist and rain which are likely even in the dry season. Bring all the food you need; you may be able to purchase some along the way, but don't bank on it.

Maps   The I.G.M. maps don't yet cover this area, but are supposed to be in preparation. Ask if sheet SE 19-15 is ready yet (scale 1:250,000). A fascinating and accurate prospectors' map of the trail, made in 1891, may be viewed at the house of Alfredo Fernholz who owns the Residencial Sorata and shop next door. Remember that Alfredo is a busy man, and should not be bothered unnecessarily. My map is based on this one.

Warnings   I saw two snakes along the trail, including a deadly coral snake. But don't panic, snakes invariably move out of the way of noisy backpackers; just avoid actually stepping on one, and be careful when clearing a tent site.

This is a malarial area, so prophylactic pills should be taken. Since some strains of malaria are resistant to certain drugs, buy your pills in La Paz before starting the hike, and ask the pharmacist's advice on the best ones to use.

Capybara

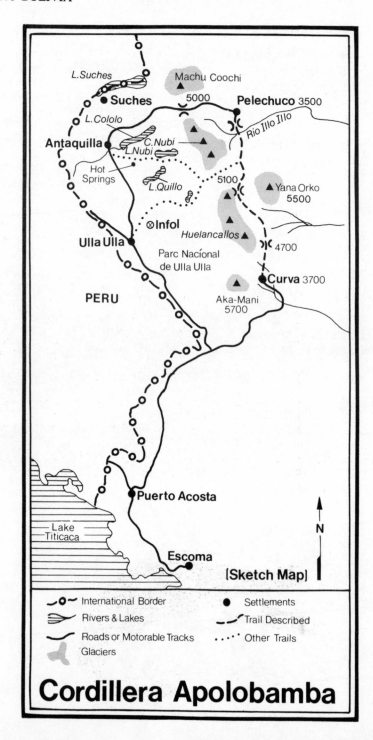

L.Suches

Suches

L.Cololo

Antaquilla

C.Nubi
L.Nubi

Hot
Springs

L.Quillo

Machu Coochi
▲
5000

Pelechuco 3500

Rio Illo Illo

▲
▲
▲

5100

▲ Yana Orko
5500

⊗Infol

Huelancallos ▲

4700

Ulla Ulla

Parc Nacíonal
de Ulla Ulla

Curva 3700

PERU

▲
Aka-Mani
5700

N

Puerto Acosta

Lake
Titicaca

Escoma

[Sketch Map]

～o～ International Border	● Settlements
🐟 Rivers & Lakes	– – Trail Described
— Roads or Motorable Tracks	···· Other Trails
Glaciers	

Cordillera Apolobamba

The Cordillera Apolobamba

Less known and less accessible than the Cordillera Real, the Apolobamba lies to the north west of that range, rising abruptly from the Altiplano, and straddling the Peruvian frontier at the northern tip of Lake Titicaca.

This is the place for truly adventurous hikers with lots of time. The beauty of the mountain scenery equals or even exceeds that of the Cordillera Real, and the glimpses of Indian life and wildlife (there is a vicuña reserve in the foothills) are even more interesting than to the south.

The Apolobamba owes its network of good trails to the Spanish lust for gold. This has been a gold mining area since the conquest, and ruined gold mines can be visited in remote valleys.

One of the biggest problems confronting the Apolobamba explorer is the lack of maps. Mine is drawn from a variety of sources and is intended as an approximate guide only. I am indebted to Pamela Holt, botanist and intrepid Apolobamba explorer, for information on areas that I haven't visited myself.

Access For those restricted to public transport, just getting to the Cordillera Apolobamba is challenging enough. It may be as easy to approach from Peru, via the northern side of Lake Titicaca as from La Paz. Puerto Acosta and Escoma are two biggish towns that can reached from La Paz or from Peru. From there you can make your way to Ulla Ulla (vicuña reserve) or to Pelechuco. Pamela Holt reports: 'Transport to Ulla Ulla and Pelechuco is via a weekly truck from La Paz which leaves on Wednesdays or Thursdays from the road near Cemetario, to the right of a petrol station. The girls at Paititi [see *Useful addresses*, page 151] made us a sketch map but we never actually found the place, although I did see the truck in the Apolobamba. We travelled courtesy of INFOL (Instituto Nacional de Fomento Lanero), Calle Bueno 444, (Casilla 732) La Paz. Tel: 379048 or 379049. They are funded by the World Bank for a five year period.'

Andean caracara

Curva to Pelechuco

Introduction I did this magnificent trek with TAWA (see *Useful addresses*) who solved the logistics of getting there, and carrying a pack over a 5,100m pass. It was a 6 day trek (one rest day) and so spectacular and interesting, I wouldn't hesitate to recommend it to backpackers who are willing to put up with the transport difficulties or to groups looking for an exceptional organised trek. The good trail runs along the eastern side of the Cordillera, ending up at Pelechuco, a village founded in 1560, which is at the crossroads of Amazon and Andean trade.

Apart from the mountain scenery, which was truly breathtaking, this trek was made special because of the contact it allowed us with the Calahuayas Indians, who are the traditional healers of the area. Highly respected throughout South America (they journey as far as Patagonia and Panama) the Calahuayas are expert in the use of herbal medicine, and the art of diagnosing disease through 'reading' a llama's entrails or scattered coca leaves. The Calahuaya language is used only for healing invocations. The Calahuayas were our *arrieros* and I am perfectly willing to to believe that their acts of propitiation to the *Achachilas* helped make this the least problematic trek I have taken in Bolivia. Bottles of the local *aguadiente*, Caiman, were opened at regular intervals, and the alcohol sprinkled around the wheels of the truck (as we approached the trail head) and around the hoofs of the donkeys, amid muttered incantations. So accustomed did we become to ritual that we too felt uneasy without it when we headed for the high pass beyond Pelechuco in a truck. One of the group commented 'Shouldn't we Caiman the wheels?'

Directions The trek begins in Curva, a Calahuayas town high on a hill top overlooking the Calaya valley and backed by the Aka-Mani mountains, the dwelling place of the local *achachilas*. We got there by chartered truck from Escoma. The jeep track to Curva branches off to the right from the road to Pelechuco after about 3 hours. It could be walked in one long day — there are plenty of good camping places with water.

From Curva, take the 'street' on the left of the church arch, and follow the trail over the left flank of the hill, then contour above the river valley. After 1½ hours drop down to the river and cross a ford to the other side and head directly up the opposite bank to a scatter of houses, Jatunpampa. The trail continues from here to a false pass (2 hours), and then in another half hour to the pass itself (4,700m) with wonderful views of the glaciers of Aka-Mani.

To descend, take the path right, east north east, down the valley to Incacanchi (Inca enclosure). There is no sign now of Inca remains here, but it is a wonderful campsite with a waterfall. From Incacanchi you cross the river via a stone bridge, and head up an amazingly steep trail that zig-zags up a seemingly vertical hillside. It will take 2 hours to reach the top of the canyon, then you continue gently uphill to the left, with more views of Aka-Mani. After dropping down briefly, you climb again to another pass and into the Sunchulli valley. Here the trail contours gently down the hillside to a perfect campsite near a deserted gold mine (fun to explore).

This campsite is 4,700m but sheltered.

The next day is a tough one. The Sunchulli pass is 5,100m high, but the views of the glaciers of Yana Orka (5,500m) and other snow peaks are ample reward. The path to the pass is clear, and follows the river valley north west. It will take about 2 hours to the top. Then it's steeply down to the valley, then gently along to the Illo-Illo river and a choice of campsites. Take the lower path down the valley, heading for a conical mountain. From Sunchulli valley campsite to the Río Illo Illo is 6 to 8 hours.

There is one more pass before Pelechuco. Cross the river by a stone bridge and climb steeply for 1½ hours to the last high point (4,700m) before dropping down for 1,000 knee-crunching metres to Pelechuco. As you descend, the vegetation and temperature changes. Foxgloves decorate the trail side, and the moist air of the Amazon basin makes everything green. You should reach Pelechuco in about 5 hours from the bridge.

Pelechuco is a quiet, pretty town, with a strongly Spanish flavour. There are cobbled streets, a fine church, colonial style courtyards, and a general air of decay. It is the perfect place in which to relax, which is a good thing since transport out is only once a week, on Saturdays. Of course, you may be lucky and find something else. In the main plaza is Pension Mexico, run by friendly Maria de Alvarez (recommended by Pamela Holt).

PRACTICAL INFORMATION
Time/Rating   A 6 day trek that could spin out much longer because of transport difficulties. Ideally, you could get the Wed/Thurs truck to within a day's walk of Curva, and be in Pelechuco in plenty of time for the Saturday truck back to La Paz. This is a strenuous trek with an exceptionally high pass (5,100m) and several others only slightly lower. Definitely only for the experienced.

Conditions/What to bring   Most days and nights will be very cold and rain is always a possibility. It will be hot enough for tee shirts and shorts on the last day. Don't forget your sunglasses against the glare of the snow. Although provisions might be obtainable in Curva, don't bank on it; bring everything you need.

Maps   There are none, apart from the middle sheet of the 3 sheet department of La Paz (1:500,000) which is very inaccurate.

Male fertility is drastically reduced during the first few days at high altitudes. Those spare condoms make excellent water carriers!

Trekking

Trekking vs Backpacking

Broadly speaking, trekking differs from backpacking in that your gear is carried by pack animals (or, in the case of the Inca Trail, porters) and that some local organisation is involved in supplying tents, food, transport, etc. In effect, a trek is a package tour which leaves you free to enjoy the mountains without worrying about any of the logistics.

There are many advantages of trekking over backpacking, not least that all the hassle and anxiety of travel in rural Peru and Bolivia is taken out of your hands. For most trekkers there is no choice: for those with only three weeks holiday a year, or who are disinclined to heave a 40lb pack around, the only way they will set foot in the Andes is with an organised group. Furthermore, it is only with pack animals that really long distances can be covered; most backpackers find a week's supply of food is all they can carry. Finally, with transport laid on, an organised trek can reach areas that are inaccessible to backpackers using public transport. Besides, it's often more *fun* than doing it on your own.

What it's like

If the trek is organised from your home country, the pampering should start shortly after the day you sign up, with pre-departure information giving you a good idea of what this particular company provides. Most likely they will deal with your airticket, send you an equipment list, and generally prepare you for what is in store.

In South America you will be met by your trip leader (or he/she may travel out with you) and will not have to think for yourself until you pass through immigration on your way out of the country! It's a wonderful chance for high-powered people to regress into complete dependancy, and the happiest trekkers are often those who do just that.

All well-organised treks will have a built-in period of acclimatisation. In Peru, this is usually a few days sightseeing in the Cuzco area, or perhaps some gentle hiking around Huaráz. You will probably be agreeably surprised at how comfortable and well-fed you are during this period, so the shock of the first day of the trek is all the greater. You are likely to travel in an open truck to the trailhead, because these are the only vehicles which can cope with the rough roads, and you will have to learn how to put up your own tent (or rather, the tent supplied by the local operator). With some of the very classy trekking companies your tent is put up for you, but the *arrieros* have so much to do anyway this only delays more important jobs — like preparing your supper.

You will be surprised at how many pack animals are needed — an average of one donkey per person. And you may likewise be surprised at the number people taking care of your needs. A typical campcrew is led by a representative of the local tour operator who is both the guide and organiser. It is he who hires the *arrieros*, buys the food, supplies the tents, decides where each night will be spent (pasture for the animals being the deciding factor), and deals with any crisis of a local nature. Your own Fearless Leader's role is to keep you happy, healthy and well-informed. Often there is a trip doctor who takes care of the healthy part, although his job is almost always limited to treating colds and diarrhoea (in the dozen or so treks I've led, there has been no case of serious illness or injury. All treks provide an impressive medicine box. Subordinate to the guide is the cook (and his helper), and the *arrieros*. The cook generally works exclusively for that particular operator, whilst the *arrieros* are contracted locally, near the trail head.

A typical day begins at dawn (about 6.00) with a wake up call, although those sleeping near the campcrew (something you learn not to do) will have been woken long before, by sounds of chattering and laughter as breakfast is prepared (the cook gets up at about 4.30 to start this chore). The concept 'I'm not a morning person' seems to be exclusively western; *all* Peruvians are morning people! Some pampered trekkers find a bowl of hot water outside their tent. Otherwise, few take washing very seriously. With outside temperatures below freezing it's a question of putting on even more clothes and staggering out to the tea tent. The tea tent is one of the joys of trekking. It's big enough to stand and walk around in, and with fifteen tightly-packed bodies, can become quite cosy. Breakfast is a substantial meal. You will usually get porridge, eggs, and bread, and sometimes even pancakes. The quality of food on a trek often comes as an unexpected pleasure.

While you are eating breakfast, the *arrieros* are rounding up the animals and starting to pack up. This is a long procedure, and you will get a head start, leaving camp at about 8.00 for the day's walk. In your daypack you will carry your picnic lunch, camera, sweater, raingear (however bright the day looks) and any other goodies you need. Your main luggage will not be accessible during the day. Lunches tend to be rather dreary — there's not much that can be done with week-old bread — and most trekkers bring their own trail snacks. The group will spread out on the trail but assemble at lunchtime, generally at a pre-arranged spot.

The day ends around 3.30 when the first walkers march into camp. There is a distinct advantage in not walking too fast. If you arrive before the pack animals and campcrew, you will have a chilly wait. If you stagger in at dusk, sobbing, at least someone will have put up your tent and tea will be almost ready. And tea is the most welcome 'meal' of the day; a chance to take your boots off and ease your aching limbs, and warm your hands round a mug of hot liquid while discussing the day. Supper comes at around 6.30 to 7.00. Meanwhile there is desultory or lively conversation, cards, Scrabble, jokes, boozing, reading, brooding ... depending on the disposition of the group. The evening meal is usually ample: three courses, often with fresh meat (chickens ride on donkeys, along with the luggage, and sometimes sheep join the trek — for a while). Most people are in their sleeping bags by 8 o'clock.

Here are a few questions that I'm often asked — and their answers:
'What if someone is too ill to walk'?   Most operators provide riding horses for emergencies, and these are often in use for off-colour trekkers. If there are no horses (as in Bolivia), there is generally a rest day built into the itinerary which can be used as a sick-day. Professional evacuation, with helicopter, etc., is very rarely possible.
'What about you know what?'   You'll get used to squatting behind bushes. Some outfitters supply toilet tents, which is much nicer for the environment, but not as pleasant as the open air. Naturally instructions on the disposal of paper, etc. should be strictly adhered to.
What about washing?   It's amazing how even shower-twice-a-day Americans settle down to a quick dab every day or so when it's freezing outside and the shower comes from a glacier. In fact, hot water for washing yourself, your hair, or your clothes is often available on request. A plastic collapsable bucket is very useful for this. Rest days are usually wash days, and you soon get in the habit, on ordinary walking days, of bringing soap, etc. for a noon-time bath when the sun is hot.

Choosing a trek

Trekking companies advertise in all the usual places: travel sections of daily or Sunday newspapers, and walking and climbing magazines (and in this book). An alternative source is *Adventure Holidays* published annually by Vacation Work of Oxford (England) and *Guide to Study, Travel and Adventure* published by the St Martins Press in New York for the Council on International Educational Exchange (USA).

More care must be taken selecting an organised trek than if you're going it alone, when you can always turn back if things don't work out. You must read between the lines of the brochure, and make sure that you can cope physically and mentally with the trek. Check the altitude gain each day, find out the height of the highest passes and the number of rest days. Do not be beguiled by talk of 'verdant rain forests and glistening peaks'; the former will be hot and wet, and the latter cold and strenuous. You can only enjoy the beauty if you can cope with the terrain. A good tour operator will put you in touch with someone who has done the trip, so you can get an unbiased account of what it's like. Remember that costs usually reflect the quality of the organisation and the comfort on the trail, so unless you are very tough and adventurous, be careful of just going for the cheapest.

There is a considerable difference between trekking in Peru and trekking in Bolivia. In Peru it is now well-established, with excellent local operators in Huaráz and Cuzco. In Bolivia, trekking is still a new concept, and much less comfortable and more adventurous. Equipment tends to be basic, there are no riding horses, and a more flexible attitude is needed. But the rewards in scenery and solitude are great.

Finally, take fitness — both mental and physical — seriously. It is no good going on a trek in the Andes if you are afraid of heights, or limited in what you can eat, or don't much like other people or foreigners or your travel companion. Fitness for trekking is more than just getting your body into shape.

Keeping up appearances. Trekker shaving at school waterfountain in Bolivia.

Appendices

Bibliography

I once asked an impressively fit woman how she had prepared for the trek. She answered 'I did a lot of reading'.

Background reading and a companion guide book will do much to enhance your trip. Here are a few suggestions, with subjective comments on those I've found particularly enjoyable or useful.

Guide books

The South American Handbook. Edited by John Brooks, Trade and Travel Publications, Bath, UK. Published annually, this is the bible for South America travellers; about 1400 pages of small print, very expensive but you'll save the purchase price within a week of SAHB-inspired travel.

BARTLE, Jim. *Trails of the Cordilleras Blanca and Huayhuash* 1980. The best hiking guide for these mountain ranges, with an excellent map. Can be purchased in Peru.

BROD, Charles. *Apus and Incas*, 1986. Subtitled 'a cultural walking and trekking guide to Cuzco', includes several hikes not described here.

FROST, Peter. *Exploring Cuzco*, Bradt Publications, 1984 (second edition). An excellent guide to the city and entire area.

JENKINS, Dilwyn. *The Rough Guide to Peru.* Routledge & Kegan Paul, 1985. Very comprehensive.

MEISCH, Lynn. *A Traveller's Guide to El Dorado and the Inca Empire: Colombia, Ecuador, Peru, Bolivia.* Penguin. This excellent and comprehensive book covers every aspect of the Andean countries likely to interest travellers rather than tourists. Information on the handicrafts and local cultures is as complete as the travel advice. Highly recommended.

RACHOWIECKI, Rob. *Peru — a travel survival kit.* Lonely Planet. Due 1987.

RICKER, John. *Yuraq Janka.* The Alpine Club of Canada and the USA (joint publication). A mountaineers' guide to the Cordilleras Blanca and Rosko. Stronger on history than climbing routes, but the best there is at present. Includes an excellent map.

Background Reading.

BINGHAM, Hiram. *Lost City of the Incas.* Various editions. A very readable account of the discovery of Machu Picchu, but don't take all the explanations as gospel truth.

BUSHNELL, G.H. *Peru: Ancient Peoples and Places.* 1956. Thames & Hudson.

DE LA VEGA, Garcilaso. *The Incas.* Avon, 1964. Written in 1609 by the son of a conquistador and an Inca princess.

HEMMING, John. *The Conquest of the Incas.* Macmillan, 1970. The most authorative and readable book on the Incas.

HEMMING, John and RANNEY, Edward. *Monuments of the Incas.* Little, Brown, 1982. A beautiful book of photographs, maps and detailed explanations of major Inca sites.

KENDALL, Ann. *Everyday Life of the Incas.* Batsford, 1978.

LANNING, Edward P. *Peru before the Incas.* Prentice-Hall, 1967.

MASON, J.Alden. *The Ancient Civilisations of Peru.* Penguin 1969.

MORRISON, Tony. *The Andes.* Time-Life Books.

MORRISON, Tony. *Mystery of the Nazca Lines.* Nonesuch, 1987.

PRESCOTT, H.W. *The History of the Conquest of Peru.* The classic work, in various editions.

STEWARD, Julian H. (ed.) *Handbook of South American Indians, Vol.2, The Andean Civilisations.* Cooper Sq. Pub.,1963.

VERGER, Pierre and VALCARCAL, Luis. *Indians of Peru.* Pocahontas Press, 1950.

Natural History

ANDREWS, Michael. *The Flight of the Condor*. BBC Publications (UK), Little, Brown (US), 1982. An excellent natural history, with outstanding photographs.

DUNNING, John S. *South American Land Birds*. Harrowood Books (US), 1982. A photographic guide to identification; illustrates over 1000 birds and describes 2740 species. Does not cover water birds.

KOEPCKE, Maria. *The Birds of the Department of Lima, Peru*. Harrowood Books, 1969. Describes 331 species with black and white drawings.

MORRISON, Tony. *Wildlife of the Andes* (provisional title. Due 1987/88). Nonesuch. A completely updated replacement for *Land above the Clouds*. .

PARKER, PARKER AND PLENGE, *An Annotated Checklist of Peruvian Birds*. Bueto Books, 1982. A complete list with notes on distribution. No illustrations.

de SCHAUENSEE, Rodolphe Meyer. *Guide to the Birds of South America*. Describes all of the 3000 species in the continent, but the illustrations are poor.

Exploration

CONWAY, Martin. *The Bolivian Andes: the Cordillera Real*. Harper Bros., N.Y., 1901. Interesting for climbers bound in this direction.

FAWCETT, P.H. *Lost Trails, Lost Cities*. Funk & Wagnalls, N.Y., 1953.

PECK, Annie S. *A search for the Apex of America*. Dodd, Mead & Co., N.Y. 1911. And she climbs Huascarán!

SQUIER, George. *Travel and Exploration in the Land of the Incas*. Harper Bros. N.Y. 1877 A fascinating book covering all aspects in depth.

MURPHY, Dervla. *Eight Feet in the Andes*. John Murray, 1983. An account of the author's walk from Cajamarca to Cuzco, accompanied by her ten year old daughter.

WRIGHT, Ronald. *Cut Stones and Cross Roads*. Penguin, 1986. A literary and well written account of an archaelogical journey in Peru.

Miscellaneous

HATT, John. *The Tropical Traveller*. Pan, 1985. Everything you ever wanted to know but were afraid to ask, and quite a bit that you had never thought of asking. The most thorough, entertaining, quotable, and useful book of general travel information ever written.

MADDA, Frank C. *Outdoor Emergency Medicine*. BioService
Corporation, Chicago, 1980. A compact and very useful guide.

TURNER, Anthony. *Travellers Health Guide*. Lascelles, 1985.

FORGEY, William. *Wilderness Medicine*. Indiana Camp Supply books,
USA. The best book I know on the subject.

Measurements and conversions

Latin America uses metric measurements and so have I throughout this book.
These conversion formulae and tables should help you.

Many people will want to convert metres to the more familiar feet. If you
remember that 3 metres is 0.84 feet, or just under 10 feet, you can do an approximate conversion quickly: to convert heights shown in metres to feet, divide
by 3 and add a zero, e.g. 6,000 m = 20,000 feet.

The error is only 1.5%.

CONVERSION FORMULAE

To convert	Multiply by
Inches to centimetres	2.540
Centimetres to inches	0.3937
Feet to Metres	0.3048
Metres to feet	3.281
Yards to metres	0.9144
Metres to yards	1.094
Miles to kilometres	1.609
Kilometres to miles	0.6214
Acres to hectares	0.4047
Hectares to acres	2.471
Imperial gallons to litres	4.546
Litres to imperial gallons	0.22
US gallons to litres	3.785
Litres to U.S. gallons	0.264
Ounces to grams	28.35
Grams to ounces	0.03527
Pounds to grams	453.6
Grams to pounds	0.002205
Pounds to kilograms	0.4536
Kilograms to pounds	2.205
British tons to kilograms	1016.00
Kilograms to British tons	0.0009842
U.S. tons to kilograms	907.00
Kilograms to U.S. tons	0.000907

TEMPERATURE
CONVERSION TABLE
The bold figures in the central
columns can be read as either
centigrade or fahrenheit.

Centigrade		Fahrenheit
−18	0	32
−15	5	41
−12	10	50
− 9	15	59
− 7	20	68
− 4	25	77
− 1	30	86
2	35	95
4	40	104
7	45	113
10	50	122
13	55	131
16	60	140
18	65	149
21	70	158
24	75	167
27	80	176
32	90	194
38	100	212
40	104	

(5 imperial gallons are equal to 6 U.S. gallons.
A British ton is 2,240 lbs. A U.S. ton is 2,000 lbs.)

Index of place names

(For other subjects see *Table of Contents*.)

PERU

Aguas Calientes, 114
Arequipa, 142-143
Auzangate (Mt), 125-140

Cabanaconde, 144
Cajamarca, 70-78
Cajatambo, 95,98
Callejon de Huaylas, 79
Caráz, 79,85
Cashapampa, 85
Cerro de Pasco, 100
Chacas, 46,89
Chachani (volcano), 142
Chalhuanca, 145
Checacupe, 135,139
Chilca, 117
Chinchero, 105-106
Chiquian, 95
Chivay, 144
Chavin de Huantar, 91-95
Choquequirau, 109
Chopicalqui (Mt), 82
Colca Canyon, 144
Colcabamba, 84
Contrahierbas (Mt), 87
Cordillera Blanca, 79-93
Cordillera Huayhuash, 95-99
Cordillera Negra, 79
Cordillera Vilcabamba, 109-124
Cordillera Vilcanota, 125-140
Cumbe Mayo, 70-72
Cusichaca (River), 111
Cuzco, 103-106

Honda (Quebrada), 89
Huancayo, 100
Huaráz, 79,95
Huari, 100
Huandoy (Mt), 82
Huánuco Viejo, 100
Huascarán (Mt), 82
Huascaran (Nat. Pk), 81,82
Huayllabamba, 105,111,117,121
Huiñay Huayna, 109,113,114
Humantay (Mt), 123

Inca Trail (the), 69,109-117

Jaguacocha (Lake), 96
Jirishjanka (Mt), 96,97
Junin, 69

Kuntur Wasi, 70

La Oroya, 100
La Unión, 100,101
Lima, 64-67
Limatambo, 119
Llamac, 95,96
Llanganuco (Lakes), 82

Machu Picchu, 110,114
Mairo (Puerto), 101
Misti (Volcano), 142
Mollepata, 119

Ocongate, 125,126
Ollantaytambo, 117
Olleros, 91
Oxapampa, 100

Pampa Galeras, 69
Paracas, 69
Paucartambo, 47
Pitumarca, 138
Pozuzo, 101-102
Pucallpa, 101,102

Punta Union, 84,85,87
Qenco, 103,104

Raqchi, 135,136

Sacsayhuaman, 103
Salinas, 107
Salinas Borax (Lake), 142
Salkantay (Mt), 120-121
Salumpuncu, 33,103,104
San Pablo (Cajamarca), 77
Santa Cruz, 85
Santa Teresa, 124
Shilla, 87

Tarahuasi, 119

Ubinas (Volcano), 142
Ulta (Pasaje de), 89
Ulta (Quebrada), 87
Urubamba, 106-107

Vitcos, 109

Wiñay Wayna (See Huiñay Huayna)

Yanahuanca, 100
Yerupajá (Mt), 96
Yungay, 82

BOLIVIA

Achacachi, 47

Chipaya, 46
Chojlla, 157
Chulumani, 167
Cordillera Apolobamba, 178-182
Cordillera Real, 149, 154-177
Coroico, 162,163,175
Curva, 180-181

Guanay, 175

Huayna Potosí (Mt), 165

Illimani (Mt), 167
Isla del Sol (Island of the Sun), 153

La Cumbre, 161,162
La Paz, 149-152
Lambate 168

Mapiri, 175

Pelechuco, 179-181

Sorata, 170-172

Takesi, 155-157
Tipuani, 171
Titicaca (Lake), 153

Ulla Ulla, 152,179
Unutuluni, 174

Yanacachi, 157
Yungus, 147,158,161,171

Zongo (Lake), 163

This is all the information I can give you, but I have one proposal: why don't you put down more clearly that you want people to write to you when there is an error or a change in the description? Tell the reader that it is fun to do it because you experience the whole trip again.

I wish ... Bradt Publications
and I hope ... mailing list.
yours ...

"WANTS YOU"

TO HELP KEEP THIS BOOK UP TO DATE!

There are spare pages at the back on which you can note any changes (give the page number) or new hikes you have found. Please send them to me at the address below. Thanks.

Hilary Bradt

Bradt Publications, 41 Nortoft Rd, Chalfont St Peter, Bucks SL9 0LA, England.

OTHER BOOKS ON SOUTH AMERICA FROM BRADT PUBLICATIONS

Backpacking in Mexico and Central America by Hilary Bradt and Rob Rachowiecki.
The second edition of the first book to cover the countryside of Central America in detail, with a particular emphasis on Costa Rica and its excellent national parks. Also information on climbing Mexico's volcanoes.

Backpacking in Venezuela, Colombia and Ecuador by George and Hilary Bradt.
Eleven treks in the northern Andes show you the national parks, take you into cloud forest and up to the snowline. Includes Colombia's Sierra Nevada de Santa Marta and Cocuy, Venezuela's Sierra Nevada de Mérida, and many other outstanding hikes.

Climbing and Hiking in Ecuador by Rob Rachowiecki.
The complete guide to Ecuador's mountains, volcanoes and trails. Includes jungle trips, an Inca trail, and a journey along the Pacific coast which combines walking with travel by bus, train and canoe.

Backpacking in Chile and Argentina by Hilary Bradt and John Pilkington.
The Lake Districts, Patagonia and Tierra del Fuego are some of the areas covered. Includes a pre-war guide to the Falkland Islands.

South America: River Trips by George Bradt.
A guide to river travel by cargo boat, rubber raft or canoe, with descriptions of eleven rivers including the Amazon.

Up the Creek by John Harrison.
An exciting account of a canoe trip up one of Brazil's least explored rivers — the Jari.

This is just a selection of the books and maps for adventurous travellers that we stock. Send for our latest catalogue.

Bradt Publications, 41 Nortoft Rd, Chalfont St Peter, Bucks SL9 0LA, England

Some of the above books are available from Hunter Publishing, USA.

NOTES

NOTES